WILD AND BEAUTIFUL

A NATURAL HISTORY OF OPEN SPACES
IN ORANGE COUNTY

ALLAN A. SCHOENHERR

Book Designer: Laura L. Liptak
Design Consultant: Paul Paiement
Photography Editor: Rick Belcher
Copy Editor: Barbara Metzger
Assistant Designer and Illustrator: Rachel D. Martin

ISBN: 10-digit ISBN: 0972854495
13-digit ISBN: 978-0-9728544-9-8

Library Of Congress Control Number: 2009929074
Natural History Orange County Open Spaces Environment Flora Fauna

Laguna Wilderness Press
PO Box 149, Laguna Beach, CA 92651-0149
www.lagunawildernesspress.com
email: orders@lagunawildernesspress.com
Tel: 951-827-1571

Printed in Malaysia

Laguna Wilderness Press is a non-profit press dedicated to publishing books concerning
the presence, preservation, and importance of wilderness environments.

Table of Contents

Table of Contents

Acknowledgments

I thank Ron Chilcote and Jerry Burchfield of Laguna Wilderness Press for encouraging me to complete this project, and I am deeply indebted to their editor, Barbara Metzger, and image wizard, Rick Belcher, for working over my manuscript and improving it. Many people helped me by providing information and reading the rough drafts of my work. In particular, I am grateful to John Gannaway, Cathy Nowak, and Harry Huggins of the Resources and Development Management Department, Orange County Parks, for providing me with outlines and maps of the county parks as well as commenting on the manuscript. Melanie Schlotterbeck and Jean Watt, local environmentalists, working with Friends of Harbors, Beaches, and Parks, provided me with all sorts of data relevant to Orange County public lands. Dr. Elisabeth Brown of the Laguna Greenbelt made suggestions on the original manuscript. Debra Clarke and Mary Thomas of the Trabuco Ranger District provided valuable commentary on the Cleveland National Forest, and Dr. David Olson and Mike O'Connel of Irvine Ranch Wildlands and Parks and Trish Smith of the Nature Conservancy provided valuable input to help me understand the confusing layers of management associated with former Irvine Ranch lands that have been dedicated to preservation. Eric Jessen of the Conservation Fund provided helpful explanations about the purchase of private properties that ultimately are turned over to public agencies for management. Angela Barlow of the California Department of Fish and Game graciously provided access to available online images of animals. Dr. Lenny Vincent of Fullerton College wrote the text and provided photos for the section on Arachnids, and Dr. Brad Dawson, also of Fullerton College, provided very important comments that improved the section on birds. Dr. Peter Bryant of the University of California at Irvine provided beautiful photos of various insects and other Arthropods, and Peter Bowler, also of that institution, contributed information on land snails and photos from the archives of the university's Museum of Systematic Biology. The graphics and photo illustrations are mine unless otherwise noted. Among the latter, figures 2.1, 2.17, 2.18, 3.10, 4.2, 7.7, and 7.32 and tables 4.1 and 7.1 were adapted from Allan Schoenherr, *A Natural History of California*. © 1992. The Regents of the University of California. Published by the University of California Press. To anyone whom I may have forgotten, rest assured that I appreciated your contribution and I apologize for any oversight.

Preface

We are very fortunate that in the midst of urban sprawl in our small county we have so many opportunities to get outdoors and experience nature. In Orange County, California, we are doubly blessed in that we have a great range of natural beauty on lands that are relatively unspoiled and are available for personal exploration.

The first part of this book is about public land, or land for which the emphasis is on preservation of the natural order of things and for which access is provided for the general public. It is a respected truth that, unless they have experienced it, people find it difficult to understand why land should be preserved in a natural state. Various parcels of public land will be described with an emphasis on what makes each one valuable or important. This book will refer primarily to the coastal or cismontane side of the Santa Ana Mountains and the adjacent coastal plain that lies in Orange County. For the purpose of continuity, however, regions south of the county line, particularly the San Mateo drainage and its wilderness, will be included. Natural landscapes are to be celebrated and appreciated. Features such as notable habitats, bird-watching opportunities, hiking trails, campgrounds, and picnic spots will be emphasized, but public places devoted entirely to recreation such as ball fields will not be discussed.

The remainder of this book is about the natural history of Orange County—about plants, animals, rocks, weather, and climate. It is not a field guide. While it may be useful for identifying various plants, animals, and rocks, it is more than mere descriptions of things. There will be an emphasis on things that are common, interesting, or significant and on the way organisms interact with the environment and each other. Beyond just learning the names of things, readers will learn how things fit together in the great scheme of life and life processes.

Chapter 1   Orange County's Public Lands

Orange County is the smallest county in southern California. Its total area is 948 square miles (2,455 square kilometers or 606,385 acres). A total of 53,836 acres, about 9%, of Orange County has already been preserved as public land or is proposed for preservation (fig. 1.1 At the base of Little Sycamore Canyon). With over 3 million residents, Orange County is the second-most-populous county in the state and the fifth-most-populous county in the United States. It is remarkable, therefore, that so much land is either in public hands or set aside for public access.

In spite of its small size, Orange County has a remarkable range of topography. Its eastern border with Riverside County lies along the summit of the Santa Ana Mountains. The high point, on Santiago Peak (fig. 1.2), is at an elevation of 5,678 feet (1,733 meters). To the north, Modjeska Peak, 200 feet lower, and Santiago Peak form a ridge known as Saddleback, a familiar landform that is visible from nearly any point in Orange County or western Riverside County. The

northwestern border of the county lies on the coastal plain of the Los Angeles Basin. To the north the border lies along the Coyote Hills, which extend eastward to merge with the Chino Hills, the high point of which is San Juan Hill (1,781 feet/574 meters) along the San Bernardino County line. The southern border lies along the northern edge of Camp Pendleton. From the western slopes of the Santa Ana Mountains the land slopes westward toward the sea, interrupted by the San Joaquin Hills, which rise to 1,164 feet (375 meters) between the El Toro Valley and the coast. Urban development is concentrated on the coastal plain, the Santa Ana River floodplain, the El Toro Valley, and coastal terraces from Newport Beach south to San Clemente.

Public lands in Orange County (fig. 1.3) are managed by a variety of agencies. Western slopes of the Santa Ana Mountains are in the Cleveland National Forest, managed by the United States Department of Agriculture, Forest Service. The federal government also manages the Seal Beach National Wildlife Refuge. There are two state parks, Chino Hills and Crystal Cove, and these, along with state beaches such as Bolsa Chica, Huntington Beach, Corona del Mar, Doheny, San Clemente, and San Onofre, are managed by the California Department of Parks and Recreation. The California Department of Fish and Game manages the Upper Newport Bay Ecological Reserve. The county itself

Fig. 1.1. At the base of Little Sycamore Canyon (Ronald H. Chilcote).

Fig. 1.2. Santiago Peak. View across El Toro Valley from the San Joaquin Hills.

manages a series of regional parks. Among them are Laguna Coast, Aliso and Wood Canyons, Irvine, O'Neill, Whiting Ranch, Carbon Canyon, Featherly, and Caspers. City parks such as the Huntington Beach's Central Park and Fullerton's Laguna Lake Park have significant natural landscapes. In addition there are privately owned lands that are managed as reserves by entities such as the Nature Conservancy, the Audubon Society (Starr Ranch), California State University, Fullerton (Tucker Wildlife Sanctuary), and the University of California at Irvine (San Joaquin Marsh). Various development companies also have set aside reserves. Among these are the Irvine Ranch Wildlands and Parks (formerly the Irvine Ranch Reserve), the Donna O'Neill Land Conservancy, and the San Joaquin Wildlife Sanctuary.

Public lands in Orange County and some private lands open for public use are managed in order to preserve plants and animals in their natural state.

Fig. 1.3. Public lands of Orange County.

FEDERALLY OWNED LANDS

Cleveland National Forest

California's southernmost national forest, the **Cleveland National Forest**, lies astride the borders of three counties—Riverside, San Diego, and Orange (fig. 1.4). The Orange County portion, at 54,521 acres, on the coastal (cismontane) side of the Santa Ana Mountains, is about 41% of the Trabuco Ranger District. The eastern (transmontane) side of the mountains lies primarily in Riverside County.

The **San Mateo Canyon Wilderness** (fig. 1.5), nearly 40,000 acres of roadless terrain, is home to southern California's only undisturbed drainage system (San Mateo Creek). Although it lies in northern San Diego County and western Riverside County, south of the Orange County line, it is of interest here because it is adjacent to Orange County, administered through the Trabuco Ranger District, and accessible by the Ortega Highway (State Highway 74).

The lower portion of San Mateo Canyon is inaccessible because it is part of Camp Pendleton; the mouth of San Mateo Creek is at San Onofre State Beach.

Travel in a wilderness has certain restrictions. Mechanized and motor vehicles including bicycles, motorcycles, and ATVs and even chainsaws are prohibited. Horseback, wheelchair, and foot traffic are permitted. Dogs must be kept on a leash. Remote camping is permitted, but otherwise camping in the national forest must be at established campgrounds. For day hikes a sign-in is provided at trailheads. For overnight travel a wilderness permit must be obtained from the Trabuco District office at 1146 E. Sixth Street in Corona or the El Cariso Visitor Information Center on the Ortega Highway. Group size is limited to 15 including livestock and dogs. Trailhead parking requires a parking fee in the form of an "Adventure Pass" for $5.00 a day or $30.00 a year. A "Golden Eagle" or "Golden Age" pass will also suffice. Day-use fee stations are located at the San Juan Loop parking lot on the Ortega Highway or at the Tenaja trailhead or the Tenaja Falls trailhead, which are accessible from Clinton Keith Road off Interstate 15.

Fig. 1.4. Black Star Canyon. Autumn view, showing Riparian community in canyon bottom, Oak Woodland on sides of canyon bottom, Lower Chaparral to left on north-facing slope, and dry Coastal Sage Scrub to right on south-facing slope. Cleveland National Forest.

Fig. 1.5. San Mateo Canyon.

Cleveland National Forest

San Mateo Canyon
Wilderness Trails

El Cariso Fire Station Visitor Center and Nature Trail

Lake Elsinore

Morgan Trailhead 1

1 Morgan Trail 2.3 m

San Juan Loop Trailhead

Ortega Oaks/Candy Store
1.0 m 2.0 m

San Juan Fire Station

2 Bear Canyon Trail 1.0 m

1.2 m

1.5 m

Bear Ridge Trail 3

Ortega Hwy

74

Sitton Truck Road

1.5 m

0.9 m — Four Corners

South Main Divide Road

Lucas Canyon Trail 4

5 Verdugo Trail 5

Tenaja Falls Trail 6

Wilomar OHV Area and Campground

6.3 m

0.6 m

2.7 m

5.4 m

0.3 m

No mechanized equipment may be used in this federal wilderness area including: mountain bikes, motorbikes, wheeled carts, all-terrain vehicles, & chainsaws. Portable camp stoves that burn propane or jellied fuels are allowed in the wilderness area. Southern California fire restrictions do not allow wood or charcoal fires, or fires that have open flames.

ons Park

Oak Flats Trail 7

0.6 m

1.0 m

6.1 m

Tenaja Falls
0.7 m

6 Tenaja Falls Trailhead

8 Bluewater Trail 3.3 m

2.0 m

Tenaja Trail (north) 9

1.0 m 1.7 m

Fisherman's Camp Trail 11

10 Indian Potrero Trail 5.0 m

0.7 m

3.3 m

9 Tenaja Trail (south) 3.5 m

Cleveland

San Mateo Trail 12

9 Tenaja Trailhead

1.5 m

Clark Trail 13

4.4 m

Legend:

Trailhead
Restrooms
Forest Service Station
Cleveland National Forest
San Mateo Wilderness
Ortega Hwy
Secondary Roads
Administrative motorized access only.
X No public access to trail across private land. Landowner permission required to pass
m miles

Map Scale
1:29,00

0   2 Kilometers
0   2 Miles

1	Morgan	Moderate
2	Bear Canyon to Sitton Peak	Moderate to Strenuous
3	Bear Ridge	Easy
4	Lucas Canyon	Moderate to Strenuous
5	Verdugo	Moderate to Strenuous
6	Tenaja Falls	Moderate
7	Oak Flats	Easy
8	Bluewater Trail	Moderate to Strenuous
9	Tenaja Trail	Moderate to Strenuous
10	Indian Potrero	Strenuous
11	Fisherman's Camp	Easy to Moderate
12	San Mateo	Easy to Moderate
13	Clark Trail	Moderate to Strenuous

Fig. 1.6. San Mateo Canyon Wilderness (courtesy of U.S. Forest Service).

The plant communities and wildlife observable in the San Mateo watershed include almost everything Orange County has to offer. At an elevation of 3,273 feet, Sitton Peak is the high point in the wilderness. This is not high enough to support Coulter Pines or Bigcone Douglas Firs, so the predominant plant communities in the wilderness are Chaparral and Coastal Sage Scrub. In the canyons, however, there are substantial stands of Southern Oak Woodland and Riparian communities that are accessible by several trails. Poison Oak is abundant along all of these trails, some of which become overgrown with vegetation from time to time.

The trails of the San Mateo Canyon Wilderness (fig. 1.6), as described by the U.S. Forest Service, are as follows:

Bear Canyon Loop. The trailhead is on the Ortega Highway at the San Juan Loop trailhead across the road from the Candy

Store, 19 miles east of San Juan Capistrano. It provides access to Chaparral, Oak Woodlands, interesting sculpted granite, seasonal flowing water, and wildflowers in the spring. A 6.5-mile round trip takes you to Four Corners and back. The return trip is along the Bear Ridge Trail. Pigeon Springs, a 5.5-mile round trip, has a stone water trough for horses. The Sitton Peak Trail, a 10-mile round trip, is accessed from Four Corners, and so are the Tenaja Trail, leading down to San Mateo Creek (5.0 miles), and the Verdugo Trail. leading to Oak Flats and the Lucas Canyon Trail (3.0 miles). The Morgan Trail branches off the Bear Canyon Loop Trail about a mile from the trailhead.

Morgan Trail. The Morgan trailhead is 2.8 miles south of the Ortega Highway on the South Main Divide Road (Killen Trail), which is accessed just east of El Cariso Station. The upper trailhead is in a grove of non-native Aleppo Pines. The upper part of the trail passes through Upper Chaparral characterized by Birchleaf Mountain Mahogany and California Scrub Oak. This scenic trail is perfect for a car shuttle. Along the way are Oak Woodland and granite boulders. The climb from the creek to a low ridge provides a scenic view of Sitton Peak. Three miles down the Morgan Trail is a junction with the Tenaja Falls Trail.

Lucas Canyon Trail. The trailhead is at the San Juan Fire Station. The trail begins at a locked gate on Forest Service Road 7S09, the Sitton Peak Road. The wilderness boundary is 2 miles up this

road, after which the trail drops into Lucas Canyon. The trail follows the canyon, crosses the creek, and climbs up to the Verdugo Trail. There are sweeping views and shady streamside areas along the way. Beyond the trail junction are Oak Flats and the 3.2-mile Bluewater Trail down to San Mateo Creek. A two-day backpack trip with a car shuttle might follow this route to the San Mateo Canyon Trail and exit at the Tenaja Falls or the Tenaja trailhead.

Tenaja Falls Trail. The trailhead can be reached by taking Clinton Keith Road west from Interstate 15 to Tenaja Road, turning right on Cleveland Forest Road (7S04) and going 5 miles (passing the Tenaja trailhead at 0.8 miles). An alternative route is via the South Main Divide Road south from the Ortega Highway 10.5 miles (passing the Wildomar Campground and off-highway vehicle area on the way). Parking is available year-round, and there is space available for horse trailers. The trail goes northward about 1.5 miles to Tenaja Falls, a spectacular sight when it is full of water. The trail continues northward to join the Morgan Trail, a total distance of 5.4 miles from the trailhead. This is also the trailhead for the San Mateo Canyon Trail, which follows San Mateo Creek.

Tenaja Trail. The trailhead is 0.8 miles from Tenaja Road on Cleveland Forest Road (7S04). From the trailhead it is 3.5 miles to Fisherman's Camp on the San Mateo Canyon Trail. This is a broad, gentle trail along shady Tenaja Creek through granitic boulders, Coast Live Oaks, Western Sycamores, and wildflowers in the spring.

San Mateo Canyon Trail. This is the premier trail in the San Mateo Canyon Wilderness. It follows San Mateo Creek through Oak Woodland, Riparian, and Grassland communities. The three major trailheads are off Cleveland Forest Road (7S04), all of which converge on Fisherman's Camp, a broad grassy area under Coast Live Oaks. The Fisherman's Camp Trail at 1.6 miles is the shortest but steepest access. Parking is available 2.4 miles from Tenaja Road.

Indian Potrero Trail. One route to this trail is to park at Caspers Park, cross the Ortega Highway, and take the road to Rancho Carillo and the trailhead. Permission to hike the two miles of county road may be obtained by calling Caspers Park. Another way is to park at the San Juan Fire Station and take the route to the Lucas Canyon Trail, go down Lucas Canyon to the Verdugo Trail, and then go south about a half mile to Rancho Carillo. From Rancho Carillo the

Fig. 1.7. Lone tree (Ronald H. Chilcote).

Fig. 1.8. Riparian Woodland in Hot Springs Canyon.

trail goes 5 miles to the Clark Trail, which crosses the San Mateo Canyon Trail in another 1.5 miles. Exit is by means of the Clark Trail or the San Mateo Canyon Trail.

In addition to these wilderness trails, the Trabuco Ranger District has a number of multiuse trails. These are single-track trails designed for hiking, mountain biking, and horseback riding. As described by the U.S. Forest Service, they are the following:

San Juan Loop. Access to this popular trail is at the parking lot across the street from the Candy Store on the Ortega Highway, 19 miles east of San Juan Capistrano. This is an easy 2-mile trail with only a 350-foot change in elevation. It loops along the edge of the Upper San Juan Campground through Riparian vegetation, Coast Live Oaks, and Chaparral and returns to the parking area. This trail also provides access to the Chiquito Trail and ultimately the San Juan Trail and Blue Jay Campground.

Chiquito Trail. This is the trail to Chiquito Basin and Lion Canyon, renowned for its oak groves and wildflowers in the spring. Lower access is from the San Juan Loop Trail, and the upper trailhead is on the North Main Divide Road (Long Canyon Road) just east of Blue Jay Campground. Total distance is 10.2 miles with an elevation change of 2,000 feet. When the stream is flowing, Chiquito Falls is a scenic highlight.

San Juan Trail. This is the primary access route to the trail system associated with San Juan Creek. The upper trailhead is at Blue Jay Campground and the lower trailhead is in Hot Springs Canyon 0.8 miles north of the San Juan Fire Station on the Ortega Highway. For the most part this trail travels through Chaparral and Coastal Sage Scrub, although the lower reaches in Hot Springs Canyon pass through a Riparian community lined with White Alders (fig. 1.8). Coast Live Oaks are scattered along the route, but for the most part this trail provides little shade. The San Juan waterfall is also viewed from this trail (fig. 3.4). It is known also as the Ortega Waterfall because it is also visible from the Ortega Highway. Most hikers choose to do a car shuttle, traveling downhill for nearly 12 miles from the Blue Jay Campground to the San Juan Hot Springs. The elevation change is 2,600 feet. An alternative route involves the Chiquito Trail and the Viejo Tie Trail, forming a loop that starts and ends at the San Juan Trail about 1.5 miles from the Blue Jay trailhead. There are several intersections with old trails along this route. Anyone traveling this trail should carry a recent map.

Falcon Trail. This is an easy half-mile crossover from the Falcon Group Camp to Blue Jay Campground.

Hot Springs Canyon Trail. This very challenging route is for the most part a cross-country trip and should not be attempted by anyone who is unaccustomed to boulder hopping and traversing unstable slopes. Viewing the waterfalls, considered the prettiest in the Santa Ana Mountains, may require two separate trips. The trail to a view point for the upper fall, a 3-mile round trip, begins on the Falcon Trail about halfway between the two campgrounds or, alternatively, at the upper San Juan trailhead below Blue Jay Campground. An experienced hiker might try the lower canyon, a 9-mile round trip, accessed by the road that leads off the Ortega Highway to the San Juan Trail. The trailhead is beyond the San Juan trailhead at the Lazy W Ranch, a church camp. Permission to cross the camp property may be requested by calling the phone number available from the Trabuco Ranger District. The goal of the hike would be to reach the lower Hot Springs waterfall, which has a 140-foot drop, the highest in the Santa Ana Mountains. This route, though rigorous, is claimed to be the prettiest in the area. It travels along and through the creek, which usually carries water, and is shaded by a substantial Riparian community. Poison Oak is abundant. At various places hikers must cross fractured metamorphic rock or slick granite.

Los Pinos Trail. This rugged trail runs along the ridge between Hot Springs Canyon and Trabuco Canyon. The upper trailhead is on North Main Divide Road (Long Canyon Road) at Los Pinos Saddle, 5.8 miles west of the Ortega Highway. This is also the upper trailhead for the Trabuco Canyon Trail. The lower trailhead is at the Lazy W Ranch church camp. Permission to cross the camp property may be requested by calling the phone number available from the Trabuco Ranger District. This 8.2-mile trail is best traversed from the top down using a car shuttle. Most of the route follows the ridgeline, where there are Coulter Pines and Big-cone Douglas Firs as well as Upper Chaparral characterized by Manzanitas. The lower part of the trail follows a brushy ridge between Cold Spring Canyon and a branch of Hot Springs Canyon.

Sitton Peak Trail. The lower trailhead is at the San Juan Fire Station. The trail to the peak is a dirt road (formerly a truck trail) that reaches the peak in about 8 miles. This is also the access route to the Lucas Canyon Trail. You can continue to the Verdugo Trail and Bear Canyon Trail to exit at the Candy Store on the Ortega Highway, a total distance of 12.5 miles. Most of this route is along ridges through Chaparral. Sitton Peak itself is composed of exfoliating granite.

El Cariso Nature Trail. This 1.2-mile loop is a self-guided nature trail that begins and ends at the El Cariso Fire Station on the Ortega Highway. It features sweeping views, an old mine, and the California Firefighters' Memorial.

Holy Jim Trail. This popular self-guided trail starts in Trabuco Canyon. It can be accessed via the dirt Trabuco Canyon Road 4.5 miles from Live Oak Canyon Road, which forks off El Toro Road at Cook's Corner. This trail follows Holy Jim Creek to a small waterfall at 2.8 miles, passing the remains of Holy Jim's old cabin and fig orchard. It continues to the Main Divide Truck Trail at 3.0 miles (Bear Spring is near this intersection). Hikers may continue along the road all the way to Santiago Peak, a round trip of 15 miles.

Trabuco Canyon Loop. Parking for the trail is 0.5 mile east of the Holy Jim parking lot. The trail follows upper Trabuco Creek through groves of White Alder, Coast Live Oak, California Bay Laurel, with its spicy odor, and a small grove of Madrones. At 1.8 miles it joins the West Horsethief Trail, which continues by means of switchbacks through Chaparral that at upper elevations consists of stands of Manzanita and California Lilac. It meets the Main Divide Road at 3.3 miles; here there are Coulter Pines and a few Big-cone Douglas Firs. It continues eastward 2.5 miles to Los Pinos Saddle. Here the Trabuco Canyon Trail heads back down to the West Horsethief Trail junction. The total mileage is about 10 miles for the whole loop. By means of a car shuttle this trail can be hiked starting at either end.

Ladd Canyon Trail. Although Ladd Canyon is accessible from the bottom by means of a short road that travels northwest from Silverado Canyon, much of the land in the canyon proper is privately owned. The Ladd Canyon Trail is a short round trip from the Main Divide Road to Ladd Canyon Spring at the upper end of Ladd Canyon. The trailhead is 0.5 mile east of the Eagle Road junction.

Silverado Road (Silverado Motorway). No longer classified as a road, this trail begins a quarter mile up the Maple Springs Road from the gate at the end of Silverado Canyon Road. It goes up the north side of Silverado Canyon to a road that runs along the Ladd Canyon Ridge. Taking that road eastward to the Main Divide Road and walking another 0.3 mile south one reaches the summit of

Bedford Peak, which, at 3,800 feet elevation, has grand views eastward toward Riverside County and westward to the Pacific Ocean. The round trip is 6.5 miles. Of particular interest along this route are outcrops of the Bedford Canyon formation (fig. 3.15), which at 150 million years of age is Orange County's oldest metamorphic rock.

The truck trails of the Trabuco Ranger District are primarily for access for Forest Service personnel and are blocked by locked gates, but they are available for biking, horseback riding, and hiking. These roads, for the most part, are along ridgelines. Therefore they pass primarily through Chaparral, and there is little shade. These multiuse trails are as follows:

Silverado Truck Trail. This trail, an abandoned road along the ridge south of Silverado Canyon, passes through private property at its lower end and is therefore largely inaccessible. At its upper end it is accessible from Maple Springs.

Fig. 1.9. Coast Live Oak in springtime (Ronald H. Chilcote).

Santiago Truck Trail. Unavailable to privately owned motor vehicles, this trail is accessed from the Modjeska Grade Road and runs along the ridgeline south of Modjeska Canyon, which technically is the upper end of Santiago Canyon. At its upper end it joins the old Joplin Trail, which extends to the saddle between Modjeska and Santiago Peaks. At 2.8 miles from the trailhead are the Vulture Crags, outcrops of conglomerate rock that are said to have once provided nesting sites for California Condors. Old Camp, the remains of an old mining camp, is down in the canyon 7.2 miles from the trailhead.

Harding Truck Trail. From the end of the paved road in Modjeska Canyon, at the Tucker Wildlife Sanctuary, there is a parking area to access this road, which leads 9.5 miles to the Main Divide Road at Maple Springs Road. From here there is access to Modjeska and Santiago Peaks via the Main Divide Road. About a mile up the road from the Sanctuary gate there is an access road down to Harding Canyon proper, a portion of the Orange County Modjeska Canyon Nature Preserve, where there is a primitive trail that leads up the creek to a small waterfall. This is a pleasant approximately 3-mile hike along a Riparian corridor marked by White Alders and Coast Live Oaks. A small pool below the waterfall could provide a cooling dip during hot weather.

Black Star Canyon Road. This gated road passes through private land at its lower end. If access is gained, this is a

Fig. 1.10. Main Divide Road. View of Santiago Peak from the south.

scenic traverse of the northern Santa Ana Mountains that joins the Main Divide Road near Beek's Place. To complete the traverse the route would travel down Skyline Drive to Corona, where access is also gated.

Roads in the national forest that are accessible from Orange County are few and may be closed during wet weather or during fire season. A phone call to the district office in Corona will produce information on the status of these roads. They are open to street-legal vehicles, mountain bikes, equestrians, and hikers. These U.S. Forest Service roads are as follows:

Main Divide Road. This road along the ridgeline of the Santa Ana Mountains (fig. 1.10) is accessible from the Ortega Highway at the El Cariso Ranger Station or by way of the Maple Springs Road in Silverado Canyon. The North Main Divide Road runs from the Ortega Highway to Beek's Place at the intersection of Skyline Drive. This road provides access to Blue Jay Campground and Falcon Group Camp as well as several of the trails mentioned above. It also provides access to several notable peaks (from south to north) including Santiago, Modjeska, Bald, Bedford, Pleasants, and Sierra Peaks. Most of the route is through Upper Chaparral and includes groves of Coulter Pine, Big-cone Douglas Fir, and Knobcone Pine. The South Main Divide Road from the Ortega Highway provides access to the Wildomar Campground and off-highway vehicle area as well as the San Mateo Canyon Wilderness trails mentioned above.

Maple Springs Road. This road starts at the gate in Silverado Canyon, 4.5 miles east of Santiago Canyon Road. It connects to the Main Divide Road 7.8 miles from the gate.

Camping is permitted only in authorized U.S. Forest Service campgrounds, many of which are subject to seasonal closures because of fire hazards or winter-weather maintenance. These campgrounds are the following:

Blue Jay. The largest and highest of the Trabuco District campgrounds, Blue Jay is often closed during winter months. Access is by means of the paved Main Divide Road, 5.1 miles west of the Ortega Highway near the El Cariso Ranger Station. A slightly shorter, also paved but steep route is by the Long Canyon Road, 3 miles from the Ortega Highway. At an elevation of 3,400 feet, there are 50 camp units and 5 group camps tucked in among Coast Live Oaks and Coulter Pines. Some Knobcone Pines have also been planted here. All amenities are available, and recreational vehicles up to 40 feet are accepted. The San Juan Trailhead is nearby, southeast of the campground.

Falcon. Three group campgrounds are available by reservation only. There is a winter-season closure. The Falcon Group camps are 0.5 miles west of the Blue Jay Campground. Parking for recreational vehicles is available.

El Cariso. The El Cariso campground has 24 units and 4 picnic sites. It is open year-round. There is room for recreational vehicles 17–20 feet in length. The south picnic area has 11 sites and is closed during the winter months.

Upper San Juan. This campground lies in a woodland of Coast Live Oaks along the Ortega Highway at 1,800 feet elevation. It has seasonal access for 18 camp sites, some of which will accept recreational vehicles to 32 feet in length.

Wildomar. This campground, at 2,400 feet elevation, has 12 camp units that cater primarily to persons who wish to use the nearby off-highway vehicle area. It is located on the South Main Divide Road about 6 miles from the Ortega Highway.

Seal Beach National Wildlife Refuge

The Seal Beach National Wildlife Refuge is operated as a partnership between the U.S. Fish and Wildlife Service and the Department of the Navy. It was established primarily as a refuge for the endangered Least Tern and the Light-footed Clapper Rail. It also provides refuge for Brown Pelicans, Peregrine Falcons, and Belding's Savannah Sparrow. It is located at the Seal Beach National Weapons Center on the Orange County line just north of Huntington Harbour. Access by the public is limited. The Seal Beach Visitor's Center has information and permits.

STATE LANDS

State Beaches

The state operates a number of popular beach parks in Orange County. It also manages several ecological reserves in which rare, threatened, and endangered species can find refuge. The beach parks are as follows:

Huntington State Beach. Extending from Beach Boulevard in Huntington Beach two miles south to the mouth of the Santa Ana River, this beach has its main vehicle access from Magnolia Street. Featuring a long sandy beach, it has a multiuse trail, a bicycle trail, volleyball courts, food concessions, and outdoor cold showers. Although this is a day-use facility, it is open until 10 PM and has 200 fire rings for nighttime ambience. It also contains a nesting sanctuary for the endangered Least Tern and the threatened Snowy Plover, two birds that nest directly on the sand. Nesting areas are closed to human intrusion during the breeding season.

Bolsa Chica State Beach. Located on Pacific Coast Highway north of Huntington Beach, this beach is connected to Huntington State Beach by a bike path and offers the opportunity for biking, skating, jogging, and surfing. It has food services, restrooms, and a lawn for picnicking. Camping is available for self-contained vehicles, and there are 200 fire rings. Bolsa Chica Ecological Reserve, an ideal site for bird watching, is across the highway.

Crystal Cove State Park. This park features three miles of coastline, wooded canyons, and coastal bluffs (fig. 1.11). It lies between Newport Beach and Laguna Beach, with its headquarters at Moro Canyon. Recently restored cliff-top cottages, dating to the 1920s, are available for rental by reservation, and a nearby restaurant offers dining with a view. The entire offshore intertidal area is an underwater nature reserve. Together with the Laguna Laurel Ecological Reserve, City of Irvine open space land in Shady Canyon, Bommer Canyon, and Quail Hill, and the county-managed Laguna Coast Wilderness Park, this is largest expanse of pristine Coastal Sage Scrub in Orange County. There are inland trails for hikers and mountain bikers and coastal trails for biking, jogging, or walking. The beaches are popular with sunbathers and picnickers, as well as scuba and skin divers.

Doheny State Beach. South of the Dana Point Marina, this beach has been a popular swimming and surfing spot for many years. It features a campground with 120 developed campsites. Its visitor center has aquariums that feature life in the intertidal zone. The privately managed educational facility known as the Ocean Institute is nearby at the northern end of the marina.

San Clemente State Beach. Off Pacific Coast Highway, near the south end of San Clemente, this beach has 157 campsites and 72 hookups for recreational vehicles. The 110-acre park has trails leading to a mile-long beach that is famous for body surfing. The park has a visitor center that emphasizes local history. It is housed in a restored 1930s cottage formerly used by the California Conservation Corps.

Fig. 1.11. Crystal Cove State Park (Ronald H. Chilcote).

San Onofre State Beach. Located off Interstate 5 south of San Clemente, this park lies on the Orange County-San Diego County line. There are two campgrounds. One of them (San Mateo) lies inland in a Riparian area along San Mateo Creek. The other (the Bluffs) is lined up along the old Pacific Coast Highway. The campgrounds have spaces for tent camping and recreational vehicles. There is a 1.5-mile trail that leads to the famous surfing beach known as the Trestles (named for the raised railroad tracks that run along its inland edge).

Chino Hills State Park. On the northern border of Orange County, this park runs from the Santa Ana River to Carbon Canyon, representing an important biological corridor that connects the Whittier Hills to the Santa Ana Mountains by means of a wildlife undercrossing that passes under State Highway 91 at Coal Canyon. The park features about 30 miles of protected habitat including Coastal Sage Scrub, Chaparral, Riparian Woodland, and Oak Woodland that contains Coast Live Oaks and one of the last remaining significant stands of California Black Walnut. Facilities include campgrounds, a picnic area, an equestrian staging area, a historic barn, and 60 miles of trails and fire roads. Most trails allow biking, horses, and hikers, but some trails are restricted to hikers. Pets are not allowed on the trails, but leashed dogs are welcome at Bane Canyon Road and McLean Overlook and in the campgrounds. The main entrance is off Highway 71 in the Chino Hills at 4721 Sapphire Road. A large fire in 2008 burned a large portion of this park.

Fig. 1.12. Newport Salt Marsh in Upper Newport Bay Nature Preserve.

Ecological Reserves

Established by the state legislature in 1968, state-managed ecological reserves are designed to protect rare plants, animals, and habitats, encourage education and scientific research, and allow recreational opportunities such as wildlife viewing and nature walking, while at the same time ensuring that these activities have no adverse effects. These reserves are as follows:

Upper Newport Bay Ecological Reserve. This reserve, operated by the California Department of Fish and Game, encompasses 752 acres of the upper bay (fig. 1.12, fig. 7.45). Adjacent to the reserve, the northwest corner of the upper bay, 140 acres of bluffs and Coastal Sage Scrub, is managed as a regional park by the county. Headquarters for the state ecological reserve are at Shellmaker Island, next to the Newport Dunes Waterfront Resort. Access is by Back Bay Road just north of Jamboree Boulevard. The Back Bay Science Center located there has a floating dock, outdoor holding tanks, and a nature trail. A new building with teaching/research facilities, a water-quality testing laboratory, and associated outdoor interpretive stations is being planned. A nesting platform for Ospreys was occupied by a mated pair that raised offspring in 2007. Over 200 species of birds are documented for the area, including rare species such as Light-footed Clapper Rails and Burrowing Owls. Habitats including Open Water, Mudflats, Salt Marsh, Freshwater Marsh, and Coastal Sage Scrub are all abundant here. Activities at the science center are geared to educational groups.

Volunteers handle thousands of people on weekend tours, and the Department of Fish and Game sharkmobile travels to local schools and libraries. Individuals have access to the southern shore of the bay by means of Back Bay Drive, which is a one-way drive eastward from Jamboree Boulevard to East Bluff Drive. Hikers, bicyclists, and photographers are welcome during daylight hours.

Bolsa Chica Ecological Reserve. With over 1,200 acres of wetlands, Bolsa Chica (fig. 1.13, fig. 7.44) is the largest "restored" wetland in southern California and one of the largest such projects ever undertaken. It is located on Pacific Coast Highway north of Huntington Beach, across the road from Bolsa Chica State Beach. With the completion in 2006 of a connection to the open sea that allows direct tidal flushing for the first time since 1899, it is anticipated that a full-scale salt marsh will repair itself with time. Meanwhile, as a work in progress, Bolsa Chica is home for hundreds of bird species including nesting Least Terns and Snowy Plovers. There is a 1.5-mile loop trail that provides close views of birds for photographers. The trails are also widely used by hikers and joggers. The Bolsa Chica Land Trust and Amigos de Bolsa Chica lead tours of the reserve on the first and third Saturday of each month. The Bolsa Chica Interpretive Center is located on Warner Avenue just east of Pacific Coast Highway. It is the starting point for a trail that leads along Outer Bolsa Bay to join the loop trail at the East Garden Grove–Wintersburg Channel. Bolsa Chica is also notable for its shell middens and mysterious "cogged stones" that testify to many years of habitation by local native Americans.

Fig. 1.13. Bolsa Chica estuary, featuring Pickleweed Marsh.

Laguna Laurel Ecological Reserve. This 76-acre reserve is contained within the borders of the 1,200-acre Laguna Coast Wilderness Park. The reserve was established primarily to protect the endemic Laguna Beach Dudleya (*Dudleya stolonifera*), which is state-listed as a threatened species. The trail starts at the Willow Canyon parking area near the intersection of El Toro and Laguna Canyon Roads. From there hikers can access Laurel Canyon, with its Grasslands, Oak Woodlands, and Riparian communities. During wet years a spectacular waterfall greets the hikers partway up the trail. A loop can be accomplished by returning through Willow Canyon, and access to the eastern end of Crystal Cove State Park is also possible.

Coal Canyon Ecological Reserve. This 953-acre reserve at the upper end of Coal Canyon on the north end of the Santa Ana Mountains is designed to protect the northernmost grove of Tecate Cypress (*Cupressus forbesii*). The trees of this grove, restricted to sandstone soils in a fog-bathed area of Upper Coal Canyon, are candidates for state listing as an endangered species (fig. 1.14). Access to this area is limited, but from time to time various agencies such as the Nature Conservancy lead tours. The lower end of Coal Canyon, formerly 663 acres of private land, was recently purchased by the state and added to Chino Hills State Park. This purchase and subsequent removal of the pavement in the undercrossing of the 91 freeway completed a very important corridor that now connects the Santa Ana Mountains to the Chino Hills, allowing wildlife such as Mule Deer and Mountain Lions to pass between these two areas of wildlife habitat. Access to this area may be provided by roads from the mouth of Coal Canyon as well as along the ridgeline north of Fremont Canyon and the North Main Divide Road of the Cleveland National Forest.

ORANGE COUNTY LANDS

County properties are managed by the County of Orange, Resources and Development Management Department, Orange County Parks (formerly known as the Department of Harbors, Beaches, and Parks). For management purposes county properties are divided into wilderness regional parks, natural regional parks, urban regional parks, nature preserves, regional beaches, coastal/tidelands properties, historic sites, and regional riding and hiking trails (a category that overlaps with trails managed by other agencies). As time passes, private reserves and mitigation lands are turned over to the county for management purposes. Often these become regional parks. As Orange County continues to be developed, new regional parks, particularly in the southern part of the county, will be authorized and opened for public use.

Wilderness Regional Parks

Wilderness regional parks are parks in which the land retains its primeval character with minimal improvements and is managed and protected to preserve natural processes. For the land to qualify as a wilderness park, the imprint of man's work must be substantially unnoticeable, it must have outstanding opportunities for solitude or a primitive and unconfined type of recreation, it must be of sufficient size as to make practicable its preservation and use in an

unimpaired condition, and it should contain ecological, geological, or other features of scientific, educational, scenic, or historical value. These regional parks are being expanded as private parcels are purchased or donated, adding to the total acreage in county hands. In addition, old landfills have been proposed as future parks. Included among these are properties in the Chino Hills (Olinda), Santiago Canyon, and south of the Ortega Highway (Prima Deshecha).

Residents of the City of Laguna Beach have voted to tax themselves in order to buy land that would form a greenbelt of relatively undisturbed land surrounding the town. By means of these purchases and land donated by various private entities such as the Irvine Company, a fairly complete Laguna

Fig. 1.14. Tecate Cypress in Coal Canyon Ecological Reserve. View down canyon toward Chino Hills State Park.

Fig. 1.15. The Laguna Greenbelt and nearby public lands.

Greenbelt (fig. 1.15) has been established in the San Joaquin Hills and includes the following entities: Aliso and Wood Canyons Wilderness Park, Laguna Coast Wilderness Park, Crystal Cove State Park, Laguna Laurel Ecological Reserve, and the Bommer Canyon/Shady Canyon Reserve (owned by the City of Irvine and managed by the Irvine Ranch Conservancy). The county's regional wilderness parks are the following:

Aliso and Wood Canyons Wilderness Park. This park is an approximately 3,300-acre U-shaped parcel that extends from Aliso Beach in South Laguna inland along Aliso Creek and Wood Canyon to include parkland

north of Alicia Parkway. Access to the park is from Alicia Parkway, Pacific Coast Highway, or Alta Laguna Park in Laguna Beach. More than 30 miles of trails along canyons and ridgelines are available for hikers, bicyclists, and equestrians. Ranger- and docent-led nature hikes are also available. Plant communities include Grasslands, Coastal Sage Scrub, Southern Oak Woodlands, and Riparian. The Orange County Natural History Museum, with its exhibits of fossils and natural history, is located near the Alicia Parkway entrance. At this entrance, the park is contiguous with Laguna Niguel Regional Park, a county urban park that has a fair-sized lake. Of special interest is the Fossil Reef or Pecten Reef, a paleontological area featuring 17-million-year-old marine seashells (Pectens). This limestone-rich shell reef is located just west of Laguna Hills on Alicia Parkway. Also of geological interest is the Topanga Sandstone, with numerous caves in which important native American artifacts have been found.

Laguna Coast Wilderness Park. This park lies north of Laguna Canyon Road (Highway 133) and is divided into four parts that straddle Crystal Cove State Park, Laguna Canyon Road, and Highway 73. It surrounds the Laurel Laurel Ecological Reserve and is contiguous with the Aliso and Wood Canyons Wilderness Park (fig. 1.16). Many miles of trails are available for hikers, bikers, and equestrians. Nature hikes led by park rangers and docents are periodically available. Of special interest are the Laguna Lakes (fig. 1.17), Orange County's only natural lakes and the source of the name "Laguna Canyon." The waterfall in Laurel Canyon is spectacular during the rainy season. It is one of Orange County's important preserves for native plant communities such as Grasslands, Riparian, Southern Oak Woodland, and Coastal Sage Scrub. It is a popular area for birders. Parking for a fee is available at three access points: one south of the intersection of El Toro and Laguna Canyon Roads, one on the east side of Highway 133 just north of Highway 73, and one at the James and Rosemary Nix Nature Center west of Highway 133 near the Laguna Lakes. The award-winning nature center features interactive displays and interpretive panels about the park's wildlife, plant communities, and native Americans. A fourth parking area, particularly for equestrian access, is on the north side of the road in Laguna Canyon at the "Big Bend."

Fig. 1.16. Entrance to Laurel Canyon.

Caspers Wilderness Park. At 8,003 acres, this is our largest county park and probably comes closest to representing a true wilderness park (fig. 1.18). It is largely roadless but has more than 35 miles of trails available for hikers, bikers, and equestrians. In addition, there is a large campground with campsites for tents, recreational vehicles, groups, and equestrians. The campsites are arranged among large Oak and Sycamore trees that can provide shade from the summer sun. There are also picnic areas and playgrounds available for day use. The nature center has a fine display of natural history information, including stuffed animals and tips on how to recognize footprints. There are ranger- and docent-led hikes, and during peak season there are campfire programs. The de facto natural areas are extended by virtue of this park's proximity to the Audubon Society's Starr Ranch Sanctuary in Bell Canyon. During the rainy season a seasonal stretch of San Juan Creek fills with water, adding a scenic touch to the surroundings. Proposed additions to this park would include adjacent portions of San Juan Canyon and Hot Springs Canyon with San Juan Hot Springs. Native plant communities include Riparian, Southern Oak Woodland, Coastal Sage Scrub, and Chaparral. The entrance is on the Ortega Highway 7.5 miles east of San Juan Capistrano.

Figure 1.17 Laguna vernal lake (Ronald H. Chilcote).

Fig. 1.18. Caspers Wilderness Park.

Limestone-Whiting Wilderness Park.
This 4,169-acre park is situated adjacent
to the Cleveland National Forest and lies
between Portola Parkway and Santiago
Canyon Road (fig. 1.19). The park features
spectacular Oak Woodlands, Riparian, and
Chaparral plant communities. Among
its most notable features are picturesque
red sandstone cliffs, representative
of the Sespe Formation, in Red Rock
Canyon and the Sinks. The trails are
available for hikers and equestrians but
are particularly favored by mountain
bikers. Ranger- and docent-led hikes
and trail rides are scheduled periodically.
Public parking is available at the corner
of Portola and Alton Parkways.

**General Thomas F. Riley Wilderness
Park.** Located at the intersection of Oso
Parkway and Coto de Caza Drive, this
548-acre park features 5 miles of multiuse
trails and has a small visitor center, a self-
guided nature trail, and a butterfly garden.
Ranger-guided tours and programs are
available. The park boasts two seasonally
flowing creeks and plant communities
such as Southern Oak Woodland, Riparian,
Grassland, and Coastal Sage Scrub.

Weir Canyon Wilderness Park. This
224-acre park includes hilltop open space
and an oak-filled canyon (fig. 1.20). Its
trails connect it to Santiago Oaks and
Irvine Regional Parks. In the future

Fig. 1.19. Limestone Canyon, Limestone–Whiting Ranch Wilderness Park (Ronald H. Chilcote).

the park is planned to extend beyond Highway 241 all the way to Chino Hills State Park and the Coal Canyon Ecological Reserve. Trails are available to hikers, mountain bikers, and equestrians. The most convenient access is through either Santiago Oaks or Irvine Park.

Natural Regional Parks

Natural regional parks feature predominantly aesthetic and passive types of activities such as picnicking, camping, nature study, and hiking. There may be limited facilities for organized recreation. Necessary utilities are available, but the areas have been left as natural as possible in recognition of the fact that natural topography and biological resources are the principal attractions of each park. These natural parks are the following:

Irvine Regional Park. Although it is classified as a natural regional park, only about half of the 477 acres of this park are maintained in a natural state (fig. 1.21). Nevertheless, this is a very old, well-established park with mature landscaping. It caters to family picnics and outings. There are good opportunities for birding. There are grassy areas, picnic areas, ball fields, playgrounds, a nature center, a zoo, a small railroad, and a lake with boats to rent and fishing opportunities. There is a bicycle rental facility and a stables where horses can be rented. The western part of the park, on a hillside, is the natural part of the park. Plant communities include Southern Oak Woodland, Coastal Sage Scrub, and Riparian (along Santiago Creek, although it is dry most of the year because it is just below the dam at Irvine Lake). Trails connect the park to Santiago Oaks Regional Park and Weir Canyon Wilderness Park. The entrance to the park is just north of the intersection of Chapman Avenue and Santiago Canyon Road.

Santiago Oaks Regional Park. Located north of Katella Avenue along Santiago Creek, this 840-acre park is mostly natural but includes picnic facilities, play areas, and a nature center. Miles of trails available to hikers, mountain bikers, and equestrians wind through Coast Live Oaks, Sycamores, and Coastal Sage Scrub. Trails connect the park to Irvine and Weir Canyon Regional Parks.

Peters Canyon Regional Park. This 340-acre natural park lies southwest of the intersection of Santiago Canyon and Jamboree Roads. Access is from Jamboree Road. The 55-acre Peters Canyon Reservoir is an important stopover for migratory birds. There are also many resident birds, making this park especially popular for birders. There is a picnic area and a 2-mile-long canyon nature trail that is available for hiking, mountain biking, or horseback riding. Some portions of the trail system are fairly steep.

O'Neill Regional Park. This large park is located along Trabuco Creek (Arroyo Trabuco) and Las Tijeras Creek. Nestled among Coast Live Oaks are a campground, picnic areas, and a nature center. The park includes 3,200 acres of natural plant communities (fig. 1.22) and only 134 acres of developed facilities. The extensive trail system is available for mountain biking, hiking, and horseback riding. This is a roughly circular park that surrounds a private golf course. It has access from Antonio Parkway or Alicia Parkway, with the main entrance off Live Oak Canyon Road 2 miles east of El Toro Road. There are ranger- and docent-led nature hikes and rides.

Fig. 1.20. Oak Woodland in Weir Canyon.

Fig. 1.21. Natural slope featuring Coastal Sage Scrub in Irvine Regional Park.

Featherly Regional Park. This 357-acre natural park is located along the Santa Ana River in one of the few sections that has not been channelized or lined with concrete. It is composed of fairly pristine Riparian habitat featuring native Sycamores, Willows, and Fremont Cottonwoods. There is a trail system available for bicycles, horses, or hikers. A 63-acre portion of the park near the Gypsum Canyon Road bridge is a privately operated park catering to recreational vehicles. Access is from Highway 91 at Gypsum Canyon near the intersection with Highway 241.

Harriett M. Wieder Regional Park. This is a park in progress. It consists of 106 acres that lie between Bolsa Chica State Beach and Huntington Beach Central Park. It overlooks the Bolsa Chica Ecological Reserve. A portion has been developed as a play park. Hiking and picnicking are available.

Urban Regional Parks

Urban regional parks are located within an urban area, but they provide a wide variety of activities such as sport centers, playing fields, golf courses, riding and hiking trails, bikeways, and swimming. Their principal attractions are man-made, but they provide opportunity for passive activities such as bird watching, educational exhibits, picnicking, and camping. These urban parks are the following:

Fig. 1.22. Coast Live Oaks and Western Sycamores in O'Neill Regional Park.

Carbon Canyon Regional Park. This park is located adjacent to Chino Hills State Park at the mouth of Carbon Canyon. Access is from the south side of Carbon Canyon Boulevard. Of its 115 acres, 40 acres, mostly on the south side of Carbon Creek, are maintained in a natural state. It has a nature trail, a redwood grove, and 12 picnic shelters. The 4-acre fishing lake also contains a population of the threatened native Western Pond Turtle.

Ralph B. Clark Regional Park. This park is located on both sides of Rosecrans Avenue at the edge of the Coyote Hills in northern Buena Park and western Fullerton. Twelve of its 112 acres are maintained as natural. There are trails in the natural area of the Elephant and Camel Hills that offer good views of the San Gabriel Mountains. One of the park's most important features is the Clark Interpretive Center, which showcases the fossils of vertebrate animals that once inhabited northern Orange County. It also has a 3-acre fishing lake and seven picnic shelters.

Craig Regional Park. This 124-acre park is located behind Fullerton Dam. It is a green oasis among rolling hills surrounded by urbanized portions of Brea and Fullerton. It has opportunities for birding and picnicking. There are nine picnic shelters and a 3-acre fishing lake. There is a small trail area north of the dam.

Laguna Niguel Regional Park. This park is located along Sulfur Creek and lies between Alicia Parkway and La Paz Road just north of Crown Valley Parkway.

Of its 228 acres of rolling hills, 103 are maintained as natural habitat. One of its dominant features is a 47-acre reservoir that has a commercial fishing concession. More than 3 miles of trails are available for mountain biking and hiking. The park's location across Alicia Parkway from the Aliso and Wood Canyons Wilderness Park provides the opportunity for extended hikes and rides.

Mason Regional Park. This 344-acre park lies in the City of Irvine at the intersection of Culver and University Drives. Within its 3-mile length is a 1-mile stretch of restored habitat. The 70 acres of natural habitat feature native vegetation such as Coastal Sage Scrub. There are six picnic shelters. Other attractions include a lake and a golf course.

Mile Square Regional Park. Located in Fountain Valley between Euclid and Brookhurst Avenues, this park is primarily devoted to active sports. There is a 4-mile-long perimeter path that offers opportunities for hiking, riding, and birding. Twenty-three of the park's 640 acres are undeveloped as a nature area.

Yorba Regional Park. This linear park is located in east Anaheim between a concrete-lined portion of the Santa Ana River and La Palma Avenue. It is composed of 175 acres of greenery, 35 of which are considered natural. There are 21 picnic shelters and four small lakes available for fishing. Access to the Santa Ana River riding and hiking trail is one of its most important features.

Nature Preserves

Preserves are county lands set aside primarily to protect natural resources. They feature interpretive programs and supervised recreational activities such as nature walks. Scientific research opportunities are also available. The preserves managed by the county are as follows:

Modjeska Canyon Nature Preserve.
This 689-acre parcel lies at the end of Modjeska Canyon Road, which technically is in Santiago Canyon. It is adjacent to the Tucker Wildlife Sanctuary and is surrounded on three sides by the Cleveland National Forest. The preserve includes portions of Modjeska and Harding Canyons. It is dedicated to the protection of Lower Chaparral, Coastal Sage Scrub, Southern Oak Woodland, and Riparian communities. Hiking and nature study are available. The preserve is open to the public by reservation only.

Talbert Nature Preserve. This 211-acre elongate preserve is located along the south side of the channelized Santa Ana River in Costa Mesa, not far from the river mouth. A self-guided trail is available for walking and bicycle riding. Picnicking and nature study are encouraged. The vegetation has been re-created to represent six different landscape types that reflect changing conditions along the river: Coastal Strand, Native Grassland, Alluvial Woodland, Wetlands, Border Plantings, and Intensive Use.

Upper Newport Bay Nature Preserve. This preserve lies along Upper Newport Bay in the City of Irvine just west of Jamboree Road. Access is from University Drive southeast of the intersection with Irvine Avenue. The preserve is made up of 134 acres adjacent to the California Department of Fish and Game Ecological Reserve. Natural communities consist primarily of Grassland and Coastal Sage Scrub. Trails along the bluffs are available for bicycles, hikers, and birders and offer panoramic views of southern California's largest estuary and Salt Marsh complex. A highlight of the preserve is the Peter and Mary Muth Interpretive Center which features multimedia nature exhibits and interpretive programs including nature walks, canoe and kayak tours, and campfire programs.

Regional Beaches

County beaches have been established and maintained to provide opportunities for swimming, wading, surfing, and sunbathing. They include the tidelands as well as the adjacent sandy shore and bluffs. County marine life refuges are usually components of these beaches. The regional beaches are as follows:

Aliso Beach. This 38-acre beach park consists of 1.5 miles of sandy beach, rocky headlands, and the mouth of Aliso Creek (fig. 1.23). It includes Thousand Steps Beach and the adjacent shoreline, accessible by staircase from Pacific Coast Highway in South Laguna. It is the coastal portion of a large area of public land that includes the Aliso and Wood Canyons Wilderness Park.

Fig. 1.23. Aliso Beach.

Salt Creek Beach County Park. This 18-acre park includes a mile of shoreline at one of Orange County's premium surfing spots. On the bluff above the beach is a small park with a lawn and picnic areas. Access is from Pacific Coast Highway north of Dana Point at the intersection of Niguel Road, near the Ritz-Carlton Hotel.

Capistrano Beach. Located south of Dana Point and Doheny State Beach, this park includes a 1/3-mile stretch of sandy beach that is accessible from Pacific Coast Highway. The beach lies on the coastal side of a row of houses.

Sunset Beach. North of Bolsa Chica State Beach, on the coastal side of the community of Sunset Beach, lies about a mile of sandy beach that belongs to Orange County. It is accessible at the end of Warner Avenue and is available for most passive beach activities.

Regional Riding and Hiking Trails

County trails are located in areas that are made accessible to the public by various managing agencies. Included are 348 miles of existing and proposed trails available for horseback riding, bicycling, and hiking. The concept is to provide links to many natural areas throughout the county. A complete list and a map is available from the county. A list of existing and proposed bikeways is also available.

PRIVATELY MANAGED PARKS, RESERVES, AND CONSERVANCIES

Several thousand acres of private property in Orange County have been set aside in some form of preserved status. In 1996 a cooperative agreement was signed between regulatory agencies, local governments, and land developers in central and coastal Orange County guaranteeing that a certain amount of land would remain in its natural state in exchange for permits to develop other parcels. This open-space conservation program takes the form of a habitat conservation plan (HCP, federal) or natural community conservation plan (NCCP, state), which philosophically is supposed to be based on a multispecies conservation format. For the most part, these plans constitute large-scale mitigation programs that enable developers to build on sensitive habitat in exchange for protecting or restoring degraded lands.

In most terrestrial habitats a developer must restore 1.5 acres for every acre that is developed. Often this consists of purchasing a parcel of degraded property such as an overgrazed pasture and converting it to a native plant community. In wetlands, every dewatered acre must be replaced by 3 acres of restored wetland. Rather than following the multispecies concept, however, these restored communities are usually designed to provide habitat for a single legally threatened or endangered species. It would be virtually impossible to restore a community to its full complement of producers, consumers,

and decomposers, and no attempt has yet been made to do so. When mitigation projects fail, it is usually because the restored habitat was not monitored.

Another form of mitigation is for a developer to purchase additional acres of previously unprotected private land in exchange for development rights on a portion of the original site. The Orange County Central and Coastal NCCP includes a portion of this type of mitigation. The idea, of course, is to increase the net benefit to conservation, with an emphasis on threatened habitats and priority species, while allowing some development of private property. After dedication, much of this acreage is turned over to various agencies, some public and some private for management purposes. The Orange County Central and Coastal NCCP/HCP set up a nonprofit organization called the Nature Reserve of Orange County (NROC) to coordinate and monitor implementation. The plan for the southern part of the county, which was signed in 2007, is still in progress. The NROC coordinates land management for the 38,000-acre reserve system of central and coastal Orange County. The reserves are as follows:

Irvine Ranch Wildlands and Parks. Of the original 93,000 acres of the privately owned Irvine Ranch, over half is now in some form of preserved status. Formerly known as the Irvine Ranch Land Reserve, more than 2,000 acres are currently managed as private conservation easements and private reserves, part of 50,000 acres of protected open space on the old Irvine Ranch. Also a part of the historic Irvine Ranch are several Orange

County regional parks, a state park, a state ecological reserve, and the City of Irvine Open Space Preserve. In 2006, the National Park Service designated 37,000 acres of the reserve the Irvine Ranch National Natural Landmark.

An umbrella organization known as the Irvine Ranch Conservancy, formerly known as the Irvine Ranch Land Trust, is a private, nonprofit land management organization that oversees 34,000 acres, the largest portion of the dedicated Irvine Ranch land. This includes 9,000 acres that is or will eventually be part of the City of Irvine Open Space Preserve. Much of the land, including Limestone and Weir Canyons, was formerly managed by the Nature Conservancy, another private nonprofit conservation agency, under contract to the Irvine Company. Some of these properties have been offered irrevocably to Orange County for future public ownership as regional parks. Lands adjacent to Laguna Coast Wilderness Park, such as Shady Canyon, Bommer Canyon, and Quail Hill,

were managed by the Nature Conservancy and now are in the City of Irvine Open Space Preserve. Other lands such as Fremont Canyon (fig. 1.24), Blind Canyon, and parts of Loma Ridge are managed today by the Irvine Ranch Conservancy and are protected under legal "conservation easements" held by the Nature Conservancy. These conservation easements are not part of the Nature Reserve of Orange County but through the easements have been placed under a permanent state of preservation. Much of the Irvine Ranch Conservancy's stewardship is focused on fire management, carnivore conservation, and restoration of sensitive natural habitats such as Coastal Sage Scrub, Native Grasslands, Oak Woodlands, and Riparian plant communities. Among the restoration methods are exclusion of non-native grazing animals, removal of invasive non-native plants, and active replanting of native species. Public access to these lands is limited to free docent-led tours for hikers, bikers, or equestrians. Programs for children, birders, and artists are also available.

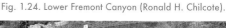
Fig. 1.24. Lower Fremont Canyon (Ronald H. Chilcote).

Windy Ridge Road. This gated preserve is accessible from below and above Irvine Regional Park by permission only. The road traverses a ridgeline north of Fremont Canyon with views down to Highways 241 and 91. It eventually connects to the Main Divide Road near Beek's Place, after passing lateral access roads that travel through Weir Canyon, Gypsum Canyon, Coal Canyon, and Black Star Canyon. Highlights along the way include the Tecate Cypress forest and Sierra Peak. The Nature Conservancy has a conservation easement to much of the land along this road; part of it is a proposed regional wilderness park, and guided access is available from time to time.

San Joaquin Wildlife Sanctuary. With over 300 acres of wetlands and 10 miles of hiking trails, this is an important sanctuary dedicated to the preservation and restoration of habitat for migratory birds and other wildlife. Trails are located on the shores of

several ponds that are bordered by natural and restored Riparian vegetation. It is managed and owned by the Irvine Ranch Water District. Information offices, avian research projects, and educational programs are funded and staffed by the Sea and Sage Chapter of the National Audubon Society. Located next to San Diego Creek near the intersection of Campus and University Drives in the City of Irvine, access is from Riparian View Drive off Michelson Avenue. Facilities at the parking area include Audubon House, which has a bookstore, a small museum/library, and an office staff. Trails in the area are only for foot traffic. The Duck Club is a large room that is available for meetings and banquets.

Starr Ranch Sanctuary. This facility, located along Bell Canyon (fig. 1.25) in the foothills of the Santa Ana Mountains, is adjacent to Caspers Wilderness Park. It is a 4,000-acre site owned and operated by the Audubon Society and dedicated to scientific research

Fig. 1.25. Riparian Woodland in Bell Canyon.

Fig. 1.26. San Joaquin Marsh.

on the biology and conservation of the local natural ecosystems. In particular, pristine Riparian, Southern Oak Woodland, and Coastal Sage Scrub plant communities are preserved here. Programs through the local universities and researchers are encouraged. Research internships for college-level students are available. Access is controlled in order to preserve sensitive study areas. General hiking, mountain biking, motorized vehicles, and equestrian use are not permitted. However, there is a public educational program associated with the Starr Ranch Field Ecology Program. Classes and special events such as family nature workshops and Natural History Day are advertised through the local media and the Friends of the Starr Ranch newsletter.

San Joaquin Freshwater Marsh Reserve. Part of the University of California's natural reserve system, the 202-acre San Joaquin Marsh (fig. 1.26) is managed by the University of California at Irvine. Historically what was known as "the marsh" included the present San Joaquin Wildlife Sanctuary as well as what is now the San Joaquin Freshwater Marsh Reserve. The two facilities are divided by Campus Drive. The present marsh is operated to enhance research and educational programs through the university. Public access to the reserve requires a permit obtained from the university.

Tucker Wildlife Sanctuary. This facility near the end of Modjeska Canyon Road is operated by the College of Life Sciences and Mathematics of California State University at Fullerton. The 12-acre facility is adjacent to the Cleveland National Forest and the Modjeska Canyon Nature Preserve. It has hiking trails, a picnic area, a small museum, a gift shop and visitor center, and an observation porch and feeding station for bird watching. The facility lies in a zone of overlapping plant communities, including Riparian, Southern Oak Woodland, Coastal

Fig. 1.27. Chamise Chaparral in Tucker Wildlife Sanctuary.

Sage Scrub, and Lower Chaparral (fig. 1.27). Its gardens also showcase drought-tolerant plants from Mediterranean regions of the world. It is operated as a research center for university students and faculty but is open to the public on a donations basis. Personnel are available to lead prearranged tours. It is widely used for educational field trips for students of all ages. It is also the point of origin for the Harding Truck Trail, which is available for hiking, mountain biking, and equestrian use.

Oak Canyon Nature Center. The City of Anaheim operates this 58-acre nature center in the Anaheim Hills. It has a permanent stream, Southern Oak Woodland, and Coastal Sage Scrub habitats. Vehicles and horses are prohibited, but its 4 miles of trails are available for hikers and educational groups. The John J. Collier Interpretive Center and Museum feature a bird-feeding station and live exhibits. Group tours and outreach programs are available. Access to the facility is from Highway 91 at Imperial Highway, south to Nohl Canyon Road, left (east) to Walnut Canyon Road, and left again to the nature center.

Environmental Nature Center. This is a 3.5-acre man-made natural area located at 1601 16th Street just off Dover Drive in Newport Beach. It features a fascinating combination of 15 California native plant communities, wildlife habitat, and walking trails. A professional staff provides the community with natural science and social science educational programs that are experienced by some 12,000 students. The new 8,500- square-foot "green" building is the first LEED Platinum certified building in Orange County, using natural ventilation, organic materials, low water usage, and its own on-site solar energy production. The museum and bookstore feature California's biodiversity and a life-size native American Tongva dwelling.

Donna O'Neill Land Conservancy. Formerly known as the Rancho Mission Viejo Conservancy, this is a 1,200-acre wilderness reserve operated by part-time staff of the Rancho Mission Viejo Company, the City of San Clemente, and Orange County. It was established as part of the mitigation for development on the historic Rancho Mission Viejo. There are plans to expand it significantly to form a much larger "reserve system." Located in the foothills of the Santa Ana Mountains in the San Mateo drainage south of the Ortega Highway, this reserve protects habitats such as native Grasslands, Coastal Sage Scrub, and Southern Oak Woodlands (fig. 1.28). Conservancy programs such as slide shows, hikes, and nature walks are available by reservation to the general public, members, and educational groups. Access is through a locked gate on the Ortega Highway about 3 miles east of San Juan Capistrano.

Huntington Beach Central Park. At 356 acres, this is the largest city-owned park in Orange County. It spans both sides of Golden West Street between Slater and Ellis Streets. Amenities include the Huntington Central Library, a large lake, 6 miles of paved trails, and additional dirt trails, as well as ball fields and other activity centers. Eighteen acres are devoted to the Shipley Nature Center, a natural area with paths and educational programs. There are opportunities for picnics, walking, and jogging. There are expansive lawn areas and a large lake. This is a very popular area for urban birders. The Eucalyptus trees provide winter roosts for migrating Monarch Butterflies.

Laguna Lake Park. Originally established in 1916 as a water source for irrigation of citrus trees, this small park in the City of Fullerton has a lake that is visited by many species of migratory birds including Wood Ducks. It is a tree-lined refuge from the surrounding urban environment. In 2004 this park was in the news as the home for the 200-pound Alligator Snapping Turtle known as Old Bob.

West Coyote Hills Nature Preserve. This 352-acre preserve on Chevron/Texaco property in the City of Fullerton is a work in progress. It is part of a development in the Coyote Hills. When completed it will include miles of trails and the 72-acre Robert E. Ward Nature Center. The Coyote Hills are an important natural area characterized by Coastal Sage Scrub. The staging area for equestrian use is located on Euclid Avenue west of Laguna Lake Park.

Olinda Oil Museum and Historical Trail. The City of Brea has established this facility in a housing tract across the road from the Carbon Canyon Regional Park. The parking area, museum, and the trailhead are off Santa Fe Avenue. The trail features historical displays and active oil wells on land associated with an oil field owned by Santa Fe Energy, a subsidiary of the Santa Fe Railroad. The trail, which is about 2 miles long, passes through Coastal Sage Scrub and Riparian plant communities and offers excellent views of Carbon Canyon and Chino Hills State Park. It is a good place to learn about the local geology, although much of the park burned in 2008.

Fig. 1.28. Native Grassland and Oak Woodland in Donna O'Neill Land Conservancy.

Niguel Botanical Preserve. This is an 18-acre botanical garden complete with specialty gardens and guided trails. It is located in Crown Valley Community Park in the City of Laguna Niguel. Access to the preserve is off Crown Valley Parkway near the intersection of Niguel Road.

Orange County Great Park. Still in its planning stages, eventually this park will replace the old El Toro Marine Corps Air Station with about 3,000 acres of public land, a portion of which has been designated a national wildlife reserve to be managed by the U.S. Fish and Wildlife Service. The City of Irvine is taking leadership in the development of this park, which will include sports complexes and restored natural areas. Of interest to nature lovers will be a botanical garden and a 2-mile-long "great canyon" planted with native trees and Mediterranean ornamentals. It will include pedestrian/bicycle paths and a perennial stream with a string of small pools. The "natural" portion of the park will include a 3-mile-long wildlife corridor that is designed to provide an important link between the parks of the Laguna Greenbelt and those in the foothills of the Santa Ana Mountains. Included in this design is what will be known as the Bee Creek Wetlands, a large pool and percolating basin for recapture and natural cleansing of the water. This wetland will be designed to attract wetland birds and should be an important facility for birders and educational field trips.

Trust for Public Land. This private conservation organization acquires parcels of private land and holds them as preserves or donates them to public agencies for management. Often these parcels are adjacent to lands that already are in public hands. Examples of these purchases include parcels in the following areas: Boat Canyon in Laguna Beach (61 acres), Porter Ranch, adjacent to Cleveland National Forest (113 acres), Fremont Canyon, next to Irvine Regional Park and the Nature Conservancy conservation easement (475 acres), and Black Star Canyon (194 acres), Harding Canyon (302 acres), and Baker Canyon (640 acres), all adjacent to the Cleveland National Forest.

Ocean Institute. This educational facility is located at the north end of Dana Point Harbor. It includes a maritime center and an 8-acre natural intertidal ecosystem. The institute sponsors educational programs for K–12 students on site, as well as trips aboard its research vessel and a replica of Richard Henry Dana's tall ship *Pilgrim*. The facility also operates a residential camp in Hot Springs Canyon where students learn firsthand about the out-of-doors.

These, then, are Orange County's wild places, preserved through thoughtful leadership so that county residents, present and future, will have access to an understanding of the way natural systems work—the way things fit together in the great scheme of life and life processes. The following chapters will present a natural history of these places, describing their important plant and animal communities against the background of their landforms and climatic conditions.

Fig. 1.29. Spring wildflowers in the wilderness reserve adjacent to the Orange County Great Park (Jerry Burchfield).

Chapter 2

Ecological Principles

Orange County lies in a region of Mediterranean climate. A Mediterranean climate is characterized by winter precipitation and long, hot, dry summers. The name refers to a similar climate that occurs in the region of the Mediterranean Sea in southwestern Europe and northwestern Africa. Other regions of the world with similar climates are in southwestern Africa, southwestern Chile, and southwestern Australia—in other words, regions at similar latitudes in the southwestern portions of every continent of the world. That is why many common horticultural plants from those countries can become naturalized locally and may even be viewed as "invasive exotics" among our native species. It also explains why many of our native plants are grown in those other countries as well.

CLIMATE AND WEATHER

A Mediterranean climate is produced by a combination of latitude and proximity to a cold ocean current. Orange County lies at about 33° north latitude, which is just north

of a belt of dry air that circles the globe. This belt of dry air is caused by predictable planetary air circulation in which air rises at the equator and descends at about 30° north and south of the equator. Moist equatorial air rises to higher elevations where cool temperatures cause condensation that leads to precipitation. This causes a belt of heavy rainfall at the equator. The opposite occurs where the air returns to earth at about 30° north and south latitude. The air is warmed as it descends, causing evaporation. Many deserts are located along this belt. These wet and dry belts move north and south with the seasons. When it is summer in the northern hemisphere and the sun is high in the sky, the wet belt moves northward so that southern Florida, at about 25° north latitude, gets lots of summer rain, a condition known as a Monsoon climate. At the same time, the dry belt moves over southern California, making summers here predictably dry. During winter in the northern hemisphere the sun moves to a more southerly position, low in the sky, at which time the southern-hemisphere dry belt moves over Chile and South Africa, causing their hot, dry summers. The southward movement of the belts allows the northern Pacific storms to move farther south, with the result that it rains in southern California during the winter.

Ocean currents along the western sides of continental landmasses move toward the equator and away from the poles. Thus, the seawater off the coast of California

Fig. 2.1. Winter snow.

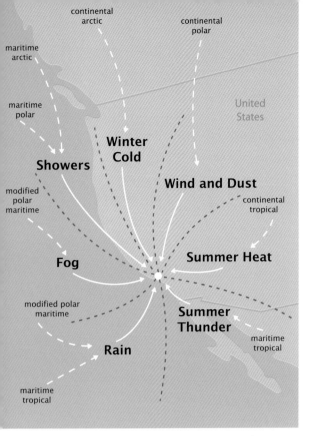

Winter Cold

Showers

Wind and Dust

Fog

Summer Heat

Summer Thunder

Rain

continental
arctic

continental
polar

maritime
arctic

United
States

maritime
polar

modified
polar
maritime

continental
tropical

modified polar
maritime

maritime
tropical

maritime
tropical

Fig. 2.2. Weather and precipitation patterns. Arrows indicate the direction and source of different weather conditions and seasons for the southern part of California. After H.P. Body. 1966. *Weather in Southern California*. University of California Press.

has come from Alaska, where it was chilled. When moist air passes over cool water, the water vapor in the air is chilled, and a cloud (fog) forms near the surface, particularly during the warmer times of the year. Orange County, therefore, also has a maritime climate, one that is influenced by the ocean. Because the water temperature of the ocean varies little, the air temperatures over the nearby land also are moderated. As a result Orange County experiences fairly high humidity and moderate temperature fluctuations on a daily and yearly basis. In contrast, Riverside County, just east of the Santa Ana Mountains, has fairly dry air and marked temperature fluctuations.

Average precipitation for various locations in Orange County is about 12 inches per year, a desert-like amount of rain. The reason that the area is not a desert is that relative humidity is usually high and temperature fluctuations are moderate. Average low temperatures are around 50°F and average high temperatures in the low to middle 70s. The range of fluctuation is only around 20°F, whereas deserts have cold nights, hot days, and extreme variations in temperature both daily and seasonally. With increased elevation and distance from the sea, temperatures become more extreme and precipitation increases. Precipitation in the mountains averages about 25 inches per year, and above an elevation of about 5,000 feet snow is common (fig. 2.1). Water temperature in Orange County varies from the 60s in the winter to the 70s in the summer, and the overnight temperature does not change significantly.

SEASONS

It is important to distinguish between "climate" and "weather." "Climate" refers to variations in temperature and precipitation that occur in predictable seasonal patterns, whereas "weather" refers to daily changes (fig. 2.2). Some people are of the opinion that we have no seasons in southern California. Our seasons do not follow the traditional pattern popularized in the old-time natural history literature, whose authors were based in the northeastern United States. They do follow a predictable pattern based on major movement of air masses. As air

Fig. 2.3. Spring fog over Orange County. Saddleback projects above fog in foreground.

heats up in the desert it rises and draws air in from the coast. This moist marine air causes fog to move over the coast and up against the coastal side of the mountains, a pattern that we associate with spring fog and summer smog. The long periods of daylight in the summer "burn off" the fog in the afternoon, but the light reacts with chemicals in the air to produce what is known as photochemical smog. During autumn and winter, in association with shorter day-length (photoperiod), cold air from the desert moves toward the coast, pushing the fog and haze out to sea. The Mojave Desert to the north of the mountains is higher than the coastal plain, and therefore the air that moves toward the coast falls downhill in the mountain passes and becomes heated by compression. This causes clear, warm days even in winter. In the autumn, the winds that follow the Santa Ana River to the sea may be so intense that they increase the fire hazard. Our seasons may be summarized as spring fog, summer smog, autumn wind, and winter rain.

Winter is a time of awakening, not a "dead time" for us. This is our rainy period, when plants awaken from their long summer dormancy. At this time our local hillsides "green up." New leaves grow and seeds germinate. In a typical winter, rain arrives every three to five days, interspersed with remarkably clear weather as warm Santa Ana winds push the haze out to sea. Tourists from snowbound climates and locals turn out in droves to enjoy the famous California sun. It is a good time to hike in our local hills. Animals such as coyotes and deer are often visible, looking fat and healthy in their winter coats. Resident birds are active all day. Lizards bask in the sun, and salamanders can be found under fallen logs and in the litter under oak trees. Many of our cactus species are in bloom. At the same time our riparian species such as Sycamores and Willows have shed their leaves, reacting to the cold weather of canyon bottoms.

As days get longer, the interior valleys and deserts heat up. Rising warm air in the deserts tends to draw cool moist air off the ocean, bringing persistent fog to coastal regions

Fig. 2.4. Summer smog from L. A. basin. Saddleback in distance.

Fig. 2.5. Chaparral fire (Geoff Smith).

(fig. 2.3). This heavy cool air tends to become trapped on the coastal side of the mountains that surround the greater Los Angeles basin. This big "puddle" of air can be viewed from an airplane or the surrounding mountains as a flat-topped layer of fog that may persist for days on end, leading to the common expression "June gloom." Many plants and animals respond to the spring by reproducing. Flowers appear, insect pollinators hatch, and migratory birds arrive. Local birds sing vociferously as they court and claim territories. Lizards and snakes emerge whenever it is sunny. Nocturnal rodents become active, gathering food to feed their babies. This is a good time to view local wildlife.

During the long, hot summer the marine layer often persists along the coast and in canyons until noon or so, and it is best to hike in the morning. The long periods of sunlight cause the fog to evaporate, but the persistent haze is "cooked" by the sun, so it is not uncommon for photochemical smog to make exercise unpleasant (fig. 2.4). Most local animals retreat to the canopy of Oaks, Sycamores, and large shrubs to wait out the midday heat. During summer many of our local plants are becoming

dormant, particularly those on south-facing slopes, where leaves turn brown or fall off completely. North-facing slopes and canyon bottoms are characterized by green foliage, whereas south-facing slopes are turning brown. In flat areas the shallow-rooted grasses and wildflowers die out completely, waiting for the rejuvenating winter rains.

In autumn, as periods of daylight become shorter and the sun gets lower in the sky, the interior deserts begin to cool off. Cool air from the high desert (Mojave) flows toward the coast, following the bed of the Santa Ana River from the San Bernardino Mountains to the coast north of Huntington Beach. Santa Ana winds, heated by compression, may produce strong, hot winds that exacerbate fire conditions. The good news is that the coastal flow tends to clear the air and cool, sunny days invite outdoor activity. This is also the prettiest time in our local canyons, because this is when the riparian vegetation puts on its display of autumn color. Lovely Sycamores backlighted by the low angle of the sun enhance everyone's photographs. Autumn-blooming plants such as Goldenbush and Tarweed plus bright red Prickly Pears add color to the landscape. Autumn is a good time for photography.

FIRES

The vegetation of Mediterranean climates is very dry by the end of the long hot summer, and the wind contributes to the probability that fires will become holocausts. In years past, autumn fires were most often started by lightning because this is the time of year when thunderstorms are most likely to occur. Nowadays, however, fires are typically started by human activity, most often arson. Factors that exacerbate fires include Santa Ana winds, encroachment of urban development upon our native ecosystems, and replacement of native vegetation by short-lived non-native species.

Periodic fires are a natural component of plant communities of southern California from Coastal Sage Scrub and Chaparral to the Mixed Coniferous Forest at higher elevations. These communities not only tolerate fire but in many cases require it (fig. 2.5). The predictable sequence of recovery from fires is a well-documented phenomenon and is well exhibited by the recovery sequence of vegetation following the 1993 Laguna Beach fire. Some plants, such as California Live Oaks, possess thick fireproof bark that helps resist the flames. Succulent plants, by virtue of their damp, water-storing pith, are also able to resist all but the most intense fires. Short-lived wildflowers and certain shrubs such as Deerweed (fig. 4.10), Bush Monkeyflower (fig. 2.10, 4.11), and Bush Mallow (fig. 4.15) come back vigorously from seed after a fire. Many factors associated with fire, such as heat, smoke, and chemicals leached from ashes by rainwater, stimulate germination of fire-following plants. Among the larger, long-lived shrubs, such as Toyon, Laurel Sumac, Lemonadeberry, Scrub Oak, and Chamise, the basic mechanism for recovery is resprouting from the root system, which survives the fire (fig. 2.6).

A typical sequence of recovery from fire for plants in Coastal Sage Scrub is as follows: In the first year short-lived annual wildflowers such as Phacelias, Lupines, and California Poppies dominate the landscape (fig. 2.7). Fire Poppy seems to be found only immediately after a fire (fig. 2.8). Remarkably, geophytes that recover from underground

Fig. 2.6. Laurel Sumac resprouting.

Fig. 2.7. Wildflowers.

Fig. 2.8. Fire Poppy.

Fig. 2.9. Catalina Mariposa Lily.

storage organs such as bulbs and rhizomes are also stimulated to grow at this time. Among these are Blue Dicks (fig. 4.52), Mariposa Lilies (fig. 2.9), and Blue-eyed Grass (fig. 4.53). During the first 4 years short-lived shrubs whose seeds are also stimulated to germinate by fires will dominate. These shrubs include Coast Brittlebush (fig. 4.8), Deerweed (fig. 4.10), and Bush Monkeyflower (fig. 2.10). Deerweed is in the Pea Family (Fabaceae), and its rapid growth is facilitated by the presence of nitrogen-fixing bacteria in the roots. This form of mutualism helps the plant produce the proteins that stimulate new growth. The largest of these shrubs, Bush Mallow, was particularly conspicuous after the 1993 Laguna Beach fire. From 4 to 15 years after a fire, mature Coastal Sage Scrub shows very little sign of a former burn. A typical interval between fires in this habitat is 15 to 25 years, but it can burn again at any time, particularly if it has been invaded by non-native annual grasses. If natural fire is artificially suppressed for

Fig. 2.10. Bush Monkeyflower.

Fig. 2.11. California Lilac.

Fig. 2.12. Chamise sprouting.

long periods of time, fuel in the form of dry, dead debris can accumulate, and this can promote a large, hot fire, particularly if it starts during a period of Santa Ana winds.

The Chaparral community is composed of evergreen, drought-tolerant plants that are larger and denser than those of Coastal Sage Scrub. Plants tend to live longer, and the interval between fires tends to be longer, but a similar sequence of recovery can be summarized as follows: For the first two years after a fire, fire-followers such as annuals (60%) and herbaceous perennials (20%) dominate. Depending on the region, these annuals can represent up to 90% of the vegetative cover. Similarly, various geophytes (bulbs, corms, and rhizomes) react to fire ultimately to represent 10–25% of the cover.

From three to ten years after the fire, short-lived shrubs that are obligate seeders, most of which respond primarily to heat, dominate the landscape. Particularly important are the California Lilacs (*Ceanothus* spp.), which contain nitrogen-fixing bacteria in their roots (fig. 2.11, 4.28, 4.41, 4.42). This feature, whereby the bacteria enhance protein

formation, ensures a quick response to the fire. Sprouters such as Chamise (fig. 2.12, 4.27) and Scrub Oaks (fig. 4.43) grow vigorously at this time as well. At higher elevations, where snow is an important environmental variable, various Manzanitas dominate on south-facing slopes. Eastwood Manzanita is a sprouter, and Bigberry Manzanita (fig. 4.46) is a seeder. On north-facing slopes a common large shrub is Mountain Mahogany (fig. 4.33), another crown-sprouter, which also has nitrogen-fixing bacteria in its roots.

Ten to 50 years after a fire, the Chaparral community begins to resemble prefire conditions. Short-lived seeders tend to die out after 10 years, and the dominant perennial woody plants will come to represent a large proportion of the vegetative cover. In many instances Chamise on south-facing slopes and Scrub Oak on north-facing slopes will appear to occur as monocultures, single-species stands. At higher elevations, Manzanitas often dominate on south-facing slopes and Mountain Mahogany on north-facing slopes. The average fire frequency in chaparral is about 35 years. After that some of the plants begin to show signs of old age.

Fig. 2.13. Knobcone Pine with closed cones.

Fig. 2.14. Knobcone Pine with open cones after fire.

Fig. 2.15. Tecate Cypress seedling.

Also found on north-facing slopes are trees such as Canyon Live Oak, Big-cone Douglas Fir, and Coulter Pine (fig. 4.34). These species are also fairly fire-adapted. The Live Oaks have thick, fireproof bark and will sprout from the base and also from lateral buds at the

bases of branches. Likewise, Big-cone Douglas Fir sprouts from lateral buds. Coulter Pine tends not to show traditional fire adaptations, and fire will kill adult plants. However, its large cones (fig. 4.48) tend to resist fire because they open slowly and the seeds drop late in the year, after the fire season is over.

In some locations where the soil is poor and fog is abundant, the dominant perennial vegetation includes some fire-adapted conifers. On Pleasants Peak, a grove of Knobcone Pine occurs on a serpentine type of soil. This is a "closed-cone pine," whose cones remain closed until the heat of a fire stimulates them to open (figs. 2.13, 2.14). In a similar fashion, the cones of Tecate Cypress, which look like golf-ball-sized juniper berries, open only after a fire. Tecate Cypress grows on sandstone at the heads of Coal Canyon, Gypsum Canyon, and the coastal side of Sierra Peak in the Santa Ana Mountains (fig. 2.15, fig. 4.37).

Since 1993 a large portion of Orange County's wildlands have burned in a sequence of large fires. Particularly hard-hit were the reserves and parks that lie along the northwestern border of the Santa Ana Mountains, where seven large fires have occurred since 1997 (fig. 2.16). Much of this land, contained within the Nature Reserve of Orange County, has been set aside to preserve natural ecosystems. The problem is not that so much of the region burned but that the interval between the fires has not been long enough to allow complete recovery. Fires require fuel and oxygen. Fuel is represented by the standing biomass of vegetation. During Santa Ana conditions in autumn, following the long hot summer, strong winds exacerbate the potential for large fires. While programs of fire suppression have increased the amount of standing fuel, Santa Ana winds create conditions that burn everything in the way, including recently burned vegetation. As urbanization encroaches farther and farther into wildlands, two things become obvious. First, human-caused sources of ignition such as car fires, house fires, downed power lines, and downright arson increase. Second, increasing numbers of homes at the urban-wildland interface increase the probability of ignition along with the cost

Fig. 2.16. Ten-year fire map in the Nature Reserve of Orange County (courtesy of the Nature Reserve of Orange County).

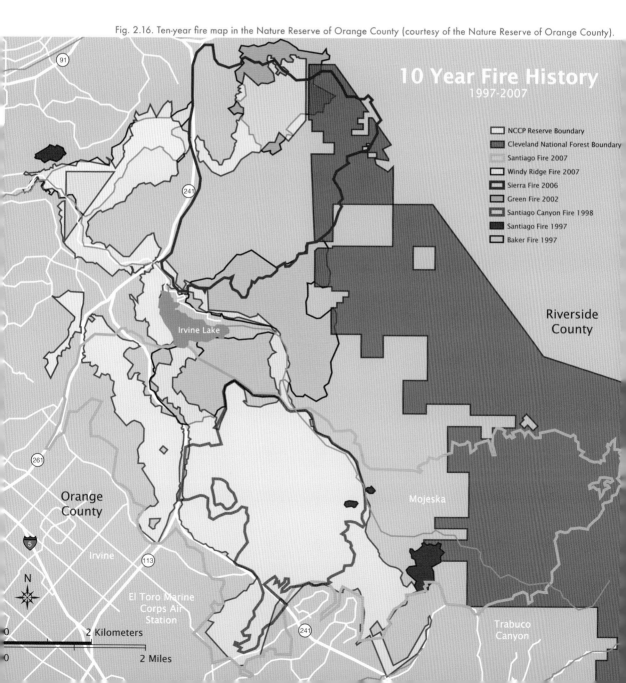

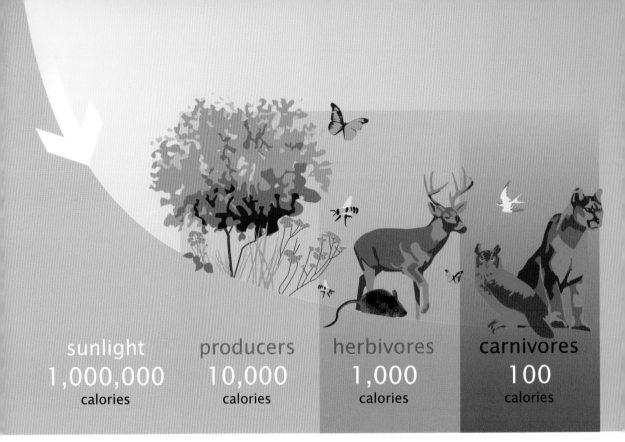

sunlight
1,000,000
calories

producers
10,000
calories

herbivores
1,000
calories

carnivores
100
calories

Fig. 2.17. Transfer of energy in ecosystems.

of fighting fires. The irony is that humans prevent fires as much as possible, but most fires are caused by humans. When fires occur too frequently, the natural sequence of recovery is interrupted. Native plants may not live long enough to produce more seeds or store enough nutrients to resprout before they burn again. Non-native weeds and grasses become established to the detriment of native plants. The effect is that the natural diversity of native plant communities is replaced by non-native grasslands that in themselves, by virtue of their dieback every summer, increase the probability of future fires. This is a textbook example of the ecological principle that instability of ecosystems is a consequence of simplification or loss of diversity.

ECOSYSTEMS

Orange County's limited precipitation is responsible both for the drought-tolerant, brushy plants that dominate its landscape and for the kinds of animals that inhabit it. The "glue" that holds the interacting living and nonliving components of an ecosystem together is the transfer of energy from one organism to another (fig. 2.17). The green plants, through the process of **photosynthesis**, convert light energy to food; in the presence of light they absorb carbon dioxide and water and produce carbohydrate (glucose) and oxygen. This transformation, which is only about 1 % efficient, in effect, converts light energy into chemical energy in the form of carbohydrate that is worth 4 calories per gram. The amount of food

a pyramid of biomass

carnivores
10,000 kg

herbivores
100,000 kg

vegetation
1,000,000 kg

Fig. 2.18. Trophic levels. The nonliving parts of an ecosystem include light, heat, water and soil. The availability of these factors dictates how much life can be supported in an ecosystem, so the factor that is least abundant is said to be an ecological limiting factor.

(carbohydrate) that can be produced in a unit of time is known as **primary production**, and the organisms that carry on photosynthesis, therefore, are known as **producers**. In general the **consumers** are animals. Animals that eat the plants are called **herbivores** and represent the **primary consumers**. **Carnivores** are **secondary consumers** because they get their energy "secondhand" by eating the primary consumers. In some very rich ecosystems or in specialized circumstances, enough energy is produced by photosynthesis to support a **tertiary consumer**, a carnivore that eats other carnivores. Some consumers are **omnivores**. They can survive on either plant or animal material. The final consumers, represented by fungi and bacteria, are known as **decomposers**. All these consumers release

energy (calories) from food by combining glucose with oxygen and excreting carbon dioxide and water, effectively a reverse of the process of photosynthesis.

It is a law of nature that energy transfer cannot be 100% efficient. Some of the energy is always lost in the process. While there is some variation in transfer efficiency, the basic rule is that only about 10% of the energy makes it from one animal to another in a **food chain**. The transfer of energy from producers to consumers in an ecosystem, therefore, is often depicted as a **food pyramid**, with the producers on the bottom and the top-order carnivores at the apex. The various layers in the pyramid are called **trophic (nourishment) levels** (fig. 2.18).

The variables that dictate how much energy is produced by plants are known as ecological limiting factors, and they are represented by minimal amounts of abiotic factors such as light, heat, water, and soil. Photosynthesis requires light, carbon dioxide, and water. Therefore, on an annual basis, low amounts of precipitation limit the primary production of a plant community, which will be reflected in the luxuriance of the foliage or biomass of plant material. Similarly, limited amounts of food will also limit the biomass of animals that inhabit the area. Obviously, light also will be a limiting factor, and therefore the short photoperiod or day-length during winter is responsible for reduced plant productivity. The irony of the climate in Orange County is that our rainy season comes during the shortest, coldest days of the year.

The average amount of primary production produced per year in our Mediterranean climate is not great. Coastal Sage Scrub on the coastal terraces, with approximately 10 to 13 inches of rain per year, produces about 3,000 pounds of glucose per acre per year or 335 grams of carbohydrate per square meter per year, and that food must be shared by all the organisms that inhabit the acre. According to the 10% rule of energy transfer, an acre of Coastal Sage Scrub (about half the size of a football field) will support only 300 pounds of herbivores and 30 pounds of carnivores. It would take at least an acre of undisturbed vegetation to support a 30-pound Bobcat if it were the only carnivore there. Chaparral, generally distributed on the slopes of the local mountains, gets more precipitation and is about three times more productive, but even at that, an acre would not produce enough food to support a solitary Mountain Lion that weighed 100 pounds. Considering all of the animals that occupy each of the trophic levels, a Chaparral ecosystem such as that which occupies the slopes of the Santa Ana Mountains will support so few top-order carnivores that a large male Mountain Lion requires about 100 square miles of undisturbed habitat for a home range and the entire Santa Ana Range supports a total of 25 to 30.

Our local plant communities are essentially food-poor because they are limited by water. The consequence of this food-poor system is not only low amounts of primary production

Fig. 2.19. Coyote.

Fig. 2.20. Gray Fox.

Fig. 2.21. California Gnatcatcher male (courtesy of UCI Museum of Systematic Biology), an endangered species.

but also a limited number of species that can survive on each trophic level. Food-rich ecosystems such as tropical forests have thousands of species per acre. They tend to be fairly stable, not easily disturbed by the loss of one or two species. Food-poor ecosystems, in contrast, tend to be easily perturbed. Loss of a single bird species may eliminate the control of an insect that, free of predation, becomes a pest that devours native vegetation. Similarly, introduction of a non-native species without a natural predator can lead to explosive growth that eliminates several native species that are unable to compete. The importance of **biodiversity** is that it tends to stabilize the ecosystem, making it more resistant to perturbation.

Some species seem to be more important to stability than others. Loss of a **keystone** species may cause a cascading series of interactions that seriously alters the natural balance of species in an ecosystem. One of the most important consequences of **habitat fragmentation** or the breaking up of large tracts of undisturbed land is that the remaining fragments are not large enough to support a keystone species. One of the most significant demonstrations of this phenomenon has been reported for scrub habitats in San Diego County. Small patches of native habitat were left in canyons as housing tracts were built on the flatter parts of the landscape. In terms of food requirements, these patches were too small for Coyotes, which became displaced through time (fig. 2.19). Coyotes are omnivores, and therefore they require less undisturbed habitat than Bobcats, obligate carnivores about the same size. As the patches were reduced in size, the Bobcats (fig. 6.115) were eliminated first and then the Coyotes. In the absence of Coyotes, **mesopredator release** occurred. Smaller omnivores, Gray Foxes (fig. 2.20), became more abundant. Gray Foxes, however, prey on birds, as do Domestic Cats, which also became more common in the absence of the aggressive Coyotes. The severe reduction in bird numbers could be attributed to the loss of the stabilizing keystone species, the Coyote. Subsequent recognition of two local bird species requiring protection was the consequence of habitat destruction and habitation fragmentation with its coincident loss of a keystone species. Thus, the California Gnatcatcher (fig. 2.21) is federally listed as threatened and the Coastal Cactus Wren (fig. 6.65) is classified by the state as a species of special concern.

The loss of keystone species and its effect on ecosystems have been demonstrated repeatedly as California has become more and more populated. Prior to the gold rush there were huge tracts of undisturbed land that supported many species. As humans pressed into these undisturbed areas, the large animals were the first to go because populations of large animals require large patches of habitat. Native herbivores such as Tule Elk and Pronghorn Antelope were replaced by domestic animals. In order to protect these animals, the large predators, such as Gray Wolves and Grizzly Bears, were hunted to extinction. The Grizzly Bear, California's largest omnivore, was a keystone species. The only large predator remaining was the Mountain Lion (fig. 6.114), which increased in numbers in the absence of competition. As Mountain Lions

increased, the number of Mule Deer (fig. 6.113) was reduced by predation. However, as patches near urban areas became smaller and Mountain Lions were displaced, the Coyotes, which require less habitat, became more abundant. The abundance of Mountain Lions and Coyotes in larger tracts of wild land today and their absence in small ones is a consequence of human activities. The remaining small patches of natural habitat are unstable and easily perturbed, and this means that more and more species are threatened with extinction. Extinctions cause a loss of diversity and lead to further instability. The disappearance of a species signals that something is wrong with its community. By protecting a rare or endangered species we can protect the entire community and its component species, and this is the function of the habitat conservation plans responsible for much of the permanently protected property available to the public in Orange County. The technical definitions of protected species are as follows: **Endangered species** have legal standing. They are protected by law, critical habitat must be designated, and a program for recovery must be initiated. **Threatened species** are also legally protected. Without protection, a threatened species could become endangered. A rare species can be rare either because it is nowhere common or because it has a very small range within which it could be common. A rare species could be classified as threatened or endangered if its habitat is threatened with destruction.

Fig. 2.22. Ducks in Barbara's Lake and Mt. Baldy (Ronald H. Chilcote).

Chapter 3

The Shape of the Land

The appearance of Orange County's topography initially is the consequence of long periods of uplift and erosion. For many millions of years the land that now makes up Orange County was submerged. Processes such as volcanism, faulting, and plate tectonics are responsible for the land as we see it today.

Rocks are made up of minerals. A mineral is composed of a single type of molecule. Quartz is a mineral composed of silicon dioxide, the same material that makes up glass. Granite is a rock, composed of several minerals including quartz, feldspar, and mica, each of which has a different chemical composition. On the basis of the way in which the rocks were formed, there are three basic types of rocks, igneous, metamorphic, and sedimentary, and they are all found throughout the county today.

IGNEOUS ROCKS

The word "igneous" refers to fire; it comes from the same root as the word "ignite." Igneous rocks have their beginning as a molten material known as **magma**. Magma

is formed by heat and pressure deep beneath the surface of the earth. A basic source of magma is **subduction**, the sliding of the ocean floor beneath a continent. Subduction is associated with the migration of geologic plates on the surface of the earth. The North American Plate is composed of lighter material than the plate that formed the ocean floor and therefore rides higher on the molten core of the earth, facilitating subduction of the ocean floor beneath the North American Plate. About 120 million years ago most of California was under seawater. Around that time our west coast looked more like the east coast of Asia. The North American Plate was sliding westward, and subduction of the Pacific Plate caused the heat and pressure that melted the rocks several miles below the surface. A large submarine trench offshore marked the zone of subduction. That magma created a series of volcanic islands very much like the area around Japan today.

When magma erupts upon the surface it cools relatively rapidly. **Volcanic** or **extrusive** igneous rocks lack visible mineral structure because the formation of visible crystals in rocks takes a long time. These rocks vary in color depending on the proportions of iron and silica (quartz). Light-colored rocks have more silica and less iron. In order, from light to dark the three common kinds of volcanic rocks are **rhyolite**, **andesite**, and **basalt**. Basalt, which is often black, is high in iron and low in silica. It

Fig. 3.1. Santiago Peak.

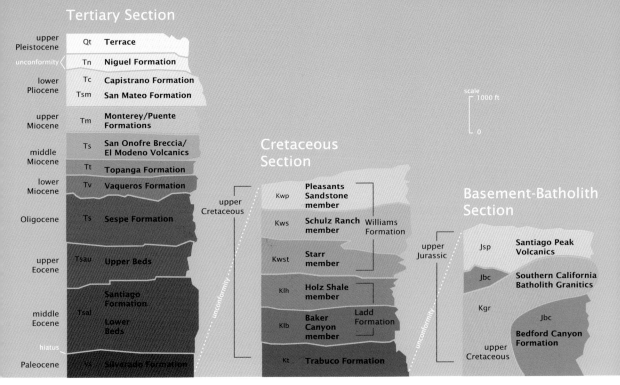

Fig. 3.2. Geologic column for Orange County (after Miller. 1992. Pacific Section AAPG Guidebook 46).

is the most common rock type on the sea floor in the vicinity of a trench. The volcanic rocks, including andesite, on Santiago Peak date back to about 135 million years ago (fig. 3.1). When old rocks are preserved on mountaintops they are called **roof pendents**. The **Santiago Peak Volcanics** have been estimated to be 2,300 feet thick.

While volcanic rocks are not common in Orange County, most of them date to the Miocene Epoch, about 14 to 16 million years ago. There were explosive volcanic eruptions that produced ash as well as lava flows. In addition to the Santiago Peak volcanics there are andesites along the western foothills of the Santa Ana Mountains. They are visible in Irvine Park and along Chapman Avenue where the road goes over the El Modena Hills. At the northwest edge of

the San Joaquin Hills, just south of Bonita Canyon Drive, there are some andesite sills and dikes that probably were erupted underwater. Along the coast from Laguna Beach northward there are about a dozen or so andesite-to-basalt outcrops that were intruded into overlying sediments about 15 million years ago. The columnar structure or "postpile" at Abalone Point just south of El Moro Beach indicates that the lava cooled rather rapidly (fig. 3.3). Another conspicuous outcrop of andesite forms the headland north of Crescent Bay.

Magma that remains deep in the earth cools slowly. Rocks formed in this way are called **plutonic** or **intrusive** igneous rocks. These rocks often have a salt-and-pepper appearance because their crystalline minerals are visible to the naked eye. They

Fig. 3.3. Columnar Basalt at Crystal Cove State Park.

Fig. 3.4. Block-jointed Granite at San Juan Fall.

vary from light to dark, depending on the proportions of iron and silica. Again, the darker rocks are higher in iron. In order, from dark to light, the common types of plutonic rocks are **gabbro**, **diorite**, and **granite**. Granitic rocks, the lightest in color and high in quartz, are the most common type (fig. 3.4). One group of plutonic rocks associated with the submarine trench is called the ophiolites. The Greek root *ophis* means "serpent," and ophiolites have a serpent-like, wavy pattern. Among these is a rock known as **peridotite,** which is the darkest of all igneous rocks. Peridotite is not often found in Orange County. The large pool of magma that was formed by subduction of the sea floor is now present as the **Southern California batholith**, and it forms an important core material for the southern California mountains. In many places it has been exposed by erosion. Grano-diorite rocks are particularly conspicuous where the Ortega Highway crosses the summit of the Santa Ana Mountains, and a mile or two south of the highway along the ridgeline road there are outcrops of the dark-colored **San Marcos Gabbro**.

SEDIMENTARY ROCKS

Weathering is a process that causes rocks to break up. Forces of weathering include ice, heat, tree roots, and chemical reactions. Erosion is the process that transports the weathered material to a new locality. Erosional processes include water, wind, and, to some degree, gravity, in the form of mass wasting. Glaciers also transport eroded materials, but there is no evidence of glaciation in Orange County. Sediments deposited by erosion are said to be unconsolidated. They are classified on the basis of size into clay, silt, sand, and gravel. When these sediments become cemented together into stone they are said to be consolidated. Consolidation requires long periods of time and usually involves significant pressure. Clays become fine-grained **shale**, silt becomes **siltstone**, and sand becomes **sandstone**. **Limestone** is a calcareous rock that may be formed as water evaporates and calcium carbonate is deposited. It also forms in shallow water with the accumulation of the calcareous shells of marine organisms.

Most of Orange County's rocks are sedimentary. These rocks, for the most part, were deposited under seawater and date to the time when most of the land was submerged. The particle size depends on the motion of the water during deposition; finer particles or clasts are deposited only in very quiet water. Shales represent deep-water muds, and the sandstones were more likely deposited in shallow water closer to the shore, where wave action and currents sorted the particles. Rivers and streams tend to leave behind a variety of particles because the water speed is variable. When a sedimentary rock contains a mixture of different-sized clasts, the rock is called a **conglomerate**. Conglomerates with rounded rocks represent old stream channels, but conglomerates with angular rocks usually represent old landslides. These conglomerate rocks are called **breccias**.

Geologists produce pictures of rock layers of different ages with oldest rocks at the bottom. The layers are called formations, and the picture is a geologic column.

From 145 to about 65 million years ago, a period of time referred to as the **Cretaceous Period**, sea level changed drastically from time to time. During inundation sedimentary material carried to the sea was deposited on the ocean floor, but during intervals when the land was above sea level erosion may have carried away a significant portion of the geologic record. When the sedimentary record is missing pieces of time, the gap is called an unconformity. Such an **unconformity** occurs in Trabuco Canyon, where the oldest sedimentary rocks in Orange

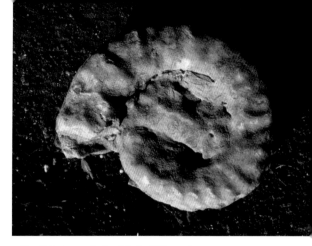

Fig. 3.5. Ammonite fossil in Ladd Formation.

County, approximately 100 million years of age, lie upon the Santiago Peak volcanics. The intervening rocks, carried away by erosion, are missing. These old sedimentary rocks are known as the **Trabuco Formation**, and they are represented by a series of red and white conglomerate rocks that were deposited on land as an alluvial fan, probably at the mouth of some large canyon. They are visible not only in Trabuco Canyon but also in Modjeska, Silverado, and Fremont Canyons.

The nature of deposition is such that the oldest sediments lie at the bottom of a sedimentary sequence, a phenomenon known as the **Law of Superposition**. Thus, when the sea once again covered the land, the Ladd Formation, representing a shallow nearshore sea, was deposited on top of the older Trabuco Formation. The **Ladd Formation**, found in Ladd Canyon, Silverado Canyon, Baker Canyon, and Fremont Canyon, is a mixture of marine and nonmarine (freshwater) conglomerates, sands, and shales, indicating that sea level changed significantly during the time of deposition from about 80 million years ago. Fossils in these sediments are

Fig. 3.6. Coal deposit in Coal Canyon.

mostly marine invertebrates, including large ammonites (fig. 3.5). These extinct animals are related to the modern Chambered Nautilus, a creature with octopus-like soft parts that lives in the outermost chamber of its coiled shell. The **Williams Formation**, with an age from 76 to 65 million years ago, includes marine and nonmarine conglomerates and silty sandstones. Many marine mollusk fossils such as snails, clams, and oysters are found here. Gradations in sediments from the Ladd Formation to the Williams Formation indicate an environment that went from a deep marine forearc deposit (**Holz Shale**) to nearshore marine and nonmarine deposits of the **Schulz Ranch member**. Representative of the "Age of Dinosaurs," Duck-billed Dinosaur (Hadrosaur) fossils found in the Ladd and Holz deposits of the Williams Formation are interpreted as terrestrial animals whose carcasses must have washed out to sea and become fossilized. The age of the Holz Member is about 89 to 76 million years. Finally, sediments deposited about 70 million years ago indicate a deeper-water continental-shelf deposit represented by the upper

Pleasants Member of the Williams Formation. The Williams Formation is well exposed in Williams Canyon, Baker Canyon, and Fremont Canyon.

After an initial unconformity, representing a gap of about 15 to 20 million years in the sedimentary record, the **Cenozoic Era** is fairly well represented in the rocks of Orange County. The Paleocene **Silverado Formation** (fig. 4.37) of the northern Santa Ana Mountains consists of interbedded sands and shales from marine and nonmarine sources. It includes low-grade coal deposits that may still be observed in the upper parts of Coal Canyon and on the northern ridge of Fremont Canyon (fig. 3.6). The lower parts of the formation include large amounts of high-quality clay. Some of the most productive clay and silica sand operations in southern California were in operation in Silverado Canyon in the early 1900s.

During the middle **Eocene Epoch**, about 50 million years ago, the shoreline lay east of the present Santa Ana Mountains. For the most part, Orange County was inundated. The **Santiago Formation**, a buff-colored sandstone found throughout much of Santiago Canyon, represents a shallow-water deposit from that time period. It reaches a thickness of 2,700 feet in some places and contains a significant number of fossil mollusks.

Overlying the Santiago Formation is a thick nonmarine layer of alluvial sediments known as the **Sespe Formation**. These deposits represent deposition on a

Fig. 3.7. Sespe Formation in Whiting Ranch Regional Park.

floodplain or delta and indicate a period of major lowering of sea level when a paleoriver system (perhaps the ancestral Colorado River) delivered sediments from an eastern source. Excellent exposures of the Sespe Formation include the red sandstone layers at the mouth of Black Star and Silverado Canyons and in the Sinks area of Limestone Canyon–Whiting Ranch Park (fig. 3.7). A spectacular exposure of both red and white layers of the Sespe Formation is conspicuous on the east side of Highway 241 just south of its convergence with Highway 91 in Santa Ana Canyon.

The **Vaqueros Formation**, marking the beginning of the **Miocene Epoch**, about 25 million years ago, is composed of light-colored sediments and contains fossils of marine vertebrates such as whales and sharks, as well as clams and oysters. The floodplain deposits contain mammal remains such as camel, horse, and rodents. Good exposures of the Vaqueros Formation are found in Laurel and Willow Canyons in the Laguna Coast Wilderness Park. Fossils of marine invertebrates such as clams and pectens are well exposed in Laurel Canyon.

About 25 million years ago the nature of plate movements on the Pacific Coast began to change. The inexorable northward movement of land west of the San Andreas Fault began. The Transverse Ranges to the north of Orange County were being rotated clockwise away from the Peninsular Ranges. The San Gabriel and San Bernardino Mountains were being pushed into the east-west alignment they exhibit today, and the Los Angeles Basin was being formed as the land subsided. The **Topanga Formation**, represented by massive cliffs with many caves, is a sandstone formed in deeper water. Native American artifacts have been uncovered in some of these caves, indicating that they were once inhabited. The large rock formations at the mouth of Willow Canyon near the parking area in the Laguna Coast Wilderness Park are part of the Topanga Formation (fig. 3.8). This formation is also visible above the Sespe Formation at Dripping Springs in Limestone Canyon.

Further deepening of the Los Angeles Basin is indicated by the finer-grained sandstones and claystones of the **Puente Formation** that occur at the northern end of the Santa Ana Mountains and underlie the Chino Hills. Up to 11,000 feet in thickness, this is a formidable rock unit, representing many years of sedimentation. The Puente Formation is visible as the colorful road-cut along the frontage road (old Highway 18) south of Highway 91 and west of the intersection with Highway 241. These softer rocks erode more easily, but they also make up most of the higher terrain in the Limestone Canyon area and on Loma Ridge. The Puente Formation, with large concretions, is also visible along the trail system of the Olinda Oil Museum and Historical Trail, near the mouth of Carbon Canyon (fig. 3.9). Contemporaneous with the Puente Formation but deposited farther offshore were the sedimentary beds of the **Monterey Formation**. This is one of California's most widespread and best-known sedimentary formations and is often associated with petroleum deposits. It is exposed throughout coastal California from Point Arena in Mendocino County south to San Onofre. Representing an interval from about 23 to 12 million years ago, this deep-

Fig. 3.9. Puente Formation with large concretions.

water deposit is composed of light-colored, thinly bedded siltstone, sandstone, volcanic tuffs, and diatomaceous shale. Signaling a period of active volcanism on land, the tuffs resulted from the aerial fallout of

Fig. 3.8. Topanga Formation at mouth of Willow Canyon.

Fig. 3.10. Monterey Diatomite at Dover Shores.

volcanic ash that sank into the water. The diatomaceous shale (diatomite) is made up of billions of glass skeletons (tests) from marine microorganisms known as diatoms. Diatoms are planktonic, microscopic, photosynthetic creatures that may be the most common organisms in the sea. They flourish during periods of upwelling, when nutrients are carried from the deep ocean to the surface. They thrive at the surface because they require light as well as dissolved nutrients, but when they die or are consumed by predators their unique glass skeletons sink to the bottom. Water depths ranged from 3,000 to 7,000 feet at the time. Because calcium carbonate dissolves under the extreme pressure of the deep ocean, the skeletal remains of other organisms disappeared, leaving behind pure deposits of diatomite. The white cliffs on both sides of Upper Newport Harbor are composed of this diatomaceous earth, which is up to 1,000 feet thick. The area on the north side is known as Dover Shores in reference to its white cliffs (fig. 3.10). Good exposures of the Monterey Formation are visible on beach cliffs such as those at Crystal Cove and Crescent Bay.

A large fossil reef, about 17 million years of age, containing casts of large Scallops (Pectens), Clams, and Snails, formerly covered about 20 square miles in Laguna Hills. The site is interpreted as a limestone-rich shell reef associated with beach sand, probably formed in a shallow tropical lagoon. Unfortunately, much of the deposit has been destroyed by construction, but a sizable sample of the formation has been preserved in Fossil Reef Park, which is located just west of the Laguna

Fig. 3.11. San Onofre Breccia in Laguna Beach.

Hills Community Center on Alicia Parkway. This material can also be observed in some of the rocks that were used to construct the mission at San Juan Capistrano.

Another distinctive sedimentary rock deposited during the middle Miocene is the **San Onofre Breccia** (fig. 3.11). This hard conglomerate resembles weathered concrete. The clasts are not rounded but angular, and many of them are quite large. These rocks cling to today's coastline, but they had their origin to the west (fig. 3.12). The coastline at the time was many miles to the east. On a large island or series of islands composed of rock materials similar to those of Santa Catalina but closer to today's coastline, landslides of rock debris, probably associated with earthquakes, coursed down the east side of the island and became cemented into solid rock. These landslides today fringe the west coast of Orange County and form some of the rocky headlands found between San Onofre and Newport Beach. These are the rough rocks that are so painful to walk over when barefooted.

Fig. 3.12. Reconstructed paleogeography of the southern California borderland during deposition of San Onofre Breccia (after S. M. Bowland. 1984. *Geology of Santa Catalina Island. California Geology 37*).

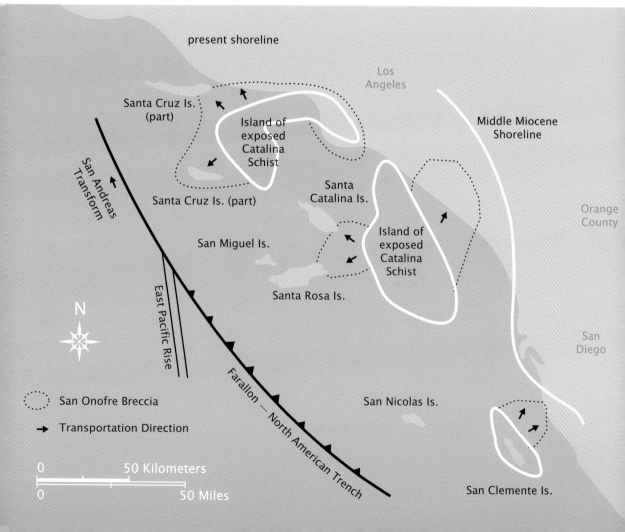

Toward the end of the Miocene and the beginning of the Pliocene, about 15 million years ago, the west coast began to be uplifted by tectonic forces. Faults became active and more pronounced. As the land rose, the sea became shallower. The coarse-grained texture of the **San Mateo Formation**, a thick-bedded, light yellow sandstone that is found near the mouth of San Mateo Canyon near San Onofre, indicates that it was deposited on a shallow ocean shelf. The nuclear power plant is built on this stable material. Farther north and about the same age as the San Mateo Formation, the **Capistrano Formation** crops out as a fine-grained siltstone on top of the Monterey Formation. It is well represented in the San Clemente and San Joaquin Hills. At the mouth of Big Canyon, on the east side of upper Newport Bay, the lighter-colored cliffs to the south are the Monterey Formation and the brown-colored cliffs to the north are the Capistrano Formation. In the Crystal Cove area the Capistrano Formation appears in resistant cliffs and roadcuts, where it may include large round concretions. It is highly visible in the cliffs along the road behind the marina in Dana Point, where it also shows a conglomerate nature indicative of the former Doheny submarine fan (fig. 3.13). The absence of carbonate fossils also indicates a deep-water environment of deposition.

The last 2 million years have been characterized by continued uplift of the Orange County coast, including the San Joaquin Hills and the Santa Ana Mountains. This uplift has placed all of the sedimentary formations above sea level, allowing geologists to re-create the ancient history of Orange County. During the last million years, marking an epoch known as the **Pleistocene** or "Ice Ages," fluctuations in sea level have been pronounced. Sea level drops as much as 300 feet during cold intervals, when much of the earth's water is frozen into glaciers. During interglacial intervals sea level is similar to or slightly higher than that of today. Evidence for these fluctuations in sea level is the presence of a series of **marine terraces** that occur along the coast (fig. 3.14). Each terrace is formed by erosion and sedimentation during a period of relatively stable sea level. This action can be seen

Fig. 3.13. Capistrano Formation in Dana Point.

Fig. 3.14. Marine terraces at Camp Pendleton represented by series of steps on hill in background.

along the beaches south of Newport Beach today. Here the action of waves creates a wave-cut bench in the hard rocks of the headlands. In between, currents deposit sand in the coves. When old wave-cut benches are uplifted they become visible as fairly flat spots in the terrain along the coast. Between Newport and Dana Point the Pacific Coast Highway has been built on the first terrace level. Older terraces may be observed on the hillsides in the area. They are particularly visible as a series of steps when viewing the ridgelines in profile. Marine fossils preserved in the sediments on these terraces indicate the temperature of the sea at the time of deposition.

METAMORPHIC ROCKS

Metamorphic rocks are those that have been changed by heat and pressure from their original form. The heat and pressure created by the subduction of the sea floor beneath the North American Plate and the intrusion of magma into the parent rock in the area altered the rock that did not melt. The original or "country" rock may have been heated to the point of plasticity,

but it did not liquify. Plutonic rock such as granite becomes a hard, banded rock known as **gneiss**. Sedimentary rocks become hardened forms that may or may not reflect the particle size of the original clasts. Fine-grained shales become **slates** and **schists**. Quartz sandstones become **quartzite**, and limestones become **marble**.

Metamorphic rocks are not common in Orange County. Those that are present are essentially roof pendents along the crest of the Santa Ana Mountains. The oldest rocks in Orange County, about 185 million years old, are known as the **Bedford Canyon Formation** (fig. 3.15). These rocks are composed of slate, schist, quartzite, and local deposits of marble. It appears that the metamorphism occurred as a result of the magmatic intrusion. The Santiago Peak volcanics, including some metamorphic volcanics, lie on top of the Bedford Canyon Formation. Offshore, west of the Newport-Inglewood Fault, most of the metamorphic rocks lie on the sea floor. They are exposed locally today primarily on Santa Catalina Island. These metamorphic rocks, predominantly blue schist and

Fig. 3.16. Serpentine on Pleasants Peak.

east of the present shoreline. Along the ridgeline of the Santa Ana Mountains in the vicinity of Pleasants Peak there are two deposits of serpentinite that effectively are roof pendents (fig. 3.16). Serpentinite is the state rock, a metamorphic form of peridotite, and in general is found in the Coast Ranges north of Point Conception and in the foothills of the Sierra Nevada along historic Highway 49. In the Santa Ana Mountains these small units are composed of shiny green to blackish-green rocks and show signs of faulting (slickensides). In addition, to the south, there is a reddish silica carbonate rock with veinlets of iron oxide that has been interpreted as hydrothermally altered serpentinite. It is upon these soils that can be found some unique plants such as Knobcone Pine (*Pinus attenuata*) (fig. 4.35).

some serpentinite, are interpreted as rocks that formerly inhabited the deep offshore trench that was formed during the period of subduction. **Serpentinite** is sometimes referred to as **serpentine**. On the mainland in Orange County those rocks are present as the clasts in the San Onofre breccia, representing materials that were shed from a former highland that lay

Fig. 3.17. Types of faults (from *California Geology*, July/August 2000).

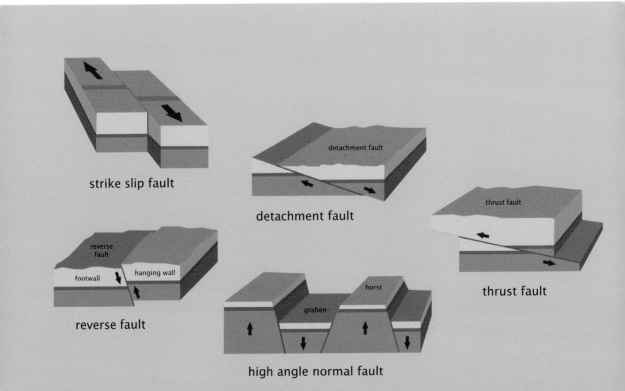

strike slip fault

detachment fault

reverse fault

high angle normal fault

thrust fault

FAULTS AND EARTHQUAKES

Cracks in the earth's crust are called **faults**. Motion along these cracks causes earthquakes and is responsible for the uplift or subsidence of landmasses. These faults are concentrated along the boundary of the North American Plate where it contacts the Pacific Plate. This boundary, in which the westward-drifting North American Plate is colliding with the northwestward-drifting Pacific Plate, is called a **transform boundary**. It began about 23 million years ago, about the time the sediment of the Monterey Formation was being deposited. Most of the major faults in southern California are **strike-slip faults**, in which the relative motion is sideways (fig. 3.17). Most of them have **right-lateral** motion, meaning that the land moves to the right from the perspective of an observer on the other side of the fault. Faults that move up and down are called **dip-slip faults**. Actually, motion can occur both ways at the same time; the Santa Ana Mountains are a fault-block range lying east of the right-lateral strike-slip **Whittier-Elsinore Fault**.

The **Newport-Inglewood Fault** lies just offshore of Orange County. It just barely touches the coastline at Little Corona del Mar (fig. 3.18). The folds in the sedimentary rocks on the sea cliff there were caused by movement

Fig. 3.18. Newport-Inglewood Fault at Little Corona del Mar.

along the fault. The magnitude-6.3 earthquake in 1933 that damaged many buildings in Long Beach and Orange County was along that fault.

The **San Andreas Fault**, which cuts through San Bernardino, runs all the way from the Imperial Valley to north of San Francisco. Other faults in this transform system continue southward into the Gulf of California. Right-lateral motion along this fault system has been responsible for dragging all the land west of it 200 to 300 miles northward. Orange County once lay at about the same latitude as Hermosillo in Sonora, Mexico.

Fig. 3.19. Santa Ana River below Prado Dam.

Movement along these faults in southern California has been responsible for the gradual uplift of the Pacific Coast and the subsequent westward retreat of the shoreline that has taken place over the last several million years. This motion has not only caused the uplift of the Santa Ana Mountains, Chino Hills, and San Joaquin Hills but exposed all of the former ocean sediments mentioned above. Meanwhile, as these landmasses were being uplifted, canyon-forming rivers were cutting through them. Where the rivers entered the sea they cut through the coastal terraces, forming estuaries such as Bolsa Chica and Newport Bay. The county's largest river, the Santa Ana, was responsible for cutting Newport Bay, although it formerly entered the bay near the present Lido Island. Upper Newport Bay may have been cut by the Santa Ana River following a more southerly course or by a river that is no longer present. Today's San Diego Creek enters upper Newport Bay at the northern end of the San Joaquin Hills, but apparently it never carried enough water to cut the channel now occupied by the bay.

The Santa Ana River today carries runoff from the western side of the San Bernardino Mountains, the San Jacinto Mountains, and the Santa Ana Mountains (fig. 3.19). The primary tributary from the Santa Ana Mountains is Santiago Creek, which enters the Santa Ana River near Tustin. Over a period of millions of years the Santa Ana River has not always entered the ocean at the same point. There was so much water in the river historically that there were large marshes where Orange and Tustin are today, and many natural springs occurred in the area known as Fountain Valley. During the time the river was meandering across the basin, it cut the channel between the Santa Ana Mountains and the Chino Hills and may have been responsible for the estuary at Bolsa Chica as well as Newport Bay. The actual river that cut Bolsa Chica is unknown. Similarly, the river that cut Laguna Canyon is no longer present. The high point in the canyon above the Laguna Lakes is today called a wind gap because there is no longer water flowing through it. The Laguna Lakes, just off Highway 133, in Laguna Coast Wilderness Park, are Orange County's only natural lakes. San Juan Creek and Aliso Creek still cut through the San Joaquin Hills. Aliso Creek heads in the El Toro Valley and San Juan Creek courses westward from its head in the Santa Ana Mountains. Along the southern border of Orange County, San Mateo Creek is one of California's few uninterrupted drainages, flowing through a natural channel from the Santa Ana Mountains south of the Ortega Highway all the way to the sea at San Onofre.

Chapter 4

Plant Communities

A **plant community** is a group of plants that tend to grow together, largely because they have similar requirements and strategies for dealing with the local climate. Many authorities have described them, but there is widespread disagreement on classification. Phillip Munz and David Keck's classic 1959 classification, published in *A California Flora*, recognized only 28 plant communities in California. Since then others have identified numerous other categories. The scheme created in 1995 by John Sawyer and Todd Keeler-Wolf, known as *A Manual of California Vegetation*, was sponsored by the California Native Plant Society in conjunction with the California Department of Fish and Game's California Natural Diversity Data Base. The system, intended to become standard, recognized about 280 units known as **series**. The second edition of that manual split California vegetation into 375 units now known as alliances and smaller variations of alliances that are called **phases**. Because recognition of the plants that define each series, **alliance**, or phase often requires

special botanical training, this volume, for the sake of simplicity, uses the traditional categories that are still in widespread use among local naturalists.

There are at least five plant communities found locally in Orange County. Each has certain important **indicator species** that seem to share **adaptations** or **strategies** that enable them to thrive under local climatic conditions. Because of the significant differences promoted by elevation, temperature, and slope effect in a Mediterranean climate, these plant communities form a pronounced vegetational mosaic that is easily recognized (fig. 1.4, 4.1). The most common scrub community that dominates slopes at lower elevations

is know as **Coastal Sage Scrub** or simply **Coastal Scrub** (fig. 4.2, table 4.1). At higher elevations in the interior, Coastal Sage Scrub is replaced by **Chaparral**, a community dominated by larger shrubs. In canyon bottoms where permanent water is present, at least close to the surface, a **Riparian** community dominated by broad-leaved, deciduous trees occurs. In canyon bottoms or on north-facing slopes where permanent water is available to deep-rooted trees there is a community of large, evergreen oaks known as **Southern Oak Woodland**. Finally, on the dry, flat areas in the valleys and on coastal terraces the native plant community is known as **Coastal** or **Valley Grassland**.

Fig. 4.1. Four plant communities in Laguna Canyon: Oak Woodland, Riparian, Coastal Sage Scrub, and Grassland.

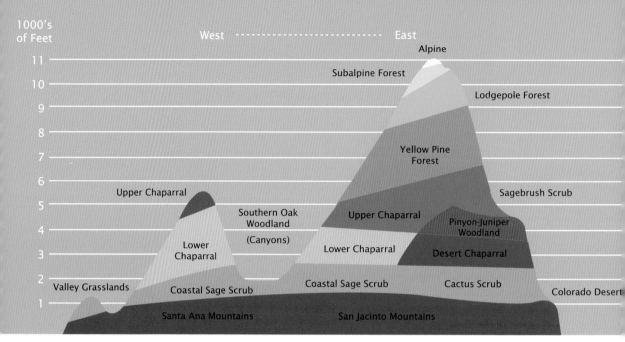

Fig. 4.2. Biotic zonation from the coast to the desert (from A. A. Schoenherr. 1992. *A Natural History of California.* University of California Press).

COASTAL SAGE SCRUB

Coastal Sage Scrub is sometimes called "soft chaparral" because the plants are mostly low-growing, flexible shrubs. The limiting factor for the distribution of this community to higher elevations appears to be cold temperatures (fig. 4.4). Where frost becomes a common occurrence, Coastal Sage Scrub is replaced by Chaparral. At lower elevations, near the coast, precipitation is desert-like, but long foggy periods, particularly during the mornings in the summer, tend to keep the relative humidity high (fig. 4.3). Because the

TABLE 4.1: PLANT COMMUNITIES			
Community	Slope Aspect	Growth Habit	Examples
Coastal Sage Scrub	South-facing	Drought-deciduous; small leaves; phytotoxins	California sagebrush, coast brittle-bush, monkeyflowers, true sages
		Succulent	Prickly pears, chollas, live-forevers
	North-facing	Evergreen; large leaves	Toyon, laurel sumac, lemonade berry, fuchsia-flowered gooseberry
Lower Chaparral	South-facing	Evergreen; small sclerophyllous leaves	Chamise, California lilacs
	North-facing	Evergreen; oval, spiny, sclerophyllous leaves	Scrub oaks, holly-leaf redberry; holly-leaf cherry
		Vines	Wild peas, honeysuckles, wild cucumbers
Upper Chaparral	South-facing	Evergreen; vertically oriented sclerophyllous leaves; sun-tracking	Manzanitas, silk-tassel bushes, Western mountain mahogany
	North-facing	Evergreen conifers	Big-cone Douglas fir, Coulter pine
Desert Chaparral	South-facing	Drought-deciduous	Desert apricot, desert almond, true sages
		Succulent	Prickly pears, chollas, Mormon teas
	North-facing	Evergreen; large leaves	Sugar bush, desert scrub oak, bigberry manzanita, jojoba

Fig. 4.3. Fog in Laguna Canyon.

slope effect is so pronounced in Coastal Sage Scrub (fig. 4.5), this community could almost be divided in two. On south-facing slopes the summer drought has a pronounced effect, and therefore the plants must be especially drought-adapted (fig. 4.6). Two common strategies characterize the plants on south-facing slopes. They tend to be either **drought-deciduous**, dropping their leaves in the summer, or **succulent**, storing water for use during the long, hot summer. Many of the drought-deciduous species have strong odors, probably to discourage herbivores, but the odors are pleasant, and the leaves of many of these species have been used to add flavor to food. For example, California Sagebrush, Black Sage, and White Sage are known to be used as flavoring. California Sagebrush (fig. 4.7) has grayish, finely divided leaves. It is actually in the Sunflower Family. The leaves of the true sages, in

the Mint Family, are long and narrow. Black Sage (fig. 4.13) has dark green leaves; it is the plant's black-colored stems that give the plant its common name. White Sage (fig. 4.12) has white leaves, and Purple Sage (fig. 4.14), which looks like a Black Sage with gray leaves, has large purple flowers. Of the succulent species, two are cacti. Coastal Prickly Pear (fig. 4.17) has flat pads, yellow flowers, and bright-red edible fruits. Coyotes and many birds eat the fruit. Coastal Cholla (fig. 4.18) has rounded stems and wine-colored flowers.

Fig. 4.4. Frost burn on Laurel Sumac.

Fig. 4.5. Slope effect in Coastal Sage Scrub.

Fig. 4.6. South-facing slope in Coastal Sage Scrub featuring drought-deciduous and succulent plants.

On north-facing and, to some degree, east-facing slopes, the plants tend to be **evergreen**. They are larger, have larger leaves, and tend not to lose their leaves in the summer. At higher elevations, where precipitation is greater and where sandy soil may have good water-holding capacity, these plants tend to grow on south-facing slopes as well. (Because many of the plants are evergreen, some authorities tend to classify them as Chaparral plants, but the plants of true Chaparral tend to have small leaves with hard, waxy surfaces.) Laurel Sumac (fig. 4.23) has large leaves that tend to fold in the form of a taco. After a period of cold weather this plant tends to die back (fig. 4.4), giving the appearance that it is dead, but it will resprout and grow vigorously in the spring just as it does after a fire (fig. 2.6). Because of its frost-sensitive nature, Laurel Sumac has been used as an indicator of climate that is suitable for planting citrus. Commonly growing along with Laurel Sumac is Toyon (fig. 4.21), which has long, dark green leaves with serrated edges. Large clumps of bright red berries adorn this shrub during the winter and provide an important food for birds, Coyotes, and Foxes. Its name is derived from an old Spanish word

that means "canyon," a location where it often grows. It also is known as Christmas Berry because it has berries at this time of year. Its third common name is California Holly, a name based on the spiny margins of its long narrow leaves. It was the presence of this plant on the hillsides near Los Angeles that led to the name "Hollywood." Many of the early settlers with European roots would adorn their homes with berry-laden branches of California Holly. Apparently the practice was so widespread that in 1920 a state law was passed that made it illegal to harvest the plant. The berries also were eaten by native Americans and early settlers, who boiled them first to remove their bitter taste. Early Spanish settlers baked the berries with sugar and used them for a filling in toyon pie. Toyon is often classified as a Chaparral plant because it is not frost-sensitive and tends to extend farther inland into lower Chaparral communities. Lemonadeberry (fig. 4.22) has thick, oval leaves, some of which may be serrated. In the spring, sticky berries with a sour flavor are produced. These berries soaked in water can be used to make a lemonade-flavored drink. The characteristics of many Coastal Sage Scrub plants are summarized here:

Drought-Deciduous Shrubs (primarily on south-facing slopes):

California Sagebrush (*Artemisia californica*). Common. Shrub with finally divided leaves and obscure greenish flowers (fig. 4.7).

Coast Brittlebush or **California Encelia** (*Encelia californica*). Frequent to common. Shrub, flowers yellow with dark centers. Blooms February to June (fig. 4.8).

California Buckwheat (*Eriogonum fasciculatum*). Common small shrub. Small oval leaves arranged in clusters (fascicles). Flowers white to creamy in tight heads. Blooms much of year (fig. 4.9).

Deerweed (*Lotus scoparius*). Frequent (particularly following fires). Low shrub. Small pea flowers yellow to orange. Blooms March to August. Has nitrogen-fixing bacteria in its roots and therefore is a good source of protein for wildlife (fig. 4.10).

Bush Monkeyflower (*Mimulus aurantiacus*). Frequent. Shrub with orange or red tubular flowers. Blooms December to July (fig. 2.10, 4.11).

White Sage (*Salvia apiana*). Occasional to frequent. Odoriferous shrub with large white leaves. Flowers white to pale lavender. Blooms April to June (fig. 4.12).

Fig. 4.13. Black Sage.

Black Sage (*Salvia mellifera*). Frequent to abundant. Odoriferous shrub with dark green lance-shaped leaves arranged opposite to each other on the stem. Flowers in whorls, white to pale lavender. Blooms April to July (fig. 4.13).

Fig. 4.14. Purple Sage.

Purple Sage (*Salvia leucophylla*). Uncommon. Odoriferous shrub with whitish lance-shaped leaves arranged opposite to each other on the stem. Flowers in whorls, bright purple. Blooms April to July (fig. 4.14).

Fig. 4.15. Bush Mallow.

Bush Mallow (*Malacothamnus fasciculatus*). Frequent (particularly following fires). Tall, rangy shrub with lobed leaves. Rose-colored flowers. Blooms April to July (fig. 4.15).

Fuchsia-flowered Gooseberry (*Ribes speciosa*). Occasional. Often on north-facing slopes. Lobed leaves and long sharp spines. Red, tubular flowers are usually pollinated by hummingbirds. Spiny fruit. Blooms January to May (fig. 4.16).

Fig. 4.16. Fuchsia-flowered Gooseberry.

Succulents (usually on south-facing slopes)

Coastal Prickly Pear (*Opuntia littoralis*). Frequent. Low-growing cactus with flattened succulent stems. Flowers yellow to orange. Bright red fruit. Blooms May to June (fig. 4.17).

Fig. 4.17. Coastal Prickly Pear.

Coastal Cholla (*Opuntia prolifera*). Occasional to frequent. Tall, cylindrical-stemmed cactus. Flowers wine-colored. Blooms April to June (fig. 4.18).

Fig. 4.18. Coastal Cholla.

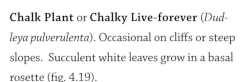

Fig. 4.19.
Chalk Plant.

Chalk Plant or **Chalky Live-forever** (*Dudleya pulverulenta*). Occasional on cliffs or steep slopes. Succulent white leaves grow in a basal rosette (fig. 4.19).

Fig. 4.20.
Chaparral
Yucca.

Chaparral Yucca (*Yucca whipplei*). Basal rosette of spiny-tipped succulent leaves. Tall stalk of white flowers after which the plant dies. Dry places in Coastal Sage Scrub and Lower Chaparral (fig. 4.20).

Evergreen Perennial Shrubs (usually on north-facing slopes)

Toyon or **California Holly** (*Heteromeles arbutifolia*). Large shrub with large, dark green, lance-shaped, serrated leaves. Flowers, small and white, clustered at the ends of the branches. Bright red clusters of berries appear from November to January. Blooms June to July (fig. 4.21).

Fig. 4.21.
Toyon.

Lemonadeberry (*Rhus integrifolia*). Frequent to common. Leaves thick and oval, often partially serrated. Flowers whitish to rose. Fruit red, squarish, and sticky, distinct sour flavor. Blooms February to May (fig. 4.22).

Fig. 4.22.
Lemonade
Berry.

Laurel Sumac (*Malosma laurina*). Common. Large shrub. Leaves lance-shaped, often folded like a taco. Winter cold weather often kills the foliage, causing leaves to turn brown, but new growth sprouts from the roots in the spring. Flowers small, creamy white. Blooms June to July (fig. 4.23).

Fig. 4.23.
Laurel
Sumac.

Coyote Brush (*Baccharis pilularis*). Occasional to frequent. Tall rangy shrub, Bright green resin-covered leaves. Flowers, small whitish sunflowers, all disc flowers. Blooms August to December (fig. 4.24).

Fig. 4.24.
Coyote
Brush.

California Scrub Oak (*Quercus berberidi-folia*). Occasional large shrub or small tree. Dark green leaves may have a wavy margin or be serrated. Leaves light-colored underneath. Acorns mature in the fall. More commonly considered a Chaparral species (fig. 4.43).

Fig. 4.25. Redberry.

Fig. 4.26. Lower Chaparral along Ortega Highway.

Fig. 4.27. Chamise.

Redberry (*Rhamnus crocea*). Large shrub with oval, dark green serrated leaves, usually flattened on the tip. Small greenish flowers in clusters. Bright red berries. Blooms March to April (fig. 4.25).

Saw-toothed Goldenbush (*Hazardia squarrosa*). Occasional. Low shrub with grasping serrate leaves. Flowers small, yellow sunflowers, all disc flowers. Blooms July to October.

Coast Goldenbush (*Isocoma menziesii*). Frequent. Low shrub or shrubby perennial. Resembles Saw-toothed Goldenbush, but leaves and flowers are smaller. Found in sandy areas. Blooms April to December.

CHAPARRAL

True Chaparral is a community of large, evergreen, woody shrubs with small, hard (sclerophyllous) leaves and large root systems. Chaparral plants dominate the landscape in the Santa Ana Mountains in the interior parts of Orange County (fig. 4.26). Chaparral is a frost-tolerant community that tends to grow at higher elevations than Coastal Sage Scrub, although there are a few localities where it grows close to the coast. In general, Chaparral requires more moisture than Coastal Sage Scrub. The above-ground growth of most Chaparral plants occurs during about four to six months in winter and spring. The rest of the year growth goes into the roots. Overall, above-ground growth seldom seems great because much of the plant's energy goes into cellular maintenance and production of chemicals such as lignins and tannins that discourage herbivory. Whereas Coastal Sage Scrub species tend to produce odors or distasteful chemicals to discourage herbivores, they have to grow a new set of leaves every year. The leaves on most Chaparral species tend to stay on the shrub for two years.

Lower Chaparral or **Warm Chaparral**, particularly on south-facing slopes, is dominated by Chamise (figs. 4.27). This is probably the most common plant on the coastal side of the mountains in southern California. It is in the Rose Family (Rosaceae), but the flowers are small, requiring close inspection to identify family characteristics. It has small, drought-adapted leaves (fig. 4.46) and a large root system and is fire-adapted. Following a fire, new shoots grow from a root crown burl (fig. 2.12). The shoots may grow a foot or more during the year following a fire. Chamise also regenerates by means of seeds, which are produced in enormous numbers. Most of the seeds are stimulated to germinate by heat.

During the first ten years after a fire, while Chamise shoots are becoming established, the landscape may be dominated by various species of California Lilac (*Ceanothus* spp.) They are so named because they have clusters of flowers that resemble Lilac shrubs. Hoaryleaf Ceanothus (fig. 4.28) has leathery leaves with spiny margins. The undersides of the leaves are whitish-gray. The leaves of Woolyleaf Ceanothus have a dense mat of white hairs on the underside

Fig. 4.28. Hoaryleaf Ceanothus.

but do not have the spiny margins. Chaparral Whitethorn (fig. 4.41) has whitish branches that end in stiff thorns and leaves with three main veins. Greenbark Ceanothus (fig. 4.42) has greenish branches that end in spines, but its leaves have only one main vein. These California Lilac species do not resprout after a fire, but their numerous seeds are stimulated to germinate by heat, smoke, or rainwater with ashes dissolved in it. Even though these plants are in the Buckthorn Family (Rhamnaceae) and not legumes, they have nitrogen-fixing bacteria in their roots that enable them to make their own amino acids, a component of proteins. Therefore, the new growth is a valuable browse for herbivorous animals, particularly deer, and the plants are quick to regenerate after a fire.

California Scrub Oak (fig. 4.43) tends to be more common on north-facing slopes. The dark green oval leaves may have spines or they may be slightly lobed. The acorns produced by these shrubs are a very important food for Chaparral animals. Scrub Jays and California Ground Squirrels bury the acorns by the thousands and in so doing inadvertently plant new oaks. Scrub Oaks also resprout after fires. Another species of Scrub Oak, known as Nuttall's or Coastal Scrub Oak, has limited distribution in Orange County, being found on Niguel Hill and the Dana Point headlands.

Plants with spiny-edged leaves and red fruit are often named after holly. Holly-leaf Redberry has bright red berries and oval leaves with serrated margins. Holly-leaf Cherry (fig. 4.29) has larger red fruit. Its leathery leaves are dark green and have distinctly spiny margins. Like commercial cherries, its fruit is sweet to the taste, but it has little pulp and a large pit. The pit when crushed releases cyanide, which should discourage foraging animals, but birds swallow the seeds whole and Coyotes appear to know not to chew the seeds because the fruit when available is important Coyote food.

Several vines occur in Lower Chaparral, particularly on north-facing slopes where there is a closed canopy among the shrubs. The vinelike habit is an adaptation for reaching the light in an area where light cannot reach the ground. Wild Cucumber (fig. 4.30) is also known as Manroot, Porcupine Egg, Chilicothe, or Marah, a biblical reference that means "bitter." The large underground

tuber, from which new growth occurs each year, may resemble a man's body, and the egg-sized, cucumber-like fruit is covered with spines. This vine, with its numerous small white flowers, grows all over the canopy where it is common. Perhaps the most attractive flowering vine is Wild Pea (fig. 4.31), which has large pea flowers resembling commercial Sweet Peas. Because it is in the Legume Family (Fabaceae), it has nitrogen-fixing bacteria in its roots.

Upper Chaparral or **Cold Chaparral** is a community of snow-tolerant species that occurs primarily at higher elevations in the Santa Ana Mountains. Various species of Manzanita are the most conspicuous shrubs. These attractive red-barked shrubs have oval leaves that rise vertically from the stem. This vertical orientation enables them to rotate the leaves to maximize light in cold weather, a process known as sun-tracking. The flowers of Manzanitas are attractive urn-shaped blossoms typical of the Heath Family (Ericaceae) (fig. 5.15). The name "Manzanita" means "little apple," referring to the red berries that adorn the shrubs in the summer and autumn. These berries are not only important food for animals such as Coyotes and birds but can be boiled to make a drink. The berries also can be used in jellies and pies or fermented to make wine. There are two common species of Manzanita. Eastwood Manzanita has dull-green mildly hairy leaves, but its most distinctive feature is a large burl at ground level from which the plant can resprout after a fire. Bigberry Manzanita (fig. 4.46) has gray-green leaves and large berries that are a favorite food for Coyotes. The Coyotes help disperse the seeds that are stimulated to germinate after a fire.

A plant that resembles Manzanita but lacks the shiny red bark is Silk-tassel Bush (fig. 4.32). It can be recognized by its gray-green leaves, which have straight hairs on their undersides. The white flowers are arranged in pendulous clusters called catkins. Dry catkins remain on the plant even after the flowers are gone.

An important forage plant of Upper Chaparral is Birch-leaf Mountain Mahogany (fig. 4.33). This is a large rangy shrub with whitish bark. Its leaves have serrated edges above the middle, but its most distinctive feature is its long feathery twisted fruit, which appears in late spring. This plant is in the Rose Family, but along with many legumes and the California Lilacs it has nitrogen-fixing bacteria in its roots, making its new twigs and leaves rich in protein.

On north-facing slopes or in canyons at higher elevations in the Santa Ana Mountains there are a number of plants that have localized distribution. Some of these are conifers, although there is no

Fig. 4.29. Holly-leaf Cherry.

Fig. 4.30. Wild Cucumber or Chilicothe.

Fig. 4.31. Wild Pea.

Fig. 4.32. Silk-tassel Bush.

Fig. 4.33. Birch-leaf Mountain Mahogany.

Fig. 4.34. Canyon Live Oak, Coulter Pine, and Big-cone Douglas Fir, in north-facing slope in Upper Chaparral.

true coniferous forest in Orange County (fig. 4.34). The most common conifer is Big-cone Douglas Fir (fig. 4.47). This relative of the Douglas Fir that characterizes the moist forests of the Pacific Northwest is locally common in canyons and on north-facing slopes. It seems to do best on steep, rocky, unstable slopes. The largest groves are in upper Trabuco Canyon. These are trees with long branches and an open growth habit. The top usually nods over. Cones are thin-scaled and pendulous, about 3–6 inches long and borne on drooping branches. The needles are about an inch long and grow all along the branches rather than in clumps or fascicles as do the needles of most pines. Seedlings grow vigorously after fires, but many adult trees produce trunk resprouts after they are burned.

The most common pine of the Santa Ana Mountains is the Coulter Pine, a large pyramidal tree with long needles in clumps of three. The cones of Coulter Pine (fig. 4.48) are the largest in California. Average cones are about the size of a volleyball and bear long curved spines on their scales. These trees are most common on interior ridges and slopes along the Main Divide Road between

Fig. 4.35. Knobcone Pine on hydrothermally altered serpentinite.

Fig. 4.36. Knobcone Pine cones and foliage, with fog drip.

the Ortega Highway and Bedford Peak. The nearest relative of the Coulter Pine is the Digger Pine or Gray Pine, a common species of the Oak Woodlands in the foothills of the Sierra Nevada and the Coast Ranges. The foliage of Gray Pines is blue-gray and thin. The cones resemble those of Coulter Pines but are smaller. Its natural distribution is far north of the Santa Ana Mountains, but there are a few specimens at the remains of the stone cabin, known as Beek's Place, on the ridge above Black Star Canyon They were probably planted by Joseph Beek, secretary of the state Senate (1919-1968), who lived from time to time at that location. He planted a number of conifers and other shade trees at the site. Believing in self-sufficiency, he stored rainwater in a cistern and for many years generated electricity with a row of windmills (now disassembled) and stored it in automobile batteries lined up in rows in a garage.

Knobcone Pine is a closed-cone pine with patchy distribution in the state. Usually it is located in a region with persistent fog and fine-grained soil. The plants depend on the fog that condenses on its needles and drips to the ground (fig. 4.36). The cones remain closed for many years, opening after a fire to disseminate their seeds (fig. 2.13, 2.14). In the Santa Ana Mountains the Knobcone Pine grows on Pleasants Peak on a peculiar hydrothermally altered soil that is said to have been derived from serpentinite (fig. 4.35). It also grows on serpentinite to the northwest. The next nearest grove is along the City Creek Road (Highway 330) in the San Bernardino Mountains. After that, the next nearest grove to the north is on Cuesta Ridge near San Luis Obispo. To the south, another grove is located in Baja California northeast of Ensenada. This is a textbook example of a species surviving on an ecological island, in this case an island marked by fire, fog, and fine-grained, depauperate soil.

Tecate Cypress is another conifer that survives today on an ecological island dictated by fire, fog, and fine-grained soil. Groves of these trees are restricted to the north side of Sierra Peak, at the upper end of Coal and Gypsum Canyons. Here they grow on eroded clays and sandstones of the Silverado Formation in a region of significant fog (figs. 4.37, 4.38). This is the northernmost location for this species. The nearest grove to the south is on Guatay Mountain in

Fig. 4.37. Tecate Cypress on Silverado Sandstone.

Fig. 4.38. Tecate Cypress and fog drip.

Fig. 4.39. Madrone.

above Coal Canyon was burned in 2002, and many seedlings were growing well in 2003 (fig. 2.15). The fire of 2006 reburned some of the area involved in the 2002 fire, but it remains to be seen how the species will survive in this, its northernmost locality.

Canyon Live Oak or Golden-cup Oak (fig. 4.50) is a large tree that is frequently associated with Big-cone Douglas Fir or Coulter Pine. It is the most widely distributed oak species in California, but in the Santa Ana Mountains its distribution typically is limited to higher elevations on canyon walls. Groves of these trees may be found on some of the steepest parts of Modjeska and Santiago Peaks. Leaves of this species are variable; some have spiny margins and some are smooth. The leaves are most easily recognized by the fact that their tops are shiny green and their undersides whitish. The acorns are large and stout, and the cups bear a golden-colored powder. The Interior Live Oak is distinguished from the Canyon Live Oak by its leaves, which are bright green on both sides. It also occurs as a shrub or "scrub oak" in some areas of Upper Chaparral.

San Diego County, and other groves are located along the international boundary near Tecate in Baja California. The cones of Tecate Cypress trees resemble golf-ball-sized juniper berries (fig. 4.49). As do closed-cone pines, these trees drop their seeds after a fire. Unfortunately, however, the trees must be about 30 years old before they have a significant number of fertile cones. The Sierra Fire of 2006 burned a grove along the ridgeline above Gypsum Canyon that was not old enough, and there has been very little regeneration in that area. The grove

Madrone is a red-barked tree in the Heath Family (fig. 4.39). It looks like a very large Manzanita with large elliptical leaves. It has a scattered distribution in shaded canyons in the Santa Ana Mountains but is most common on the north slope of Trabuco Canyon at about 3,000 feet elevation.

The characteristics of many Chaparral plants are summarized here as follows:

Lower Chaparral Plants (primarily on south-facing slopes)

Chamise (*Adenostoma fasciculatum*). Large shrub with red twigs and shredding bark. Leaves small, in clusters. Small white flowers in branching clusters. Highly flammable. Blooms in July and August (fig. 4.40).

Hoaryleaf Ceanothus (*Ceanothus crassifolius*) (fig. 4.28). Leathery leaves curled on edges between spines, distinctly whitish underneath. Leaves opposite. Flowers in small white clusters. Blooms in March and April.

Woolyleaf Ceanothus (*Ceanothus tomentosus*). Three main veins in leaves, serrated edges, dense wooly hairs underneath. Leaves alternate. Flowers blue to white, conspicuous and showy. Blooms in March and April.

Hairy Ceanothus (*Ceanothus oliganthus*). Resembles Woolyleaf Ceanothus but underside of leaves has short hairs. May be treelike in stature. Flowers deep blue. Blooms in March and April.

Deer Brush (*Ceanothus integerrimus*). Resembles Woolyleaf Ceanothus, but leaf edges are smooth and flowers are white. Blooms in March and April.

Chaparral Whitethorn (*Ceanothus leucodermis*). Small leaves with three main veins. Whitish stems end in spines. Flowers blue. Blooms in March and April (fig. 4.41).

Fig. 4.40. Chamise foliage.

Fig. 4.41. Chaparral Whitethorn.

Fig. 4.42. Greenbark Ceanothus.

Greenbark Ceanothus (*Ceanothus spinosus*). Leaves shiny green on upper surface, one main vein. Green stems end in spines. Flowers pale blue to white. Blooms in March and April (fig. 4.42).

Lower Chaparral Plants (primarily on north-facing slopes)

California Scrub Oak (*Quercus berberidifolia*). Leaf blades wavy or spine-tipped, upper surface green and shiny, lower surface paler with minute hairs. Acorn cup thick with small wartlike bumps. Flowers in slim stringy catkins. Blooms from March to May (fig. 4.43).

Nuttall's or **Coastal Scrub Oak** (*Quercus dumosa*). Resembles California Scrub Oak, but hairs on underside of leaves are visible to the naked eye. Found in Orange County near the coast on Niguel Hill and Dana Point headlands.

Holly-leaf Redberry (*Rhamnus ilicifolia*). Leaf blades have spiny edges, but the leaves are fairly flat. Resembles Redberry of lower elevations, but the leaves tend to be pointed, not flattened on the tip. Plants become covered with bright red berries in late spring to summer. Blooms in March and April.

Coffeeberry (*Rhamnus californica*). Leaf blades are oblong and 1 to 3 inches in length with pronounced veins. Abundant small flowers greenish and borne on small stalks. Berries brown to dark red. Blooms in May and June (fig. 4.44).

Holly-leaf Cherry (*Prunus ilicifolia*). Leaves are shiny and spiny-toothed. Small white flowers in elongate clusters. The red fruit has a thick pulp layer around a large stone. Blooms from March to May (fig. 4.29).

Flowering Ash (*Fraxinus dipetala*). Frequent small tree with pinnately compound, deciduous leaves, usually with seven leaflets. Clusters of small white flowers in spring. Flattened, helicopter-like seeds.

Heart-leaved Penstemon (*Keckiella cordifolia*). Rangy shrub with heart-shaped leaves and scarlet, tubular flowers.

Yellow Penstemon (*Keckiella antirrhinoides*). Rangy shrub with linear leaves and yellow two-lipped flowers in pairs (fig. 4.45).

Upper Chaparral Plants (primarily on south-facing slopes)

Eastwood Manzanita (*Arctostaphylos glandulosa*). Oval leaves dull green, mildly hairy. Small branches hairy or glandular. Berries generally smaller than ½ inch. Large burl at base of shrub, a source of new sprouts. Flowers white. Blooms from February to April.

Bigberry Manzanita (*Arctostaphylos glauca*). Oval leaves gray- green, hairless. Small branches hairless. Berries generally ½ inch. No large burl at base of shrub. Flowers white. Blooms from December to April (fig. 4.46).

Pale Silk-tassel Bush (*Garrya flavescens*). Elliptical leaves opposite on stem, hairless above and hairy below. Young twigs white and wooly. White flowers borne in long pendulous catkins (fig. 4.32).

Birch-leaf Mountain Mahogany (*Cercocarpus betuloides*).Leaf blades dark green and oval, serrated above the middle. Bark generally whitish. Open growth habit. Flowers small. Fruit twisted and feathery. Blooms from March to May (fig. 4.33).

Fig. 4.43.
California
Scrub Oak
leaves and
acorns.

Upper-Elevation Plants (primarily north-facing slopes)

Big-cone Douglas Fir (*Pseudotsuga macrocarpa*). Tall tree with thin vegetation and long branches. Needles approximately 1 inch long arranged along drooping stems. Pendulous cones 3–6 inches long with thin scales and three-pointed bract above each scale (fig. 4.47).

Fig. 4.44.
Coffeeberry.

Coulter Pine (*Pinus coulteri*). Large, full pyramidal tree with long needles (6–12 inches) in clusters (fascicles) of three. Very large cones up to 14 inches in length with large hooked spine on each scale (fig. 4.48).

Fig. 4.45.
Yellow
Penstemon.

Knobcone Pine (*Pinus attenuata*). Small, multiple-trunked tree with 4-6-inch needles in fascicles of three. Cones closed, 4–6-inch long, asymmetrical with large knobs on each scale, arranged in whorls on the stems. Cones open after fires. Limited to hydrothermally altered serpentinite of Pleasants Peak (fig. 4.36).

Fig. 4.46.
Bigberry Manzanita leaves
and fruit.

Tecate Cypress (*Cupressus forbesii*). Small pyramidal tree with irregular spreading crown. Bark peels in strips revealing red color underneath. Scale-like leaves arranged in circular pattern on stems. Fleshy, round cones approximately 1 1/4 inch in diameter with eight to ten scales. Limited to clays and sandstones on Sierra Peak at the heads of Gypsum and Coal Canyons (fig. 4.49).

Fig. 4.47.
Big-cone Douglas Fir foliage
and cones.

Fig. 4.48.
Coulter Pine
foliage and
cone.

Fig. 4.49. Tecate Cypress foliage and cones.

Fig. 4.50. Canyon Live Oak acorn and leaves.

Canyon Live Oak or **Golden-cup Oak** (*Quercus chrysolepis*). Large spreading evergreen tree. Leaves dark green on top and whitish underneath. Some leaves with smooth margins and some with spiny margins. Stringy male catkins appear March–May. Large, fat acorns appearing in the fall have a golden powder on the cup (fig. 4.50).

Madrone or **Madroño** (*Arbutus menziesii*). Attractive, open tree with polished red bark and large oval, leathery leaves 3–5 inches long. White to pinkish urn-shaped flowers in nodding 5–6-inch long clusters. Berries red to orange. Limited to shady locations in Upper Trabuco Canyon (fig. 4.39).

Chaparral Bear Grass (*Nolina cismontana*). A yucca-like species that more nearly resembles a tall bunchgrass. Related to certain desert plants that reach spectacular size with great plumes of white flowers. Endemic in the Santa Ana Mountains, although its taxonomic status is still controversial. Often associated with Manzanitas, Knobcone Pines, and Tecate Cypress. Unlike Chaparral Yucca, does not die after sending up its stalks of white flowers (fig. 4.51).

VALLEY OR COASTAL GRASSLAND

Our grasslands dominate flat areas on coastal terraces or broad valley floors. These are among the most disturbed communities in the state. Our native grasses have largely been replaced by Mediterranean weeds. Formerly our grasses mostly included perennial bunchgrasses that would die back each year and return from a perennial root system. The non-native grasses that dominate our grasslands today are mostly ephemeral or annual species that return each year from seeds that are stimulated to germinate by winter rains. Our natural grasslands also contained many species of wildflowers or forbs that provided a remarkable display of color after years with adequate precipitation. Many of these wildflowers are also fire-followers, providing a colorful ground cover the first year after a fire. Some common grassland plants include the following:

Fig. 4.51. Chaparral Beargrass on ridge above Gypsum Canyon.

Native Grasses

- **Bent Grass** (*Agrostris* spp.)
- **California Deergrass** (*Muhlenbergia rigens*)
- **Giant Wild Rye** (*Leymus condensatus*)
- **Needlegrasses** (*Nasella [Stipa]* spp.)
- **Small-flowered Melic Grass** (*Melica imperfecta*)

Introduced Grasses

- **Brome Grasses** (*Bromus* spp.)
- **Italian Ryegrass** (*Lolium multiflorum*)
- **Meadow Barley** (*Hordeum brachyantherum*)
- **Wild Oats** (*Avena fatua*)

Geophytes

- **Blue Dicks, Wild Hyacinth** (*Dichelostemma capitatum*) (fig. 4.52)
- **Blue-eyed Grass** (*Sisyrinchium bellum*) (fig. 4.53)
- **Catalina Mariposa Lily** (*Calochortus catalinae*)
- **Golden Stars** (*Bloomeria crocea*)
- **Shooting Stars** (*Dodecatheon clevelandii*)
- **Splendid Mariposa Lily** (*Calochortus splendens*)

Wildflowers (often mixed with grasses in sandy or disturbed areas)

- **California Everlasting** (*Gnaphalium californica*)
- **California Goldfields** (*Lasthenia californica*)
- **California Poppy** (*Eschscholzia californica*)
- **Caterpillar Phacelia** (*Phacelia cicutaria*)
- **Clovers** (*Trifolium* spp.)
- **Dove Weed, Turkey Mullein** (*Eremocarpus setiger*)
- **Fascicled Tarweed** (*Hemizonia fasciculata*)
- **Fiddleneck** (*Amsinckia menziesii*) (fig. 4.54)
- **Ground Pink** (*Linanthus dianthiflorus*)
- **Gumplant** (*Grindelia camporum*)
- **Miniature Lupine** (*Lupinus bicolor*)
- **Plantain** (*Plantago erecta*)
- **Popcorn Flower** (*Plagiobothrys nothofolvus*)
- **Purple Owl's Clover** (*Castilleja exserta*) (fig. 4.55)
- **Wishbone Bush** (*Mirabilis laevis*)
- **Yarrow** (*Achillea millifolium*)

Fig. 4.52. Blue Dicks.　　　Fig. 4.53. Blue-eyed Grass.　　　Fig. 4.54. Fiddleneck.

SOUTHERN OAK WOODLAND

Majestic **Coast Live Oaks** (*Quercus agrifolia*) dominate the **Southern Oak Woodland** community (fig. 4.56). They have huge root systems that tap deeply into the soil so that they are able to draw water to their leaves all year long. These large green oaks are common on canyon floors and north-facing slopes in shady canyons. The shiny green oval leaves are curled and have spiny edges (fig. 4.57). The undersides of the leaves have tufts of hair at the juncture of the main veins. The bark on these trees is fire-proof, but fires may burn off the leaves. The trees, however, can resprout from lateral buds or from the roots at the base

Fig. 4.55. Purple Owl's Clover.

of the trunk. Fog is important for these large trees; it condenses on the leaves and drips onto the ground, helping to keep the soil moist even in summer. Shade provided by the canopy of the large oaks produces

Fig. 4.56. Southern Oak Woodland with Coast Live Oaks and Western Sycamores in Emerald Canyon.

Fig. 4.57. Coast Live Oak foliage.

a refuge for many animals escaping the summer heat, and cavity-nesting birds establish homes in hollows in the trunks. In Chino Hills State Park and along the Santa Ana River and lower San Juan Creek, **California Black Walnut** (*Juglans californica*) may be found as well (fig. 4.58), and in coastal canyons large evergreen shrubs such as **California Scrub Oak** (*Quercus berberidifolia*) may intermingle with the canopy. **Poison Oak** (*Toxicodendron diversilobum*) is often an important understory species that is recognizable by its clusters of lobed leaves in groups of three. Poison Oak is winter-deciduous. Its bright red leaves add a touch of autumn color to this community. The naked stems are less recognizable in the winter but still can produce dermatitis.

Fig. 4.58. California Black Walnut foliage and fruit.

RIPARIAN WOODLAND

Trees of the **Riparian Woodland** require permanent water. They often border running streams, although they may do well in canyon bottoms where water is readily available but may not be visible on the surface. Most of the riparian species are winter-deciduous, dropping their leaves in the fall (fig. 4.59), often with a colorful display. Orange County's best display of autumn color takes place in the canyons when these trees start to go dormant during the cold season (fig. 4.60). Many riparian trees also have wind-blown seeds, which helps explain how they are distributed from one wet place to the next.

Fig. 4.59. Riparian Woodland in winter, White Alder.

Fig. 4.60. Pacific Willow in autumn.

At lower elevations **Western Sycamore** (*Platanus racemosa*) is a conspicuous species (fig. 4.56, 4.61). Sycamores have large palmately lobed leaves, and in the fall spiny golf-ball-shaped fruits adorn the tips of the stems. Farther inland and at higher elevations **Big-leaf Maple** (*Acer macrophyllum*) occurs along the streams. These trees also have palmately lobed leaves, but these are arranged oppositely on the stems. The helicopter-like fruits of these trees are called samaras. **White Alder** (*Alnus rhombifolia*), with large oval leaves, and **Fremont Cottonwood** (*Populus fremontii*), with heart-shaped leaves, are important species here as well. **Black Cottonwood** (*Populus balsamifera*) has larger, darker green leaves than Fremont Cottonwood. The cottony seeds blown from these trees sometimes cover the ground in the fall. Several species of willow also occur in this community. Along larger streams in the Santa Ana Mountains one may find **Red Willow** (*Salix laevigata*) or **Gooding's Black Willow** (*Salix goodingii*). Closer to the coast, **Arroyo Willow** (*Salix lasiolepis*) is the dominant species. Willows all have long, narrow leaves.

A fairly common evergreen species is a large odoriferous tree known as **California Laurel** or **California Bay Laurel** (*Umbellularia californica*). The dark green leaves are 3–6 inches long and emit a peppery odor when torn or crushed (fig. 4.62). Similar to commercial bay leaves, they may be used to flavor food. This is a member of the tropical Laurel Family (Lauraceae) which includes Avocado, Camphor, and Cinnamon trees. It is fairly common in the Pacific Northwest, where it is also known as Pepperwood. In Oregon the attractive wood is used to produce many carved objects and is sold as Myrtlewood. A large evergreen shrub that is common in this community is **Mule Fat** (*Baccharis salicifolia*). Mule Fat also has long narrow leaves like a willow, but it is more closely related to Coyote Brush and also has whitish rayless sunflowers.

Fig. 4.61. Western Sycamore.

Fig. 4.62. California Bay Laurel foliage and fruit.

Fig. 4.63. Mustard and Wild Chrysanthemum at Pelican Point, former site of stables, Crystal Cove State Park.

At lower elevations where stream channels widen out to alluvial flats, Sycamores are joined by **Mexican Elderberry** (*Sambucus mexicana*). This is a winter-deciduous shrublike tree that appears to have long narrow leaves, but close inspection will reveal that these are compound leaves with many leaflets. Elderberries produce purple berries and flat sprays of white flowers in the spring. Wines can be made from the berries and the flowers. In general, trees of the Riparian Woodland are winter-deciduous.

INVASIVE PLANT SPECIES

Non-native or nonindigenous plants are also called alien, exotic, or introduced species. Historically, non-natives have become established at the rate of two to four species per year. Usually they are undesirable because they tend to choke out native species. Sometimes an undesirable non-native can succeed in eliminating many native species and thus reduce the biodiversity of an entire plant community. Invasive species

Fig. 4.64. Artichoke Thistle, a significant invasive plant.

but when the die in the summer, along with dead annual grasses, they increase the fire hazard by adding significantly to fuel (fig. 4.63). It has been said that Mustard seeds were spread by Gaspar de Portolá so that he could retrace his route as he located sites for the first Spanish missions. Mustard leaves are apparently allelopathic, inhibiting the germination of native seeds. **Tumbleweed** or **Russian Thistle** (*Salsola tragus*) was introduced in a shipment of winter wheat from Russia to western Canada in the 1920s. It only took a couple of decades for wind to blow them to southern California.

can replace natives by outgrowing them, by introducing chemicals that inhibit growth (allelopathy), or by adding nitrogen to soil that normally supports species that have adapted to nitrogen-poor soils.

Non-native grasses such as **Wild Brome** (*Bromus* spp.) and **Wild Oats** (*Avena* spp.) are perhaps the most egregious of the introduced species. They rapidly replace native grasses and wildflowers to the detriment of diversity in our native Grasslands. These plants were introduced along with domestic livestock in their feed and fur. The wild **Mustards** (*Brassica* spp.) that invade our grasslands are attractive when they bloom,

Among the most invasive of our non-native species are **Artichoke Thistle** (*Cyanara cardunculus*) (fig. 4.64), **Star Thistle** (*Centaurea melitensis*), **Fennel** (*Foeniculum vulgare*), **Pampas Grass** (*Cortaderia selloana*), and **Fountain Grass** (*Pennisetum setaceum*), all of which invade our Grasslands, primarily by means of wind-blown seeds. Several poisonous species are invasive, among them **Tree Tobacco** (*Nicotiana glauca*), **Poison Hemlock** (*Conium maculatum*), **Jimson Weed** (*Datura stramonium*), and **Castor Bean** (*Ricinus communis*). Attractive shrubs in the Pea Family that have invaded our shrublands include the ornamental species **Spanish Broom** (*Spartium junceum*) and **French Broom** (*Genista linifolia*). **Giant Reed** (*Arundo donax*) and **Tamarisk** (*Tamarix chinensis*) are serious invaders in our Riparian habitats, where they rob native species of water.

Chapter 5

Invertebrates

Invertebrates are animals without backbones and include most of the animals in the world. Among these, the Arthropods (Insects, Crustaceans, Arachnids, Centipedes, and Millipedes) are the most conspicuous, particularly on land.

Native animals that live in southern California must cope with three basic stresses: low primary productivity, hot, dry summers, and cold, wet winters. Because low amounts of precipitation mean low amounts of photosynthesis, local animals have to survive in a food-poor ecosystem as well as be able to cope with drought and temperature extremes. These characteristics favor animals with low metabolic requirements. Small animals eat less food and require less space. Cold-blooded (ectothermic) animals require less food because they do not have to use food calories to heat their bodies; they move into or out of the sun to regulate their body temperatures. Don't expect to meet many big, fierce animals in Orange County.

Small, cold-blooded animals such as Insects and Spiders have a distinct advantage in our climate. They require small amounts of food, and their life cycles enable them to spend long periods of time in a state of dormancy or hibernation in which they conserve energy by lowering their body temperatures and metabolic rates.

INSECTS

Because of the 10% rule of ecosystems, insect herbivores are about ten times as common as carnivores and the creatures that prey on carnivorous insects are about a hundred times less common than the herbivores. Probably the most common native insect, therefore, is the seed-eating **California Harvester Ant** (*Pogonomyrmex californicus*). It tends to occupy sandy areas where annual plants produce large numbers of seeds. Its underground nests are easy to find by virtue of the pile of seed debris that rings the entrance to the burrow (fig. 5.1). The greatest threat to our native ants is the introduced **Argentine Ant** (*Iridomyrmex humilis*). This small black ant is omnivorous, feeding on almost any kind of food, and has become the most common ant in our homes and yards. Originally introduced to New Orleans in a coffee shipment, it has become one of the most common pests in the United States. In coastal areas, where the climate is less extreme, it out-competes the native ants, and once established it quickly eliminates native ant colonies. It does require

Fig. 5.1. California Harvester Ant nests.

Fig. 5.2. Grasshoppers mating.

year-round water, however, so environments without artificial water supplies should not support these non-native ants for long. A non-native ant that is more feared is the **Red Imported Fire Ant** (*Solenopsis invicta*). When disturbed, these swarm-stinging ants will swarm out of their underground nests and deliver painful stings to the unsuspecting human who inadvertently sits or steps on the burrow. These ants are moisture-dependent, so they thrive where there is a well-watered landscape such as a lawn. They may, however, inhabit picnic areas or campgrounds in our local parks. Fortunately, they apparently do not survive away from irrigated areas, so our natural landscapes should remain free of these pests.

Plants provide food for insects in many forms. Among the leaf-eaters, the **Rattlesnake Grasshopper** (*Opeia obscura*) is probably the most conspicuous. It tends to produce a loud rattling sound by rubbing peglike protrusions on the inner side of its hind leg against its forewing, and when it flies it makes a crackling sound. There are several other common species of grasshoppers. A number of them have colorful wings ranging from bright yellow, orange, and red to blue; the colors are important for sexual displays. They are particularly common in our local Grasslands (fig. 5.2). **Field Crickets** (*Gryllus* spp.) are also leaf-eaters. They live on the ground in cracks or under debris. Their conspicuous songs are produced by males' elevating their wings above their abdomens and rubbing together long roughened veins at the base of the forewings. The chirp rates of crickets are a function of temperature, increasing when it is warmer. Along with certain grasshoppers, crickets can become agricultural pests by invading fields in great numbers.

Where leaf debris falls to the ground there will be a community of detritus feeders. Among the insects a number of beetles fill this niche. The **Stink Beetle** (*Eleodes* spp.) is particularly common. Because the front wings (elytra) of these shiny black beetles are fused shut they cannot fly, but they can be seen busily walking about our trails. Skunklike, when disturbed they may squirt a bad-smelling liquid from their hind ends. They stand on their heads with their abdomens raised as a threat (fig. 5.3).

Fig. 5.3. Stink Beetle in defensive posture.

Fig. 5.4. Cicada molting exoskeleton.

Some insects live underground and feed on roots or underground storage organs such as tubers and bulbs. Probably the one that evokes more comment than any other is the **Jerusalem Cricket** or **Potato Bug** (*Steno-pelmatus* spp.), a large wingless cricket with a shiny bald head. It can deliver a painful bite, but it is not venomous. Its large size (up to 2 inches in length) and big bald head give it an "other-worldly" appearance and make it the subject of much superstition. It is nocturnal but spends drier months buried deep in the soil. It is most active on the surface in the spring, after significant winter rains.

Larvae of **Cicadas** (Family Cicadidae) live underground and eat roots, as do many beetle larvae known as grubs. Larval Cicadas emerge from the earth and shed their final exoskeleton to become winged adults (fig. 5.4). **June Beetles** of various species range from brown to striped. The adults emerge in the spring and often fly to lights at night. **Green Fruit Beetles** (*Polyphylla* spp.) are often erroneously called "**June Bugs**." Originally native to Arizona and New Mexico, these large green beetles spread westward to become common in

areas with orchards such as Orange County. When the orange groves were replaced by malls and housing tracts they shifted to residential areas with backyard fruit trees. Youngsters used to play with these beetles by tying a long piece of thread to one of the hind legs and letting it fly along like a sort of small self-propelled kite.

The role of insects as pollinators is well known. Plants produce colors and odors to attract pollinators, and the nectar is the reward. Among the nectar-feeding insects, butterflies and bees are the most conspicuous. About 96 species of butterflies live in Orange County. While the adults may feed on a number of different kinds of plants, often the eggs are laid and the larvae mature on certain required food plants. For example, the larvae of **Monarchs** (*Danaus plexippus*) and **Queens** (*Danaus gilippus*) (Family Nymphalidae) feed on poisonous Milkweeds (fig. 5.5). The larvae and adults are therefore poisonous, if not distasteful, and are avoided by birds. This avoidance has produced a form of mimicry whereby many orange look-alike butterflies that are not poisonous are also protected from

Fig. 5.5. Monarch Butterfly on Milkweed.

winter they roost at night in great numbers in these trees. In the morning they spread their wings and warm up, making the trees appear to have blooming butterflies. During the day they fly about feeding on nectar. These communal roosts can be observed in Mile Square Park and in certain trees near Emerald Bay in Laguna Beach.

predation. Monarchs are long-distance migrators. The adults leave in the spring and travel northward, ultimately to Canada. The butterflies return the following fall to the same areas of southern California. What is remarkable about this is that the butterflies that return are not the same ones that left the previous year. In fact, the butterflies reproduce several times during the year, with the result that the returnees are actually the great-grandchildren. They gather in the same roosting trees, usually Monterey Pines or Eucalyptus. In the

Swallowtail butterflies also are common (fig. 5.6). Many of them feed on various species in the Parsley Family (Apiaceae). The **Pale Swallowtail** (*Papillo eurymedon*) larva feeds on California Lilacs. Another group of interesting butterflies is the Blues (Family Lycaenidae), a number of which occur in localized wetland habitats near the coast, and because of destruction of that habitat these butterflies are classified as endangered. The **Pygmy Blue** (*Brephidium exilis*), considered by many to be the smallest butterfly in the world, feeds on saltbushes in coastal marshes and beach cliffs.

Fig. 5.6. Tiger Swallowtail.

Whites and Sulfurs (Family Pieridae) are familiar to gardeners. White ones generally are known as **Cabbage Butterflies** (*Pieris* spp.). The larvae generally feed on various species of Mustard. The yellow ones may be **Alfalfa Butterflies** (*Colias* spp.) because they feed on alfalfa, or they can be **Senna Sulfur** (*Phoebis sennae*), which feed on various species of *Cassia* or *Senna*, common horticultural legumes (figs. 5.7, 5.8). The **California Dogface** (*Colias eurydice*), which has black-and-white forewings and yellow hindwings, is the official state insect (fig. 5.9). It is common in the Santa Ana Mountains, where it feeds on purple flowers such as thistles.

Moths are night-flying butterflies. **Millers** (Family Noctuidae), also known as **Owlet Moths**, are the most common moths locally (fig. 5.10). The adults can be seen at night flying around lights. In the daytime they rest inconspicuously on the walls of houses or on tree trunks. The larvae are sometimes called cutworms, and many are agricultural pests that live underground feeding on roots. They are called Millers because the powder from their wings resembles flour. **Sphinx Moths** (Family Sphingidae) are also called **Hawk Moths**. Their name comes from their caterpillars' habit when disturbed of rearing back and curling their heads down in such a way that they resemble an Egyptian sphinx. These are large moths with swept-back wings. The **White-lined Sphinx** (*Hyles lineata*) is

Fig. 5.7. Cloudless Sulfur Butterfly.

Fig. 5.8. Sulfur Caterpillar on Senna.

Fig. 5.9. California Dogface (Peter Bryant).

Fig. 5.10. Miller Moth.

Fig. 5.11. White-lined Sphinx Moth.

Fig. 5.12. Hornworm, White-lined Sphinx Moth larva.

Fig. 5.13. Ctenucha Moth (Lenny Vincent).

Fig. 5.14. Honey Bee (Lenny Vincent).

a common sight in the summer, when it may be found resting on the walls of buildings (fig. 5.11). These moths are the Hummingbirds of the insect world. They hover over flowers and dip their long tongues into deep white flowers such as Jimson Weed (*Datura stramonium*). The **Tobacco Hornworm** (*Manduca sexta*) is the large green caterpillar with the horn on its rump that feeds voraciously on domestic tomato plants (fig. 5.12). The adult is a Sphinx Moth. Larvae of these moths pupate underground and emerge to feed at night, usually on white or light-colored flowers. Yuccas are plants that are pollinated by Yucca Moths (Family Incurvariidae). In our area the Chaparral Yucca (fig. 4.21) is pollinated by small white **Yucca Moths** (*Tegeticula maculata*). The moths deliberately carry pollen from one flower to the other, and the only place a female will lay her eggs is in the ovary of a Yucca Flower. The Yucca plant grows a tall stalk with a large white clusters of flowers to attract the moths. This example of mutualism is famous in the biological world. As the larvae mature they eat some of the seeds of the Yucca fruit, and when the larvae pupate they fly out to mate and repeat the process. Our Chaparral Yucca, having accomplished reproduction, blooms once and then dies. The **Ctenucha Moth** (*Ctenucha multifaria*) (Family Arctiidae) is a beautiful day-flying moth (fig. 5.13). Its abdomen is a brilliant metallic blue-green and the head is bright red. The larvae seem to feed on grasses, but the adults can be seen in great numbers from May to September feeding on a variety of flowers in Coastal Sage Scrub, particularly in the San Joaquin Hills.

There are native bees that feed on nectar, but the most common bees are the **European Honeybees** (*Apis melifera*) that were introduced to the Americas by English colonists and Spanish missionaries (fig. 5.14). The swarms of workers that appear in the spring are led by the queen in search of a new hive. New hives are often formed in the hollows of trees, particularly Coast Live Oaks, but the bees will also swarm in rock crevices or in the walls of houses. European Honeybees have displaced many of our native bees, but now they are becoming displaced by Africanized Bees, with which they hybridize. Originally introduced to Brazil, Africanized Bees made their way rapidly to the United States. They are copious honey producers, but they fiercely protect their nests by swarm-stinging and therefore can be dangerous to humans when they are disturbed. **Drone Flies** or **Flower Flies** (*Eristalis tenax*) also feed on nectar (fig.

5.15). Some are so similar in appearance to European Honeybees that most people cannot tell the difference. Sometimes they are called **H-bees** because the first two bands on the abdomen are connected by a longitudinal bar, forming the letter H. Flies have only two wings (Diptera) whereas Bees (Neuroptera) have four (two pairs) of wings. The flies are stingless, but they mix with the honeybees, taking protection from their mimicry. Larvae of the Drone Flies live in sluggish streams or small ponds, but larvae of most Flower Flies (Family Syrphidae) are predaceous; many feed on aphids.

There are many kinds of wasps in our area. Most are predaceous, but **Tarantula Hawks** (*Pepis* spp.) feed on the nectar of Milkweeds (fig. 5.16). The adults are large and black, with orange wings. Females sting a Tarantula and then drag the paralyzed spider down a burrow and lay an egg on it. The larva upon hatching feeds on the Tarantula for weeks. When the Tarantula is fully eaten, the larva pupates and hatches to emerge from the burrow. **Paper Wasps** or **Yellow Jackets** (*Vespula*

Fig. 5.15. Flower Fly pollinating Manzanita.

Fig. 5.16. Tarantula Hawks on Milkweed.

pennsylvanica) make nests of wood fibers mixed with saliva. While these nests are often visible under the eaves of houses, they more commonly are placed in burrows underground. Adults are attracted to fruit and meat and can be pests at picnics. **Mud Daubers** (*Sceliphron caementarium*) make mud nests, also under eaves or rocks. The adults are large, black-and-yellow wasps with long slim waists. Larvae are fed paralyzed spiders. **Sand Wasps** or **Digger Wasps** (*Bembix* spp.) make shallow underground burrows in which each lays a single egg. The adults are greenish-blue with black abdominal bands. The larvae are provisioned with a diet of paralyzed flies and other insects. These wasps occur in sandy areas such as beach bluffs and sand dunes. **Velvet Ants** (*Dasymutilla* spp.) are actually wasps (fig. 5.17). Females are wingless and can deliver a painful sting. Males have wings. These furry-bodied wasps in our area are usually reddish-orange. They may be seen scurrying about on the ground. They lay their eggs in the nests of ground-nesting bees and wasps, and their larvae feed on those of the ground-nesters.

Insects that suck sap have piercing mouth parts. Most of them are true Bugs (Hemiptera). Many resemble beetles, but they have a visible triangular scale between the wings known as a scutellum. Real **Stink Bugs** (*Chlorochroa* spp.) are bright green. They are common in the summer in grasslands. The black-and-orange **Harlequin Bug** (*Murgantia histrionica*) is fairly common on wild Mustards, and the **Milkweed Bug** (*Lygaeus kalmii*) is orange and gray with a black rump. It prefers milkweeds but may be found on various members of the Sunflower Family (Asteraceae) as well.

There are several species of Aphids (Family Aphididae) in our area, but most of them are found on garden and agricultural plants. One that occurs in Riparian habitats is the **Willow Aphid** (*Pterochlorus viminalis*). This is a fairly large species with black spots on its back. Aphids suck sap from the stems of plants and produce a nutrient-rich excrement known as honeydew. Ants are particularly fond of this substance and carry it back to their burrows, where they use it to grow a fungus that they use for food. Argentine Ants are notorious for farming the aphids, moving them from

Fig. 5.17. Velvet Ant.

Fig. 5.18. Lady Bird Beetles.

place to place to protect them from predators such as **Lady Bird Beetles** (fig. 5.18). **Cochineal Scale Insects** (*Dactylopius opuntiae*) form a protective mass of sticky white filaments on Coast Prickly Pear (fig. 5.19). The insect itself is a bright carmine red. Cochineal or Spanish red is a pigment that may be extracted from the insects by crushing dried specimens and boiling the powder in water. The dye has considerable commercial value.

Because their food is only 10% as abundant, carnivorous insects are much less common than herbivorous ones. The wasps mentioned above are carnivores in at least part of their life cycles. One carnivorous bug is the **Bee Assassin** (*Apiomeris crassipes*). This is a black bug with ruby-red markings and thick strong legs. It is an ambush hunter; it waits near flowers and ambushes any insect that comes near, including Honeybees. It often is found on California Buckwheat. It can use its piercing mouth parts to deliver a painful "bite." The **Praying Mantids** are perhaps our best known predacious insects. The **California Mantis** (*Stagmomantis californica*)

Fig. 5.19. Cochineal Insects on Prickly Pear cactus (Lenny Vincent).

is a large brownish mantid that is most often found in Coastal Sage Scrub (fig. 5.20). It waits motionless for other insects or spiders and captures them with its powerful front legs, which are held in a "praying" position when at rest. Males have long wings that extend beyond the abdomen, whereas the wings of females are only about half as long.

Pit-making Ant Lions (*Myreleon* spp.) and **Surface-dwelling Ant Lions** (*Brachynemurus* spp.) (fig. 5.21) are seldom seen as adults, but their larvae and their funnel-shaped pits are commonly found along trails in sandy areas. Larvae of the pit-making forms, with oversized mandibles, lurk in the bottoms of these pits waiting

Fig. 5.20. Praying Mantis (Lenny Vincent).

Fig. 5.21. Ant Lion (Lenny Vincent).

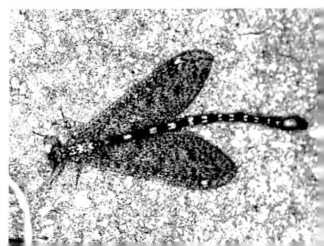

Fig. 5.22. Scud, an Amphipod (Peter Bryant).

Fig. 5.23. Water Boatman (Peter Bryant).

to prey on hapless insects, particularly ants that stumble into them. Larvae of the surface-dwelling forms are more common. They merely lie under the surface of loose soil and wait for prey to wander by. They make surface trails by walking backward. Ant Lions are one of the very few insects that are able to do this.

Blood-sucking insects prey on the blood of vertebrate animals, including humans. Perhaps the most feared is the **Western Cone-nosed Bug** or **Kissing Bug** (*Triatoma protracta*). It is in the same family (Reduviidae) as the Bee Assassin, but it usually preys on Wood Rats. It is called a Kissing Bug because it has a tendency to bite humans around the mouth. In tropical America there are species of Kissing Bugs that carry a trypanosome protozoan known to cause Chagas' disease. This disease is unknown in Orange County or the Los Angeles Basin at the present time, but the bite is painful and some people have an allergic reaction ranging from itching and swelling to anaphylactic shock. The main reason these bugs come in contact with humans is that they are attracted to lights.

AQUATIC ARTHROPODS

Crustaceans are aquatic counterparts to the insects. They are extremely common and thrive in nearly every habitat, including those in Orange County. The ubiquitous **Copepods** are arguably the most common animals in the world. These are microscopic shrimplike crustaceans that feed on very small photosynthetic organisms and are very important in most aquatic food chains. **Scuds** (Amphipods) are detritus-feeders often found in algal mats along the edge of slow-moving water (fig. 5.22). They appear to be small versions of **Pill Bugs** or **Sow Bugs**, terrestrial crustaceans found in most suburban gardens. **Crayfish** are lobster-like animals up to 8 inches in length. Common in almost all warm-water habitats, they ingest crustaceans, worms, insect larvae, and small fishes. They also feed on carrion and are therefore the scavengers of an aquatic ecosystem. Crayfish are not native to Orange County, but they have been introduced as fish bait and as food; the meaty tails and claws are eaten by many people. In some places crayfish are sold under the name "Langostino," which means "little lobster." Another name for them is Crawdads.

Insects are common in freshwater habitats but generally absent in association with seawater. True bugs (Hemiptera) include several families of common aquatic insects. **Water Striders** (Family Gerridae) are long-legged bugs about 1 inch in length. They move about on the surface of slow-moving water, feeding on small prey items. They are kept from sinking by the presence of many tiny water-repellent hairs on their feet. The effect of these hairs can be appreciated by watching the shadow of a Water Strider on the bottom of a shallow pool. On the shadow it appears that each foot terminates in a circular disc that looks like a small satellite dish. **Backswimmers** (Family Notonectidae) get their name from the fact that they swim on their backs (upside down). These fast-swimming predators feed on small crustaceans, aquatic insect larvae, and small fishes. Most numerous of the aquatic bugs are the **Water Boatmen** (Family Corixidae). They get their name from their oarlike hind legs, which they use to propel themselves (fig. 5.23). While underwater, in order to breathe, they carry a bubble of air on the undersides of their bodies, which gives their underneath surfaces a silvery appearance. These are extremely important insects in aquatic communities because they are shredders of leaf litter and debris. **Gi-**

ant Water Bugs (Family Belastomatidae), large predatory insects also known as **Toe-biters**, may reach 2 inches in length. They can capture and consume a variety of prey including insects, tadpoles, and fishes.

There are about ten families of **Water Beetles** (Coleoptera). The most common are the **Diving Beetles** (Family Dytiscidae). These predatory beetles swim with oarlike hind legs and carry air under their wing covers (elytra) (fig.5.24). They refill these cavities by surfacing rump first or backing into bubbles formed by aquatic plants. **Water Scavenger Beetles** (Family Hydrophylidae) differ slightly in appearance from Diving Beetles; they are flattened instead of rounded on the underside. More important, they are herbivorous instead of carnivorous, but they often are found in the same water.

There are several kinds of insects that are aquatic during their immature stages (larvae or nymphs) but terrestrial flying forms as adults. Adult **Caddisflies** (Trichoptera), **Mayflies** (Ephemeroptera) (fig. 5.25), and **Stoneflies** (Plecoptera) are similar

Fig. 5.24. Diving Beetle (Peter Bryant).

Fig. 5.25. Mayfly adult (Peter Bryant).

Fig. 5.26. Dragonfly nymph (Peter Bryant).

Fig. 5.27. Dragonfly.

Fig. 5.28. Damselfly.

in appearance, with large membranous wings. Usually the adult stage is of short duration, and the adults may not feed at all. The larvae or nymphs spend their lives underwater, coming out of hiding to feed on detritus or algae at night. They commonly live in streams, so they are equipped with hooks and are often flattened or streamlined to withstand the current. The emergence of adults is known as the "hatch." At this time, trout fishermen attempt to catch fish by offering dry flies that mimic whatever is hatching. Some larvae of Caddisflies are known as case builders. They pick up bits of debris from the bottom and build protective shells around themselves. Different species in different habitats use different materials. Some larvae cut up bits of leaves, others use pine needles, and some use small stones.

Dragonflies and **Damselflies** (Odonata) prey on mosquitoes and other flies. Immatures (nymphs) are totally aquatic (fig. 5.26). As adults, **Darners** (Family Aeshnidae) and **Skimmers** (Family Libellulidae) rest with their four wings spread open (fig. 5.27), whereas the smaller Damselflies (Zygoptera) tend to rest with their wings folded back (fig. 5.28). The **Green Darner** (*Anax junius*) is over 3 inches long. Like other Dragonflies, Green Darners mate while flying, and they may be observed some distance from water. The **Big Red Skimmer** (*Libellula saturata*) is often seen near streams and ponds. Its length is about 2½ inches and its wings are bright orange-red over the basal half. The **Violet Dancer** (*Argia vivida*) is an intense blue. It may be seen flitting along near aquatic vegetation, particularly along mountain streams. After the female mates it crawls down the stem of an emergent sedge or cattail and inserts the eggs into the stem. Immatures, with three feathery gills on the ends of their abdomens, crawl around in leaf litter and debris underwater.

Mosquitoes (Family Culicidae) are small blood-sucking flies (Diptera) that represent a major irritation to humans. Male and female adults feed primarily on nectar; only females suck blood. They need at least one blood meal to stimulate ovarian development and reproduction. Because they are annoying and carry disease, there are intense programs for Mosquito abatement. Malaria is virtually non-existent in Orange County, but up until the 1920s it was a significant disease in California, particularly in the Central Valley, where there were abundant marshes and wetlands for breeding. The primary concern today is that some Mosquitoes (*Culex* spp.) carry the virus responsible for strains of equine encephalitis, incorrectly referred to as sleeping sickness. Typically, the virus is carried by birds, so in areas where encephalitis occurs, vector control officers periodically sample the blood of chickens for presence of the virus and educational programs advise residents to eliminate standing water in which the larvae (wigglers) develop. The best technique for preventing the bite of a mosquito is to use a mosquito repellent that contains toluamide or DEET. Mosquitoes locate vertebrate prey by a combination of heat, the odor of nitrogenous waste (urea), and carbon dioxide. DEET works by blocking the odor receptors on the mosquito's proboscis. The mosquito may find you by the heat you produce, but it won't recognize you as a source of blood.

ARACHNIDS

Arachnids include Spiders, Ticks, and Scorpions. As far as biomass is concerned, these represent the most abundant predators in our local habitats. They are seldom seen because they are small, well camouflaged, or simply rare. All of them are ambush hunters. As described by Lenny Vincent of Fullerton College, the Arachnids of Orange County are as follows:

Spiders

All spiders are carnivorous, and almost all have venom that is used to subdue their prey. The prey is digested externally and only liquefied food is ingested. Silk figures prominently in the life history of spiders. Silk, which is made of protein, may be used to line burrows, wrap prey, cover eggs, aid dispersal during breezy days (ballooning), and construct webs. Some spiders do not use webs to capture prey but rely on keen eyesight to actively hunt their victims. At least 166 species of spiders are known locally from Coastal Sage Scrub. Some of the common ones are the following:

Orb Weavers (Family Araneidae) are represented by several species. Two species of large and colorful garden spiders are obvious daytime ambush predators that hang head-down in the centers (hubs) of their large and conspicuous orb webs. Heavy zigzag bands of silk known as stabilimenta are often visible in the webs. The adult female **Banded Garden Spider** (*Argiope trifasciata*) has an oval

Fig. 5.29. Banded Garden Spider (Lenny Vincent).

Fig. 5.30. Silver-backed Garden Spider (Lenny Vincent).

abdomen that is marked on top by alternating transverse silvery-white or yellowish bands and narrow dark bands (fig. 5.29). The top (dorsal) surface of the cephalothorax has silver hairs. The legs have dark spots on a yellow background. Females are up to 1 inch long. Adult males, which are seldom seen unless they are in the female's web preparing to mate, are about one-quarter the size. The abdomen of a **Silver-backed Garden Spider** (*Argiope argentata*) has three pairs of lateral lobes (fig. 5.30). The front half of the abdomen is yellowish while the back half has a triangular pattern that is dark with a few white marks. Adult females are about $^3/_4$ inch in length; males are very small and seldom seen.

Cyclosa turbinata is a small Orb Weaving Spider about $^1/_4$ inch long (fig. 5.31). Its abdomen, mottled white, gray, and black, is distinctive in having a large conical hump at the posterior end and two small humps at the anterior end. The vertical orb web of females is also distinctive because of the thick, central vertical stabilimentum that extends from the top frame thread through the hub of the orb. The spider nestles within this stabilimentum along with her numerous egg sacs, which are covered with the insect remains of past meals. **Labyrinth Spiders** (*Metepeira* spp.), depending on the species, range in size from $^1/_5$ to $^1/_2$ inch in length (fig. 5.32). The first body segment, the carapace, is brown. The abdomen is also brown but with a pretty leaflike pattern

Fig. 5.31. Orb web of *Cyclosa turbinata*, a small Orb Weaver (Lenny Vincent).

Fig. 5.32. Labyrinth Spider (*Metepeira* sp.) (Lenny Vincent).

Fig. 5.33. *Agelenopsis*, a Funnel-web Weaver (Lenny Vincent).

Fig. 5.34. Black Widow (Lenny Vincent).

of white, black, and specks of red. Behind the vertical orb web, this spider constructs a maze-like tangle web from which it gets its name. In the center of the maze *Metepeira* builds a distinctive little tentlike retreat. Egg sacs are laid within the tent and covered with pieces of insect remains. The best place to look for these webs is in patches of Prickly Pear.

Funnel-web Weavers (Family Agelenidae) are represented by at least four genera in our area (fig. 5.33). Only the large webs of *Agelenopsis* are easy to spot. Some species build their webs in vegetation, for example, between Prickly Pear pads, while others build on the ground. The nonsticky webs are flat horizontal sheets that extend out from a funnel. It is common for the funnel to originate in a vacated rodent burrow. These spiders are sensitive to vibrations and if disturbed will retreat into the depths of the funnel.

Cobweb Spiders (Family Theridiidae) are a very diverse group of relatively small oval or globose spiders with 62 genera known worldwide. Many species make conspicuous irregular three-dimensional nonsticky webs both in and around the house as well as in the field. Their webs may be found under road-cut

overhangs, in tree holes, between the large forking branches of Oaks and Sycamores, and in rodent holes or cracks in the soil. The **Black Widow** (*Latrodectus hesperus*) is one of five species of widow spider in the United States and the only one found throughout California (fig. 5.34). The less dangerous **Brown Widow** (*L. geometricus*), first found in Los Angeles County in 1999, is now recorded as of 2008 in more than 30 cities in Southern California, including several in Orange County. Away from habitation it is most often found in a rodent burrow hanging upside down with its hourglass clearly visible. Black Widow webs are unusually strong. When an insect is caught in the web, the spider uses its last pair of legs to cast sticky silk from its spinnerets over the prey.

Sheetweb Weavers (Family Linyphiidae) are represented by more than 4,000 species worldwide. Our most conspicuous species produce a sheet of silk that is slightly domed in the center. The spider hangs upside down below the dome, and prey caught in the web are bitten from below and pulled through the sheet to be consumed. Webs are found in Prickly Pear patches and on the outer portions of shrubs.

Fig. 5.35. Wolf Spider with egg sac (Lenny Vincent).

Fig. 5.36. Green Lynx (Lenny Vincent).

Fig. 5.37. Jumping Spider.

Fig. 5.38. Sac Spider *Cheiracanthium*.

Cursorial Spiders are spiders that appear to spend much of their time on the ground and do not spin webs. "Cursorial" means "running." **Wolf Spiders** (Family Lycosidae) in our area hunt on the ground and can most easily be seen moving about in road cuts during the day. They have excellent vision and an acute sense of touch. In many cases they may employ an ambush hunting technique, rushing prey at close proximity. At times an adult female can be seen with a large egg sac attached to spinnerets at the tip of her abdomen or with spiderlings riding high on her cephalothorax (fig. 5.35). Two genera of **Lynx Spiders** (Family Oxyopidae), *Peucetia* and *Oxyopes*, are found in our Coastal Sage Scrub. They are typically found on vegetation rather than on the ground. Lynx Spiders have good eyesight and are active day hunters. They can run and jump, sometimes over an inch, to grab prey upon or flying over vegetation. They are easily identified by the prominent long spines on their legs and, upon closer examination, the hexagonal arrangement of six of their eight eyes. Both genera have long tapering abdomens. The carapace of our local *Oxyopes*, depending on the species, may be yellowish with indistinct longitudinal gray bands or reddish brown on the sides and yellow in the center. The more commonly seen *Peucetia*, aptly named the **Green Lynx**, is mostly green with some small red spots interspersed and is about ¾ inch long (fig. 5.36). It is often found on California Buckwheat.

Jumping Spiders (Family Salticidae) are the largest spider family in the world, with over 5,000 species (fig. 5.37). They actively hunt their prey during the day, taking advantage of their excellent eyesight. Their eyes are

Fig. 5.39. *Misumenopsoides*, a Flower Spider (Lenny Vincent).

also important in mating behavior, which involves a courtship dance including leg and palp waving. Our most conspicuous salticids belong to the genus *Phidippus*. They can be recognized easily by their bright red-and-black coloration.

Sac Spiders (Family Miturgidae) when not hunting rest in a pillow-shaped silk sac. They live in Coastal Sage Scrub and are not seen often. An exception is *Cheiracanthium*, which can be found hunting in vegetation. *Cheiracanthium* is about ¼ inch long with a slender pale yellow to pale green body (fig. 5.38).

Crab Spiders (Family Thomisidae) have a flattened crablike appearance and tend to scuttle sideways like crabs. They are mostly cryptically colored diurnal spiders and are often found motionless in flowers, where they patiently await the arrival of unsuspecting pollinators such as bees. Many species have powerful front legs and venom that allow them to catch prey many times

larger than themselves. Yellowish Crab Spiders belonging to the genus *Misumenops* or *Misumenopsoides* are common locally (fig. 5.39).

Tarantulas (Family Theraphosidae) of the genus *Aphonopelma* are often seen walking about in the fall (fig. 5.40). In almost all cases, it is the adult male that is seen. These males are likely searching for female burrows, not hunting for prey. Females remain in their burrows all year long. Relying on their sense of touch, Tarantulas hunt at night near the burrow entrance. In captivity, the females can live 30 or so years.

Fig. 5.40. Tarantula.

Fig. 5.41. Scorpion.

Scorpions

Like Spiders, all Scorpions are carnivorous. They are usually only seen at
night, near their retreats, foraging or
waiting for prey to approach. They feed
on insects, spiders, and other invertebrates including other scorpions.
During the day, they hide in their burrows or under bark or rocks. Depending on their size relative to the prey,
they may use pedipalps (pinchers) or
the venomous stinger to subdue their
prey (fig. 5.41). Most Scorpions will
use their stingers in defense. The total
number of species of Scorpions found
in Orange County is not known. *Ser-
radigitus gertschi, Paruroctonus silvestrii,
Anuroctonus pococki, Pseudouroctonus
angelenus,* and *Vaejovis puritanus* are the
most likely to be encountered.

Ticks

Ticks live on blood acquired from mammalian prey. Feeding takes place in the spring
and summer months. Adults hang on vegetation and wait until a mammal passes near
enough for them to latch on. They feed
until satiated and then drop off. Soft ticks
(Family Argasidae) are seldom encountered
by humans; hard ticks (Family Ixodidae) are
those we usually concern ourselves with.
The **Western Black-legged Tick** or **Deer
Tick** (*Ixodes pacificus*) is of some concern to
humans because it carries several diseases,
including Lyme disease. The **Pacific Coast
Tick** (*Dermacenter occidentalis*) is the most
likely to be encountered by a local hiker. It
is the vector for Rocky Mountain spotted
fever in some parts of the western United
States. The **American Dog Tick** (*Dermacenter variabilis*) is the one that is most likely

to become attached to your dog while hiking in local brushy areas (fig. 5.42). When it becomes engorged with blood it can be the size of a peanut.

Chiggers

Contrary to popular belief, **Chiggers** or **Harvest Mites** (Family Trombiculidae) do not burrow under the skin of their host. **Belkin's Chigger** (*Eutrombicula belkini*) is found in a few localities in southern California, particularly in Ventura and Orange Counties near the coast. Larval chiggers, about the size of a pinpoint, wait in fresh grasses and crawl up the legs of an unsuspecting hiker, where they tend to stop at a restriction such as the sock line or waist line. The larva injects digestive juices into the skin, causing an itchy red bump that may last for several days. After its blood meal, it drops off. Insect repellents applied to the skin of the lower leg and under the socks usually will deter chiggers.

A fairly new science is being used to document the presence or absence of suspected criminals at the scene of a crime. The science could be called "forensic entomology." In June of 2007 a murder suspect claimed that he was in a Midwestern state at the time his family members were murdered in California. Entomologists identified a large grasshopper, a paper wasp, and two true bugs that were taken from the radiator of an automobile rented by the suspect. The entomologists testified that the car was used in the Western states because those insects did not occur in the Midwest. A similar situation occurred involving chiggers in California. Because chiggers are known from so few places in California, a murder suspect with chigger bites was placed at the precise location where the body of his murdered girlfriend was found.

CENTIPEDES

Centipedes are long slender Arthropods with a pair of legs on each body segment (fig. 5.43). They are carnivorous, feeding on a variety of prey that they capture by means of venom produced by their fanglike jaws, known as chelicerae. Centipedes rarely bite humans, but their clawed legs may produce perforations on the thin skin of some people. Six species have been reported from Orange County. One common form, the **Tiger Centipede** (*Scolopendra polymorpha*), may be found under rocks, logs, and bark.

Fig. 5.42. Dog Tick (Lenny Vincent).

Fig. 5.43. Centipede.

Fig. 5.44. Millipede.

MILLIPEDES

Two species of Millipedes have been reported for Orange County (fig. 5.44). Millipedes have two pairs of legs on each body segment. They have an appearance like an elongate Pill Bug. These are detritus feeders and harmless to humans. They are found in moist places on the ground or in rotten logs. They seem to glide along smoothly with wave-like movements of their many legs. When disturbed they secrete an odorous substance that contains a drug that acts like a tranquilizer. If a Spider preys on a Millipede, the Spider falls asleep. If it survives being immobilized, it is unlikely to prey again on a Millipede. Although the Millipede may die from the Spider bite, it has "altruistically" protected other millipedes from predation.

LAND SNAILS

Of the three most conspicuous land snails in Orange County, two are non-natives. The common **Garden Snail** (*Helix aspersa*) was originally introduced from France as an exotic food. Its present distribution is more or less restricted to irrigated land-scapes associated with urban settings. It is suitable for human consumption but first must be purged of its gut contents. The typical procedure is to keep the snails in a container of corn meal. As the snails consume the corn meal their gut contents are replaced with the edible material, making them more palatable. Steamed and drenched in garlic butter, they make a fine addition to a gourmet meal. The **Spanish Milk Snail** (*Otala lactea*) is also native to the Mediterranean region. It is hardier than the Garden Snail, able to withstand long-term exposure to direct sun. Where it occurs it may be seen clinging to fence posts, shrubs, or dead sticks. The only conspicuous native snail is the Southern **California Shoulder Band** (*Helminthoglypta tudiculata*), a large olive-colored species with a single light-colored stripe along the length of the coil. It is associated with coastal habitats such as Coastal Sage Scrub and Grasslands.

There is a species of freshwater snail that might be recognized in slow-moving water. The **Pond Snail** (*Physella virgata*) is a small species in which the shell coils to the left. These snails feed on algae and detritus. There are also some freshwater snails in which the shell coils to the right. The non-native **New Zealand Mud Snail** (*Potamopyrgus antiipodarum*) has been reported from several local streams, particularly Trabuco Creek. Its presence is considered undesirable because it tends to replace the native species.

Vertebrates are animals with backbones: fishes, amphibians (frogs, salamanders), reptiles (lizards, snakes, turtles), birds, and mammals. The vertebrate animals of Orange County are surprisingly diverse. The ones that are likely to be seen or are most interesting from the perspective of a naturalist are described below.

FISHES

Most of our native freshwater fishes are in the Minnow Family (Cyprinidae) or the Trout Family (Salmonidae). For the most part these are fishes of running-water habitats. In Orange County these habitats are severely threatened by channelization, pollution, and groundwater overdraft. Lower reaches of the Santa Ana River and San Juan Creek are good examples of channelization. There is nothing natural about a concrete-lined watercourse. The Santa Ana River historically would dry up in the summer and flow to the sea during the rainy season. Today its flow is regulated by Prado Dam in order to protect homes and businesses that have sprung up

along its banks between Riverside County and the ocean, and it flows year-round. This water is primarily secondary effluent from sewer treatment plants in Riverside and San Bernardino Counties but also includes urban and residential runoff from all the cities upstream. In the Anaheim area much of this water is trapped in percolation ponds that allow the water to sink into the earth and recharge the water table. Water districts in Orange County then pump out the groundwater for residential and industrial consumption. This type of pumping ultimately lowers the water table and promotes the drying of surface water in small streams. The only natural stream that runs all the way to the sea undisturbed is San Mateo Creek, which runs from the Santa Ana Mountains to San Onofre State Beach just south of the Orange County line. As might be expected, this creek contains a good representation of native aquatic species. The effect on this creek of the proposed routing of Highway 241 remains to be seen.

The **Coastal Rainbow Trout** (*Onchorynchus mykiss*) is one of the most widely distributed species in the state (fig. 6.1). It has been introduced as a game fish in many places. Its distribution is spotty in Orange County, but one never knows where it will show up. Historically one form of this species was known as the **Southern Steelhead Trout**. This was a sea-run form that spent most of its adult life at sea and returned to coastal drainages

Fig. 6.1. Rainbow Trout.

such as the Santa Ana River, San Juan Creek, or San Mateo Creek to spawn. Old photos of these fish show that they reached large size; some reports say that they were "as long as a man's leg." Recently they have been discovered spawning in San Mateo Creek, and there are unofficial reports of them in San Juan Creek as well. There is a move among some biologists to enhance the lower reaches of San Juan Creek with fish ladders to encourage Steelhead once again to migrate upstream to perceived ancestral spawning grounds.

Other than Rainbow Trout, our most common native fish is the **Arroyo Chub** (*Gila orcutti*), although it is only locally common in San Juan and San Mateo Creeks (fig.

6.2). Chubs are in the Minnow Family. They lack the adipose fin and speckled appearance of the Rainbow and seldom exceed 3 inches in length. They appear to be the only fish species at the Audubon Sanctuary in Bell Canyon, a tributary of San Juan Creek. There is some question whether they were introduced to San Juan Creek along with Rainbow Trout. Likewise, the **Threespine Stickleback** (*Gasterosteus aculeatus*) is often introduced along with trout. This small species with three sharp spines in front of its dorsal fin was formerly also a sea-run species, mating in shallow waters of coastal streams. Male sticklebacks develop bright red bellies during the breeding season.

Fig. 6.2. Arroyo Chub.

Fig. 6.3. Speckled Dace.

An estuary species that was once documented in the freshwater of San Juan Creek is the **California Killifish** (*Fundulus parvipinnis*) (fig. 7.47). This is a common small fish in estuaries throughout the state. It is a top-feeder, recognizable by the upward tilted mouth, placed at the front and top of its head. The San Juan Creek population was entirely an inhabitant of freshwater, but it has been extirpated since the creek in that area has been concrete-lined. Another estuary species that spent limited time in freshwater is the **Tidewater Goby** (*Eucyclogobius newberryi*). This 2-inch fish is recognized as a Goby by its ventral cone-shaped suction cup, formed by the union of its pelvic fins. This is a seriously endangered species that formerly occurred in the mouths of Orange County rivers. Lately it has been recorded only in San Mateo Creek. It is threatened by habitat destruction and the introduction of non-native fish such as Large-mouth Bass.

The **Speckled Dace** (*Rhinichthys osculus*) was once the most common minnow in the western United States (fig. 6.3). In the Los Angeles area today the Santa Ana form occurs only in headwaters of the Los Angeles, San Gabriel, and Santa Ana Rivers.

Fig. 6.4. Santa Ana Sucker.

In Orange County it is found only in certain permanent pools in Santiago Creek. This minnow species is recognized by its 3-inch length, pointed nose, and dark speckles on its sides and top. It is a candidate for listing as an endangered species.

The **Santa Ana Sucker** (*Catostomus santaanae*) looks like a minnow, but its ventral, sucker-shaped mouth indicates that it is in the Sucker Family (Catostomidae) (fig. 6.4). Large specimens of this species have reached about 6 inches in length. This species, federally listed as threatened, occurs today mainly in the headwaters of the San Gabriel and Los Angeles Rivers and in the lowland floodplains of the Santa Ana River, particularly in the vicinity of Riverside. Formerly it occurred all the way to the mouth of the Santa Ana River and in Santiago Creek, but its habitat there has been seriously disturbed by gravel mining.

AMPHIBIANS

Amphibians are cold-blooded vertebrates without scales, feathers, or fur. Most of them can live either in or out of water. Because their skin is permeable to water they need to remain near water, but they secrete mucus on the skin to inhibit evaporation. Being small and cold-blooded, they do not require large quantities of food. Although they seem ill-suited to our hot, dry climate, Orange County has a surprising diversity of amphibians.

Salamanders are amphibians with tails and four legs of similar size. The **Coast Range Newt** (*Taricha torosa*) is our only member of the Newt Family (*Salamandridae*). This

Fig. 6.5. Coast Range Newt.

is a rough-skinned salamander that is light-brown on the top and orange underneath (fig. 6.5). The larvae are aquatic and resemble the adults, but the aquatic forms have oarlike tails that they use for swimming. During summer, adults may move away from water and become dormant, resting under rocks, logs, or even wood rat nests. After the winter rains begin they migrate to nearby streams and ponds, where they mate. Fertilized egg masses are deposited in slow-moving pools. Larvae hatch in about four to six weeks. The skin of newts is poisonous, containing a chemical known as tetrodotoxin, the same chemical that makes Puffer Fishes poisonous. It deters predators, which may die from it, but it also serves as a sex attractant during the mating season.

Most of our salamanders are Lungless Salamanders (Family Plethodontidae). These are terrestrial salamanders that breathe through their skin, particularly on the underside of their bodies and through their toe tips. They spend most of their time under some form of cover where they can remain moist. Our most common Lungless Salamanders look like earthworms with legs. They are known as

Slender Salamanders. The **Garden Slender Salamander** (*Batrachoseps major*) is about the size of a pencil, up to 6 inches in length, with a tail about twice its body length (fig. 6.6). It is brownish-black on top and grayish underneath. These salamanders are found in many habitats including suburban gardens from the foothills to the coast. After the first rains of the year they begin to appear in moist locations, under rocks, logs, boards, and trash cans. During the dry season they retreat to cracks where they remain dormant until it rains again. They are active mostly at night, when they crawl about feeding on small insects such as termites. The **Black-bellied Slender Salamander** (*Batrachoseps nigriventris*) is smaller than the Garden Slender Salamander. It is recognized by its blackish belly with light speckles. Often associated with Oaks, it occurs farther inland and at higher elevations than the Garden Slender Salamander. Its southernmost distribution in Orange County is at Aliso Creek and at Tenaja Creek in the Santa Ana Mountains. It coexists with the Garden Slender Salamander in parts of Laguna Beach and the San Joaquin Hills.

The **Arboreal Salamander** (*Aneides lugubris*) is a large robust salamander with a body length up to 4 inches (fig. 6.7). It is purplish-brown with yellow spots on top and creamy to gray underneath. Its toe-tips are visibly expanded. Most often associated with Oaks or Sycamores, it tends to inhabit the canyons in the Santa Ana Mountains. It is often found under logs or in leaf litter but may crawl up into cavities in the trees or in hollow logs to lay its eggs. It is known to eat Ants, Caterpillars, Spiders, and Centipedes.

The **Monterey Salamander** (*Ensatina eschscholtzii*) is a reddish, smooth-skinned salamander with large dark eyes (fig. 6.8). It is often found on roads in the canyons during rainstorms and may be active in the daytime. It occupies a variety of habitats, but particularly Oak and Coniferous Woodlands above 1,000 feet elevation. Its food habits are similar to the Arboreal Salamander's, and sometimes the two species are found in the same hollow log

Frogs and Toads have no tails as adults, but their aquatic larvae, known as tadpoles, have tails. Metamorphosis of these amphibians is well known, and many people have watched captive tadpoles lose their tails and grow legs. Toads are more terrestrial than frogs. They tend to have roughened, warty skin, and their hind legs are shorter than those of frogs. The webs between their hind toes are not as well developed as the webbed feet of frogs. Toads have large oval glands, known as parotoid glands, behind their eyes. These glands secrete a distasteful, sometimes poisonous mucus as a deterrent to predation.

The Spadefoot Toad Family (Pelobatidae) has only one representative in Orange County, the **Western Spadefoot Toad** (*Spea [= Scaphiopus] hammondi*) (fig. 6.9). The adults are blunt-nosed and have large golden-colored eyes with vertically elliptical pupils. They are greenish on top and whitish underneath. The hind foot has a dark digging spur. This nocturnal toad spends most of the year underground. It emerges

Fig. 6.6. Garden Slender Salamander.

Fig. 6.7. Arboreal Salamander.

Fig. 6.8. Monterey Salamander.

Fig. 6.9. Western Spadefoot Toad.

Fig. 6.10. Western Toads mating.

Fig. 6.11. Pacific Treefrog.

in winter, when it breeds and lays eggs in temporary pools. While the adults are seldom seen, hikers sometimes see the larvae in puddles on dirt roads in the San Joaquin Hills. They were formerly common along Santiago Creek, but gravel mining and other activities have destroyed much of their habitat. The state has listed this toad as a species of special concern.

The True Toad family (Bufonidae) includes our most commonly observed amphibian, the **Western Toad** (*Bufo boreas*). This toad is fairly large, up to 5 inches in body length. It is easily recognized by a distinct yellow stripe down its back (fig. 6.10). Its parotoid glands are larger than its eyelids. These toads occur in a great variety of habitats, sometimes quite a distance from water. It is not uncommon to find them on wet suburban lawns at night. The breeding call is a repetitive birdlike chirp.

The **Arroyo Toad** (*Bufo californicus*) is an inhabitant of sandy streambeds in the foothills, in association with Oaks and Sycamores. During the dry season these toads remain in burrows on stream terraces, but

during the rainy season they become active along streams. They are primarily nocturnal, so they are seldom seen. Adults can be recognized as having no mid-dorsal stripe, and the parotoid glands are bicolored, dark in back and light in front. This species is federally listed as endangered. Its most serious threat is habitat destruction.

Two kinds of treefrogs are found in Orange County. The **Pacific Treefrog** (*Pseudacris [= Hyla] regilla*) is the most common, occurring in a variety of freshwater habitats from the foothills to the coast (fig. 6.11). These are small frogs with expanded toe tips that, acting like suction cups, enable them to climb even the smoothest of surfaces. They do not need to be associated with trees; it is not uncommon to find them on the walls of the restrooms in our coastal parks. They come in a variety of colors but are easily recognized by their dark eye stripe. In the spring they gather in large numbers in slow-moving pools of water. Their mating calls are easily recognized as the familiar "ribbit" that produces the din emanating from the local canyons at night. The **Cali-**

Fig. 6.12. California Treefrogs mating.

Fig. 6.13. Western Pond Turtle and Red-eared Slider.

fornia Treefrog (*Pseudacris [= Hyla] cadaverina*) is most often found in the foothills of the Santa Ana Mountains along streams with large boulders (fig. 6.12). These treefrogs have no eye stripes and are usually grayish, matching exactly the color of the boulder on which they perch. They seldom occur in large aggregations. Their call resembles that of the Pacific Treefrog but is a single note rather than the two-syllable "ribbit" sound.

REPTILES

Reptiles are cold-blooded vertebrates that usually are recognized by their scaly skin. They lay shelled eggs and have internal fertilization, adaptations that enable them to live away from water. Usually we think of lizards and snakes in this group, but turtles also are reptiles.

Our only native **Turtle** is the **Western Pond Turtle** (*Actinemys [= Clemmys] marmorata*). This turtle, which may reach 7 inches in length, is a uniform brown to khaki color (fig. 6.13). It is usually seen sunning itself beside slow-moving water in

a stream or pond. No longer common in our foothill streams, it formerly inhabited the lower Santa Ana River. It may be seen at the San Joaquin Marsh, lower Aliso Creek, San Mateo Creek, or Carbon Canyon Regional Park. It is classified as a species of special concern by the state and the federal government. Its most serious threats are habitat destruction and introduced turtles such as the **Red-eared Slider**, which has a red stripe on the side of its head, and the **Western Painted Turtle**, which has yellow stripes on its back and orange markings on its belly.

Another non-native turtle with a patchy record in Orange County is the **Spiny Softshell Turtle** (*Apalone spinifera*). These aquatic turtles, with a round flattened shell and a long neck, have been documented for the Santa Ana River and the lower San Diego Creek near the University of California at Irvine. They float or paddle along with just their long pointed noses and eyes above the surface. They may reach 18 inches in length. From time to time there are reports of Snapping Turtles in Orange County waters. The most famous case involved a 100-pound **Al-**

ligator Snapping Turtle (*Macrochelys temmincki*) that in September 2004 was finally removed from Laguna Lake in Fullerton. For years there were tales of a monster that pulled ducks underwater, and the mystery finally was solved with the capture and removal of the Snapping Turtle.

Lizards, in general, are active in the daytime. In Orange County, all of our lizards are insectivorous. They eat termites, ants, earwigs, beetles, and spiders. Most are inactive during the winter, hibernating under debris, logs, rocks, or in cracks, and become conspicuous by basking in the sunlight while warming up. Many disappear on cold days and reappear when it is warm.

One of the most common is a small species known as the **Side-blotched Lizard** (*Uta stansburiana*). Just a bit over 3 inches in total length, it is distinguished by a black blotch on its side just behind its front legs (fig. 6.14). It prefers open spaces and is frequently seen basking beside a trail or scurrying into cover. Usually seen as brown with blotches on their backs, breeding males can be quite colorful, with small blue or orange spots on their backs and a blue patch on the throat that they display to other males or breeding females. Recent research shows that orange males have larger breeding ranges and mate with a greater number of females, whereas the blue males mate with fewer females and guard their mates. Yellow males resemble females and are able to sneak up and mate with them without being noticed by dominant males. Side-blotched Lizards are short-lived, with high reproductive rates. Numerous juveniles appear in early summer and are able to reproduce the following spring.

Most common overall is the **Western Fence Lizard** (*Sceloporus occidentalis*), also brownish with dark blotches (fig. 6.15). Breeding males may be black with white, green, or blue spots on their backs. The belly and throat of these males is a bright iridescent blue that is exposed to breeding females or other males by doing "pushups." The brilliant blue of the belly is responsible for the common name "Blue-bellied Lizard." Western Fence Lizards may be seen throughout the county. They tend to seek habitats with more cover and larger boulders than

Fig. 6.14. Side-blotched Lizard.

Fig. 6.15. Western Fence Lizard.

the Side-blotched Lizard, but the two species coexist throughout much of their range. An interesting feature is a protein in their blood that kills the infectious bacterium carried by ticks that causes Lyme disease.

At higher elevations, particularly in association with large rock outcrops in the Santa Ana Mountains, the **Granite Spiny Lizard** (*Sceloporus orcutti*) may be found. It resembles the Western Fence Lizard but has a dark band on each side of the neck (fig. 6.16). In addition to the blue coloration on the belly, breeding males often have an iridescent violet stripe down the center of the back. These attractive lizards are quite wary and retreat into a crack in the rocks when approached by humans.

The **Coast Horned Lizard** (*Phrynosoma coronatum*) was fairly common in years past, particularly in Coastal Sage Scrub (fig. 6.17). Although commonly called a "Horned Toad," it is a reptile, not an amphibian. It is adept at camouflage, matching the background on which it rests and pressing its flattened body against the ground so as to make no shadow. When molested, it may squirt blood from a sinus in front of its eyes, giving it the appearance of being injured. Presumably this behavior discourages a predator that would prefer live prey. However, the blood apparently is rendered distasteful by formic acid, a by-product of the lizard's diet, consisting mostly of Ants. In addition, the spines on the back of its head make it difficult for a predator, particularly a snake, to swallow it whole. The Coast Horned Lizard is classified by the state and federal governments as a species of special concern. The major problem has been loss of preferred habitat in Coastal Sage Scrub, but its major food, the native Harvester Ant, is being replaced by the invasive, non-native Argentine Ant. Another problem is that Coast Horned Lizards were common in sandy areas along dirt roads where they ate the ants feeding on the seeds of annual weeds there. When a Horned Lizard perceives a threat it tends to "freeze" in place, relying on its camouflage to conceal it, and may be squashed by the tires of a passing automobile or bicycle. Horned Lizards like warm weather. When it is cold they tend to remain buried. They are often active when the soil temperature is in the 100s.

Fig. 6.16. Granite Spiny Lizard.

Fig. 6.17. Coast Horned Lizard.

Fig. 6.18. Western Skink adult male.

Fig. 6.19. Western Skink juvenile.

Fig. 6.20. Gilbert's Skink adult male.

Fig. 6.21. Western Whiptail.

Skinks are highly secretive. They are remarkably common but seldom seen. They are somewhat elongate with small legs, and when they move they tend to resemble small snakes. In contrast, the lizards mentioned above, which possess conspicuous scales, skinks have small shiny scales. Juveniles and subadults have two whitish stripes that run from the head to the base of the tail; adults generally tend to lose the stripes. The **Western Skink** (*Eumeces skiltonianus*) is more common in lowland habitats close to the coast, and it may be found in Coastal Sage Scrub, Oak Woodland, or Riparian settings (fig. 6.18). Juveniles have a bright blue tails that are easily broken off (fig. 6.19). A broken tail bounces and writhes, distracting the predator while the skink escapes. A new tail can be regenerated in less than a year. Breeding males have pink or orange throats, and the stripes may be indistinct. In contrast, **Gilbert's Skink** (*Eumeces gilberti*) tends to occur farther inland, occupying Chaparral, Oak Woodland, and Coniferous habitats (fig. 6.20). Juveniles have reddish-pink tails and adult males orange or red heads.

Whiptail Lizards are also elongate and tend to resemble skinks, but their legs are longer and they do not move in the serpentine fashion of a skink. Whiptail Lizards seem to move incessantly. They can be seen running across a trail or foraging in leaf litter under a shrub. The **Western Whiptail** (*Aspidocelis [= Cnemidophorus] tigris*) is fairly large, up to 10 inches in total length (fig. 6.21). It has a dark ground color with interrupted light stripes that gives it a checkered appearance. Its long slender tail is often

Fig. 6.22. Orange-throated Whiptail.

Fig. 6.23. Southern Alligator Lizard.

black. Western Whiptails are most common in Chaparral, but overall they are distributed from the coast to the mountains. They are quite wary and escape easily when approached. The **Orange-throated Whiptail** (*Aspidocelis hyperythra [= Cnemidophorus hyperythrus]*) is smaller than the Western Whiptail (fig. 6.22). It resembles a Western Skink in that the adult male has an orange throat and the juvenile has a blue tail, but Orange-throated Whiptails have five yellowish stripes running from the head to the base of the tail, and adults retain the stripes. Primarily associated with open areas in Coastal Sage Scrub, the Orange-throated Whiptail is also a federally and state-listed species of special concern. It prefers warm weather, and it tends to prefer termites over other insect prey.

The **Southern Alligator Lizard** (*Elgaria multicarinata*) is a large elongate lizard with small legs (fig. 6.23). Because of its serpentine locomotion and large size, it often is mistaken for a snake. Its ground color may be brown, yellow, or reddish. The adult is marked with dark crossbars, and males have a large triangular head. A prominent fold runs lengthwise along the side of its body. Its unbroken tail is over twice its body length, so it may be up to a foot in total length. Southern Alligator Lizards are found in many moist habitats including suburban gardens. They are large enough to take prey larger than insects and have been known to raid birds' nests. They are well known to bite when handled, and they often defecate on the handler.

In the same family (Anguidae) as the Alligator Lizard is the **California Legless Lizard** (*Anniella pulchra*). These burrowing lizards, about the size of soda straws, when unearthed appear to be small silvery snakes. They have black lines running the length of the body. They live in soft soil, typically along the coast, but they also occur in suburban gardens. They feed on small insects such as termites. Close inspection reveals that they are lizards and not snakes; snakes have no eyelids or ear holes and legless lizards do. Like the other uncommon lizards of Coastal Sage Scrub, California Legless Lizards are listed by the state and the federal government as a species of special concern.

Snakes are top-order carnivores; they feed at the top of the food pyramid. It is understandable, therefore, that they are not very common. Even though snakes are seldom seen, there is a wide diversity of species. Most snakes feed on rodents. Some snakes feed on lizards or other snakes, and the smaller snakes eat insects and salamanders. Over-

Fig. 6.24. California Whipsnake.

all, they are beneficial animals, helping to maintain stability in a fairly harsh ecosystem. Most snakes hibernate in the winter and are most active on warm days in the spring.

The **California Whipsnake** or **Striped Racer** (*Masticophis lateralis*) is our most common snake (fig. 6.24). This is a slender black snake with two white or yellow stripes that run the length of the body. This is a favorable color pattern for an active snake. When it moves through vegetation, only part of its body is visible at a time, and because the stripes run lengthwise it does not appear to be moving. Whipsnakes are active diurnal predators. They move rapidly, generally with the head raised for better vision. They have large eyes and excellent vision. They feed on a variety of foods from lizards to rodents, which are eaten live upon capture without constricting. They are difficult to capture and often bite when handled. They are most common near the coast but occur inland in virtually all habitats.

The **Red Coachwhip** or **Red Racer** (*Masticophis flagellum*) is similar in shape to but larger than the California Whipsnake (fig. 6.25). It has a black neck with white rings, and the remainder of its upper surface is reddish.

Behavior and food preferences also are similar, although Coachwhips are known to feed on other snakes as well. The Red Coachwhip is no longer common in Orange County and may have been extirpated. It prefers open Coastal Sage Scrub and Grassland habitats. Apparently it is another victim of habitat destruction.

The **Western Yellow-bellied Racer** (*Coluber constrictor*) is a rare slender snake that is bluish or olive on top and yellowish underneath. Juveniles with brown crossbars resemble small Gopher Snakes. Like the other racers, these are active predators, and they prefer Grassland or open Riparian habitats, where in undisturbed situations they may take cover under rocks or debris. This is one of the snakes that is known for communal nesting, in which several snakes inhabit a single den.

Our largest snake is the **Gopher Snake** (*Pituophis catenifer*) (fig. 6.26). Full-sized specimens may reach almost 6 feet in total length. This snake has a yellow or tan ground color with dark brown squarish blotches along its back. A dark brown line between the eyes is an important feature of recognition that is absent in a rattlesnake. When a coiled snake under a shrub is disturbed it may vibrate its tail in such a way that it may disturb the leaf

Fig. 6.25. Red Coachwhip.

Fig. 6.26. Gopher Snake.

Fig. 6.27. California Kingsnake, banded pattern.

Fig. 6.28. California Kingsnake, striped pattern.

litter and make a noise that resembles that of a rattlesnake. Gopher Snakes are important for rodent control. Because they are slow-moving, they tend to be ambush hunters, but they will go down ground squirrel or gopher burrows in search of prey. They are found in all habitats, wherever rodents are located, including urban areas. Because of their large size and slow locomotion they are the most common snakes killed on roads. During hot weather they may become nocturnal.

Another common diurnal snake is the **California Kingsnake** (*Lampropeltis getula*). In Orange County the most common color pattern is brown and yellow rings or bands (fig. 6.27). In desert areas these snakes tend to be black-and-white. Kingsnakes are primarily snakes of the lowlands, inhabiting Coastal Sage Scrub, Grasslands, and Chaparral, but they are not unknown in urban areas. Toward the southern part of Orange County an alternative, very different color pattern may occur: a solid brown background with a single long yellow stripe down the back (fig. 6.28). Both color patterns are known to occur in the same litter, and some snakes show a mixture of the two

Fig. 6.29. California Kingsnake, hybrid pattern.

Fig. 6.30. Mountain Kingsnake.

Fig. 6.31. Coastal Rosy Boa.

(fig. 6.29). The banded pattern is usually associated with ambush hunting; it makes the snake difficult to see when it is not moving or lying still in filtered light that is a mixture of light and dark shadows. Interestingly, the striped forms tend to be active predators. Kingsnakes may be active during the day or night, and their diet varies widely, including insects, amphibians, reptiles, and rodents. They are called Kingsnakes because they will eat other snakes including Rattlesnakes. In fact, Rattlesnakes exhibit a distinctive defense posture in the presence of a Kingsnake.

The **Mountain Kingsnake** (*Lampropeltis zonata*) is our most beautiful snake (fig. 6.30). Its pattern of red, black, and white rings leads some misinformed individuals to think that it is a venomous **Coral Snake**, which does not occur in California. Mountain Kingsnakes occur in the mountains in association with Live Oaks and Conifers and particularly rock outcrops. They also occur in canyon bottoms. These secretive snakes are most active in the spring, when they seek their favored prey, Western Fence Lizards and Skinks. Most of

their time is spent under logs, rocks, or in crevices. They are seldom seen locally but sometimes spotted on trails in Holy Jim, San Juan, Silverado, and Santiago Canyons. These are such beautiful snakes that people are tempted to take them home, but possession of a Mountain Kingsnake is illegal. Because of their rarity, they are classified by the state and the federal government as species of special concern.

An unusually docile snake is the **Coastal Rosy Boa** (*Charina [= Lichanura] trivirgata*) (fig. 6.31). This is a heavy-bodied snake with a blunt nose and tail, a small head, and small eyes. Its background color is grayish, and it has three broad longitudinal stripes that may be brown, orange, or reddish. It may roll into a ball when disturbed. These snakes are most commonly observed in the spring in Coastal Sage Scrub or open Oak Woodlands, particularly in the vicinity of rodent burrows. During the hottest or coldest times of the year they tend to remain underground. They feed primarily on rodents, which they capture in their burrows. This is a federal species of special concern because it is popular in the pet trade.

Fig. 6.32. Two-striped Garter Snake.

Fig. 6.33. Western Ringneck Snake.

In Riparian communities with permanent water the **Two-striped Garter Snake** (*Thamnophis hammondii*) may be found basking among the rocks or in ambush position underwater as it waits for a frog or fish to come near (fig. 6.32). This is the only garter snake that occurs in Orange County. Its background color is olive-brown or brownish-gray with a pale yellow stripe on each side of the body. There is no central stripe. During winter this snake spends its time in burrows or rock crevices, sometimes a significant distance from water. When handled it is likely to coil around a handler's wrist and deposit a foul odorous musk on the skin. It is listed by the state as a species of special concern.

Some snakes are fairly small. The small snake most likely to be seen in Orange County is the **Western Ringneck Snake** (*Diadophis punctatus*) (fig. 6.33). About the size of a pencil, it is olive to brown-ish on the back and has a yellow to orange neck-band that is the source of its name. Its belly is bright orange, a color that is revealed when it is disturbed as it twists its body and coils its tail with the belly side

up. This might be interpreted as a threat posture, because these snakes are mildly venomous--a mechanism that is used to subdue prey. These are secretive snakes that live in moist areas in Coastal Sage Scrub, Chaparral, Oak Woodland, and urban areas. They feed on Earthworms, Slender Sala-manders, Treefrogs, and other small snakes and are probably most active at night.

There are three kinds of **Rattlesnakes** in Orange County. Rattlesnakes are pit vipers; they have heat-sensitive pits below their nostrils on each side of the head. They use this extra sense receptor to locate and strike at warm-blooded prey, small birds and mam-mals. Rattlesnakes are to be respected, not feared. They are not interested in wasting venom on a human who is too big to eat, although when molested they will use their venom in defense. The sound of the rattle is a warning to stay away. When a rattlesnake is encountered it simply needs to be avoided by backing up and walking around it. Most snakebites occur because someone insists on handling one. Since these animals are ambush hunters, however, a person may inadvertently step on one that is hiding

Fig. 6.34. Southern Pacific Rattlesnake.

Fig. 6.38. Patch-nosed Snake.

Fig. 6.35. Red Diamond Rattlesnake (Chuck Leavell).

Fig. 6.36. Speckled Rattlesnake.

Fig. 6.37. Long-nosed Snake.

behind a rock or log. A bite may be painful but seldom causes more than a small amount of tissue damage at the site of the wound. Sometimes there is a more serious reaction that requires monitoring or hospitalization. There is no need to cut and suck or to freeze the site. Immobilization of the limb is always a good idea. A person who is bitten, however, should visit a doctor as soon as possible and explain the circumstances of the bite.

The **Southern Pacific Rattlesnake** or **Western Rattlesnake** (*Crotalis helleri [= C. viridis]*) is our most commonly seen venomous reptile (fig. 6.34). It is brown to black with light borders to the diamond patterns on its back. It does not have black and white rings on its tail. It can be found in most habitats and is often seen basking in open areas during the spring and summer months. This is seldom a docile animal.

The **Red Diamond Rattlesnake** (*Crotalis ruber*) is our largest rattlesnake (fig. 6.35). It is a heavy-bodied snake that may reach 5 feet in length. Its ground color varies from pinkish to brick-red, and the diamond pattern is outlined in

Fig. 6.39. Lyre Snake.

Fig. 6.40. Spotted Night Snake in defensive posture.

white. Its tail has alternating black and white rings, leading to the common name "Coontail." Red Diamond Rattlesnakes are fairly common in low-elevation habitats, particularly Coastal Sage Scrub and Chaparral. They are most active in the spring and in winter months retreat to refuges under logs, rocks, or in rock cracks. Sometimes several of them are found in a common den. These are fairly docile snakes, usually found curled up under overhanging rocks, in cactus patches, or under shrubs.

The **Speckled Rattlesnake** (*Crotalus mitchelli*) has been associated with rocky habitats at higher elevations in the Santa Ana Mountains, but apparently there have been few sightings of this species in recent years (fig. 6.36). Most recently specimens have been observed at Tenaja Fall on San Mateo Creek and on the floor of Fremont Canyon. This rattlesnake has highly variable coloration, from pink to tan to dark brown. Markings on its back range from speckled to banded. The pupils of the eyes are vertically elliptical. If there are black and white rings on the tail, they should be indistinct and only just in front of the rattle. This is generally not an aggressive snake.

There are a number of snake species for which there are historical records but that seem to be rare or absent today in Orange County. Among these are the **California Glossy Snake** (*Arizona occidentalis [= A. elegans]*), which resembles a smooth, shiny Gopher Snake; the **Long-nosed Snake** (*Rhinocheilus lecontei*) (fig. 6.37), which resembles a Mountain Kingsnake without the distinctive white bands; and the **Patch-nosed Snake** (*Salvadora hexalepis*), which resembles a racer with a single dorsal stripe and a leaflike scale on the tip of its nose (fig. 6.38). Several small burrowing snakes are also rare or absent, including the **Black-headed Snake** (*Tantilla planiceps*) and the **Blind Snake** (*Leptotyphlops humilis*). Two species of rear-fanged snakes, recognized by their vertically elliptical pupils, are known to occur in exfoliating rocks. These rare or extirpated species include the larger **Lyre Snake** (*Trimorphodon biscutatus*) (fig. 6.39) and the pencil-sized **Spotted Night Snake** (*Hypsiglena torquata*) (fig. 6.40). Anyone who believes he has observed one of these reptiles should notify the public land manager as soon as possible.

Fig. 6.41. Turkey Vultures in Monterey Cypress.

Fig. 6.42. Turkey Vulture sunning.

BIRDS

Birds are the most conspicuous of our vertebrate animals. Most of them are active in the daytime. They are fun to watch, and many of them are attractive. If one includes waterfowl, seabirds, shorebirds, and migrating species there are over 400 kinds of birds that could be observed in Orange County. Bird watching, or "birding," is a fast-growing hobby. On any weekend in Orange County's parks birders and bird photographers can be found scanning trees and shrubs with binoculars or "scoping" mud flats and estuaries looking for rare or interesting birds. Because the common names of birds have been standardized by the American Ornithologists' Union, the scientific names of birds will not be included in this volume. The birds of Orange County's public lands (excluding the inhabitants of the intertidal region, which are listed in Chapter 7) are as follows:

Raptors

Birds of prey are called raptors (formerly raptores). Two orders of birds, Falconiformes (Hawks, Eagles, Vultures) and Strigiformes (Owls), are commonly included. Lately the term "raptor" is reserved for diurnal birds of prey such as hawks and eagles, which would exclude the owls. Even though Turkey Vultures and Condors are in the same order as Hawks and Eagles, they also might not be called raptors because they eat carrion and do not capture their prey alive. It is unfortunate that we cannot come to an agreement on the use of a word that is such a common part of our language.

Birds of prey are equipped with stout, hooked beaks for tearing flesh and large, powerful feet with long, curled claws that they use to grasp and kill prey. The size of

Fig. 6.43. Red-tailed Hawk.

Fig. 6.44. Red-shouldered Hawk.

their wings and tail in proportion to their body points to their preferred technique for pursuing prey. Birds that soar have long, broad wings, whereas those with shorter wings are more maneuverable and catch their prey while in flight. Even though many of these hawks seem to coexist they are separated by different hunting behaviors and food preferences, an ecological concept known as **niche partitioning**.

Turkey Vultures are most often seen soaring as they search for carrion. These large black birds with naked red heads sometimes roost at night in large numbers in trees (fig. 6.41). They have excellent vision, and in contrast to most birds they have a fair sense of smell, particularly for odorous decay products. (Gas company employees have long noticed that they can locate gas leaks by watching where the Turkey Vultures are soaring.) In the air they may be recognized soaring with their wings in a V. In the morning, Turkey Vultures often are observed sunning themselves with their wings spread. Although warm-blooded, they use solar energy for a quick warm-up (fig. 6.42). The feet of Turkey Vultures are more like those of a chicken. Their claws are fairly straight, more for standing or walking on the ground than for grasping prey. They often nest on the ground behind shrubbery at the base of cliffs or in cavities in trees or cliffs. The **California Condor**, one of the state's most endangered birds and no longer an inhabitant of Orange County, is a very large vulture.

Large soaring hawks are known as Buteos. Our largest hawk, the **Red-tailed Hawk**, is our most common raptor (fig. 6.43). It has been estimated that we have at least 75 nesting pairs in the county. In the air this hawk can be distinguished from a Turkey Vulture because it soars with its wings on a flat plane, and adult specimens have a recognizable red tail. When it is perched it can be identified by a broad brown band across its lower breast. It is found throughout the county. It makes a large stick nest in a tree or a cavity in a cliff. It feeds primarily on rodents and snakes, and sometimes it can be seen feeding on road kill.

Another common hawk in our area is the **Red-shouldered Hawk** (fig. 6.44). While this bird certainly soars, it also commonly hunts from a perch. When it is perched it is apparent that it is smaller than a Red-tailed Hawk: its shoulders are red, and its tail has narrow black and white bands. The breast in juveniles is streaked and in adults is marked by orange bars. This is the noisiest hawk our area. In the air it may repeatedly emit loud, high-pitched shrieking vocalizations. It occurs from the foothills to the coast and is more likely than the Red-tailed Hawk to establish a home range in an urban area.

Ospreys are fish-eating hawks (fig. 6.45). They may be observed near lakes, reservoirs, and estuaries such as Upper Newport Bay and Bolsa Chica. In the air with a wing-spread up to 5 feet, they may be recognized by their long wings. They tend to fly with their wings crooked, gull-like. They catch fish with their feet, often positioning the fish head-first like a torpedo while they fly to a perch to eat it. Like owls, Ospreys have the ability to rotate their third toe either forward or back, so they can catch prey or perch with two toes forward and two toes back. While on a perch the distinguishing field marks are a black eye-stripe on the otherwise white face. Ospreys, victims of DDT, are recovering in numbers. Histori-

cally, nesting has been observed in Laguna Canyon, Irvine Lake, and, unexpectedly, on the mast of a sailboat in lower Newport Harbor. At the Upper Newport Bay Ecological Reserve, a nesting platform was constructed in 1993 with the hope it would attract a breeding pair of Ospreys. It was not until 2007 that it worked. Three young Ospreys hatched and fledged from that platform.

The **Northern Harrier** is about the same size as a Red-shouldered Hawk (fig. 6.46). It is typically seen flying low over marshes and open country, including agricultural fields. Its former name **Marsh Hawk** attests to this favored habitat. Its wings are longer and narrower than a Red-shouldered Hawk's, and when it glides it rocks back and forth with its wings in a V and its tail feathers not spread. In the air it is easy to identify by its buff-colored rump. This bird nests on the ground and therefore is particularly sensitive to disturbance.

Of the group of hawks known as Accipiters, the three California species differ primarily in size and are not easy to tell apart. In Orange County we have only the two smaller

Fig. 6.45. Osprey.

Fig. 6.46. Northern Harrier flying over Salt Marsh.

forms. In flight they can be separated from Buteos by short, broad wings and a long tail. They seldom soar. The tail is black-and-white banded, but the white bands are broader than those of the Red-shouldered Hawk and the birds are significantly smaller. They are brownish to gray, and adult birds have orange bars on the breast. Both are pursuit hunters, catching other birds on the wing. The **Cooper's Hawk**, with a wing-spread of about 30 inches, is known to nest in Riparian or Oak Woodlands (fig. 6.47). It is not a common bird, but it may visit feeding stations. The **Sharp-shinned Hawk** is smaller and less common than the Cooper's Hawk and more likely to be observed in suburban areas. These birds are primarily seen in the winter; they nest farther north. The two species are so difficult to tell apart that local birders are known to simplify a sighting by calling a bird of dubious identity a "Coop-shin" or *Accipiter* sp.

Falcons are raptors with fairly narrow, pointed wings and a tail that is narrow in flight. The only falcon common in Orange County is the **American Kestrel** (fig. 6.48). Formerly known as a **Sparrow Hawk**, this dove-sized bird preys primarily on mice, insects, and lizards but has been known to take small birds such as Sparrows. This colorful bird has a rufous body and blue-gray wings. There is a pattern of black and white vertical bands on each side of the head. Kestrels may be seen perching on high branches, wires, or on fences along a roadway. In rural areas, they commonly hunt in roadside vegetation and can be seen with their wings fluttering, hovering in place as they stalk potential prey. When they first land on a perch, they often pump their tails up and down as if catching their balance. The other three falcons that could potentially be seen have a historical record in Orange County but must be considered rare these days. The **Merlin**, once known as the **Chicken Hawk**, is slightly larger than a Kestrel. The **Prairie Falcon**, more often seen in desert or grassland areas, has been recorded from the Santa Ana Canyon and the upper parts of Gypsum Canyon, but there are no known nesting pairs in Orange County today. These are fairly large birds with a wingspread of about 40 inches. Their distinctive black "armpits" are visible when the bird is in the air. The **Peregrine Falcon** is about the same size as a Prairie Falcon. It is

Fig. 6.47. Cooper's Hawk with House Sparrow in talons.

Fig. 6.48. Kestrel.

Fig. 6.49. White-tailed Kite (Chuck Leavell).

Fig. 6.50. Golden Eagle.

Fig. 6.51. Bald Eagle.

the world's fastest bird, having been clocked in a dive at speeds over 200 miles per hour. Peregrines are on the state endangered-species list. They never were common in Orange County and disappeared in the 1960s, apparent victims of egg-thinning associated with DDT. In recent years they have been noted occasionally along the coast, but no nesting has been observed. Sometimes they are observed with jesses on their feet, indicating that they have escaped from captivity; they are very popular among falconers.

The **White-tailed Kite**, formerly known as the **Black-shouldered Kite**, is a medium-sized falcon-shaped raptor (fig. 6.49). Its underparts are mostly white with dark wing tips, making it resemble a gull in flight. When it is perched, its black shoulders are conspicuous. Its preferred prey is the California Vole or Meadow Mouse. Apparent fluctuation in populations of White-tailed Kites have been related to inexplicable cycles of Vole populations. Kites get their name from their hunting behavior, which usually consists of hovering over a field with wings fluttering, giving them the appearance of a kite. They may be observed countywide wherever there are open fields.

With a wingspread of over 6 feet, **Golden Eagles** are our largest raptors (fig. 6.50). When soaring with their wings in a V, they may resemble Turkey Vultures. Nesting pairs, up to four per year, are often recorded in the Santa Ana Mountains and the Chino Hills. Sometimes they are spotted along the coast, although they tend to take rodents, not fish, as their prey. In contrast, **Bald Eagles**

Fig. 6.52. Great Horned Owl.

Fig. 6.53. Great Horned Owls on nest.

mostly eat fish and would most likely be seen along the coast (fig. 6.51). About the same size as a Golden Eagle, with their pure white heads adult Bald Eagles are easy to spot. Juveniles, however may resemble Golden Eagles. Also having suffered a decline associated with DDT, Bald Eagles have been reintroduced to Santa Catalina Island, where they are successfully nesting. Recently, birds from Santa Catalina have been observed in Laguna Beach. As years go by we should see them more often along the Orange County coast. It should be gratifying to see recovery of populations for this bird, the symbol of the United States.

Owls are not always included in lists of raptors, presumably because they are in a different order (Strigiformes) and because most of them are nocturnal. However, similar to those of hawks, the feet and beaks of owls are adapted for the capture of prey. Owls also are well adapted for hunting at night. Their hearing and vision are superb. Their eyes are positioned forward, and there is a dish of feathers around each eye that acts like the external ear of a mammal (which gathers sound and directs it toward the ear hole). Because a dish surrounds

each forward-facing eye, movements created by the prey are stereoscopically transmitted to the same point on the face. Owls are able to hunt in complete darkness, using only sound cues to locate their prey. Unlike many hawks, owls tend to swallow their prey whole. In many birds there is an enlarged portion of the esophagus called a crop where fur and bones accumulate. Owls and some hawks regurgitate this material in a flattened gob called a pellet. Owl pellets are often found on the ground in the vicinity of a preferred perch, often a cavity in a cliff or a hollow tree. Examination of the skeletal material in these pellets reveals what the owl has been eating. As might be expected, most of the bones are from nocturnal rodents.

Our largest owl is the **Great Horned Owl**, easily recognized by its large size and the tufts of feathers that resemble mammalian ears (fig. 6.52). There are an estimated 20 pairs of breeding adults in Orange County. Instead of building their own nests, Great Horned Owls use the stick nests of hawks and ravens (fig. 6.53). Their favored prey includes larger rodents such as Cottontail Rabbits, Wood Rats, and Gophers. They are distributed countywide and are not uncommon in well-wooded suburban areas. This

Fig. 6.54. Barn Owl (Ted Schoenherr).

Fig. 6.55. Burrowing Owl.

is the owl that makes the familiar "ha-who-who-who" sound at night. Sometimes it emits a clicking noise while on a perch, a sound that has been interpreted by some ornithologists as a form of echolocation.

Barn Owls are fairly common from the foothills to the coast (fig. 6.54). They are found around woodlands of all types, cliffs, barns, Eucalyptus rows, and suburban areas with enough trees. They emit a distinctive call, a long hissing shriek, while flying at night. Road-killed Barn Owls are often found along

rural roads. Apparently they fly low over road-ways while searching for prey and inadvertently get hit by motor vehicles, particularly large trucks. During years with abundant food, Barn Owls can raise two or three broods in a year.

The **Western Screech Owl** is a common resident of Oak and Riparian Woodlands in the foothills and mountains. These are small owls, with a body length of about 8 inches, and they have a pair of short, feathered "ears." They commonly nest in cavities of Oaks and Sycamores. Up to two pairs per half mile of streambed have been documented. A sort of burbling, tremulous quaver of these small owls is a familiar nighttime sound in these wood-lands. The sound is sometimes compared to that of a bouncing ball. They eat small rodents, insects, and on occasion small birds.

The **Burrowing Owl** is a small, long-legged, short-tailed owl that is the only owl likely to be seen in the daytime (fig. 6.55). It is about 10 inches tall and has no ear tufts. When these owls are seen they are likely to be in the vicinity of abandoned burrows of California Ground Squirrels, in which they make nests. While they were formerly quite common in Grassland areas, including agricultural fields, in recent years they have been sighted at the Seal Beach National Wildlife Refuge, Upper Newport Bay, and near the campus of the University of California at Irvine. One interesting sighting was near an abandoned ground squirrel burrow in small patch of uncultivated land between Highway 55 and an on-ramp. In natural settings near pastures, these birds are known to decorate the entrance to their burrows with the dung of livestock, presumably to disguise

Fig. 6.56. Black Phoebe.

Fig. 6.57. Ash-throated Flycatcher.

their odor from predators. An interesting instinct in young birds further helps to protect them from predators. If an intruder is heard entering the burrow, young owls clack their bills together, making a sound that resembles the rattling of a Rattlesnake and is sometimes enough to send a mammalian predator fleeing.

Other owls for which there are historical records include **Spotted Owls**, **Long-eared Owls**, **Short-eared Owls**, and **Northern Saw-whet Owls**, all of which must be considered rare. Spotted Owls, residents of wooded canyons, were last seen in Upper Trabuco Canyon. Nesting Long-eared Owls were last seen at four localities—Irvine Lake, Limestone Canyon, Gabino Canyon, and Weir Canyon—where they were using hawk and crow nests. Recent sightings of Short-eared Owls were at Seal Beach National Wildlife Refuge and Preusker Peak in the Santa Ana Mountains. Northern Saw-whet Owls, which resemble Screech Owls without ear tufts, have been observed in upper Silverado, Harding, and McVicker Canyons in the Santa Ana Mountains. A person who believes he has observed one of these birds should report his observation to the land manager or the local chapter of the Audubon Society.

Flycatchers

Because habitats in a Mediterranean climate tend to be food-poor, small, ectothermic (cold-blooded) animals such as insects tend to be common. It should not be a surprise, therefore, that insect-eating birds are fairly common in Orange County. Flycatchers are conspicuous because of their habit of sitting on a high perch or fence and flying off repeatedly to catch insects on the wing. The easiest flycatcher to identify is probably the **Black Phoebe**, a year-round resident (fig. 6.56). It has a black head, breast, and back but a white belly, as if it were wearing a tuxedo. It is a common bird in Riparian areas, canyons, and suburban areas from the foothills to the coast. Its nearest relative, the **Say's Phoebe**, is an uncommon summer resident of Grasslands and Scrub habitats. It has a grayish-brown bird with a black tail. It has light-colored throat and breast, but the belly is a pale rufous color. The **Ash-throated Flycatcher**, a summer resident, superficially resembles Say's Phoebe but lacks the black tail: its throat is white, and its belly is pale yellow (fig. 6.57). As do many flycatchers, the Ash-throated Flycatcher also has a small crest. It is fairly common in wooded parts of the interior of Orange County. The **Western Kingbird** and

Fig. 6.58. Cassin's Kingbird.

Fig. 6.59. Cliff Swallow nests.

Cassin's Kingbird are difficult to tell apart (fig. 6.58). These flycatchers have gray heads, bright-yellow bellies, and a black eye-stripe. Cassin's Kingbird is a year-round resident, but both species may be present in the summer. The Cassin's Kingbird is probably the more common, nesting in wooded areas including Eucalyptus trees. Both species tend to avoid the more urbanized areas of northern Orange County. When they are present in groups they tend to make a racket of raspy calls consisting of two notes repeated over and over.

There are at least 11 kinds of small related flycatchers known collectively as *Empidonax* flycatchers. They look so much alike that it takes an expert to spot the differences. They are plump, greenish to grayish birds with small slender beaks, two pale wing bars, and a white eye-ring in most species. Most of them have a pale yellow breast. The most likely to be observed in our wooded canyons in spring and summer is the **Pacific Coast Flycatcher**, formerly called the **Western Flycatcher**. Another small flycatcher known as the **Western Wood Peewee** resembles the *Empidonax* flycatchers, but its throat and belly are gray and the wing bars are grayish and less distinct. The eye ring is also less distinct.

Swallows and Swifts

Although they are not closely related, Swallows and Swifts have similar body morphology and hunting habits. Swallows and Swifts, like flycatchers, catch insects on the wing, but they do not hunt from a perch. While they are feeding, they fly rapidly and sometimes erratically, often in groups. Swallows are smaller and fly with a more rapid wing beat. Our common swallows are about $5 \frac{1}{2}$ inches long, and compared with those of Swifts their wings are fairly short. The **Cliff Swallow** is our most common swallow through spring and summer. This short-tailed swallow can be recognized by its buff-colored rump. While Cliff Swallows are widespread in Orange County from the coast to the foothills, they are best known as the swallows that return each year to build gourd-shaped mud nests (fig. 6.59) on the San Juan Capistrano Mission. Legend has it that they miraculously appear each year on Saint Joseph's Day, March 19, and then disappear on October 23, the Day of San Juan, the mission's patron saint. While it is true that the birds are most common between these dates, this best represents a migratory phenomenon associated with day

Fig. 6.60. Barn Swallows on nest.

length. Migratory animals are stimulated to migrate in response to changes in the amount of light. These small birds actually fly all the way to South America to spend the summer (our winter) and return to breed here during our summer. Their dates of arrival and departure are not as exact as legend would have it, but they are fairly close because the schedule is innate. Early arrivals are called scouts, and late arrivals are called stragglers. Throughout Orange County they can be found building nests on cliffs and bridges. In recent years they have been less common at the mission than

in those other places. Part of the problem seems to be that San Juan Creek is now concrete-lined, and the mud that the birds need to build their nests is no longer abundant there. There is also some evidence that the birds are being evicted from their nests by non-native House Sparrows.

Northern Rough-winged Swallows superficially resemble Cliff Swallows, but they are browner and lack a buff-colored rump. They also use bridges for their mud nests, and they coexist with Cliff Swallows at several locations along the Santa Ana River and San Diego Creek. The other common swallow is the **Barn Swallow**, easily recognized by its long forked tail (fig. 6.60). These are pretty birds with dark blue-black backs, orange throats, and pale orange bellies. They make open half-cup mud nests under the eaves of buildings and are fairly common along the coast. The **Tree Swallow** nests in tree cavities (fig. 6.61) and sometimes in Bluebird boxes. Less likely to be

Fig. 6.61. Tree Swallow.

seen than the other three, it can be found near water and reservoirs such as the one in Peters Canyon. It has a blue-green back and a white belly. All four swallow species can be seen at the San Joaquin Marsh near the University of California at Irvine and along San Diego Creek.

Swifts are larger than Swallows and have long pointed wings. The **White-throated Swift** is our most common species. It is most likely to be seen in the vicinity of cliffs in our local foothills. Recently these swifts have been observed roosting on the Humanities Building at California State University, Fullerton. They often fly quite high in a group. Their key identifying feature is the white throat. These birds can be found year-round, and there is some evidence that they are among the few bird species that can hibernate in the winter. They are conspicuous by their voices in the spring, when the call, a long series of high-pitched twitterings, can be heard as males chase females in small wheeling flocks. They mate in mid-air; a pair of birds, pressed together in flight, seems to fall from the sky in a suicide dive, only to pull out and fly off before it hits the ground.

Goatsuckers

Goatsuckers, ground-nesting birds that behave like bats, are represented by two species in Orange County. They are active at dusk, when they may be seen as long-winged birds flying erratically as they catch flying insects. During the day they often rest on the ground, relying on their brown, mottled color to conceal them. When walking through brushy areas people are sometimes startled by the sudden flight of one of these birds seemingly from under their feet. The name "goatsucker" refers to their very large mouths, which enhance their ability to catch flying insects. Legend has it that these birds would creep up on nanny goats during the night and suck milk from their teats. This story is not to be confused with that of the "Chupacabra," which means "goat-sucker" in Spanish. Chupacabra is a legendary blood-sucking animal that is supposed to kill an animal by puncturing its neck, vampire-style, and sucking out its blood.

The **Common Poorwill** is the most likely goatsucker to be seen or heard in Orange County (fig. 6.62). It is fairly common in the brushy foothills, where its two-note mournful call, described as "Poor Will," can be heard at night during spring and summer. These birds are inactive during winter. They are the first birds to be documented to lower their body temperature and enter a state of hibernation during the cold season. In the spring, they emerge from a protected cavity and may be found lying on the ground in the sun with their wings spread as they warm up. The **Lesser Nighthawk** is a rare summer inhabitant of washes from the foothills to the coast. It resembles the Poorwill but has a large white patch on each wing that is revealed only when it flies. "Flash marks" like this are important as a distraction to a potential predator that might come upon the bird in its daytime retreat.

Gleaners

Gleaning is a form of feeding in which birds scavenge small insects from the bark and leaves of plants. Many of these birds are seldom seen because they spend most of their time gleaning deep inside the cover of foliage. Often these are birds of Scrub habitats with short wings and long tails, adaptations for maneuvering in flight. Many of these birds are a drab brown color, but they may overcome their hidden lifestyle by having loud distinctive calls or songs, a way of communicating without being seen. Typically they have slender beaks, useful for extracting small insects from cracks in bark.

The **California Gnatcatcher** does not catch insects on the wing; it is a gleaner. This is a small blue-gray bird, and males have a black cap during the breeding season. During the spring and summer months its kitten-like mewing call reveals its presence even though it may not be seen. This federally listed threatened bird has become the "poster child" for Coastal Sage Scrub as an endangered habitat. Furthermore, it has become symbolic of controversies in the interpretation of the U.S. Endangered Species Act. In Orange County it occurs on some of the most expensive privately owned real estate in the world, where suburban sprawl has destroyed and fragmented its native habitat and in so doing threatened its very existence. Like a canary in a coal mine, California Gnatcatchers have become indicative of the health of the Coastal Sage Scrub ecosystem. Mitigation

Fig. 6.62. Common Poorwill warming up.

associated with habitat conservation plans has targeted the California Gnatcatcher, often ignoring whether the "restored" habitat has any of the other species that make up a complete community. The **Blue-gray Gnatcatcher** resembles the California Gnatcatcher. It has no black cap and has extensive white under the tail. It is most likely to be seen in Chaparral and Oak Woodlands.

Vireos are small plump gleaners that superficially resemble *Empidonax* flycatchers. They have white eye rings and two white wing bars. **Hutton's Vireo** is the most likely to be seen locally. It is a common resident of Live Oak and Willow woodlands. They are not uncommon in well-wooded urban parks. The **Least Bell's Vireo** is an inhabitant of Riparian areas, where it typically nests in low Willows. It resembles Hutton's Vireo but tends to be a lighter gray and to have a white spot in front of the eye and above the bill. Destruction of its streamside habitat has led to its being listed as endangered by both the state and the federal government. Like the California Gnatcatcher, this is a target species for mitigation and restoration projects. The **Ruby-crowned Kinglet** is a vireo look-alike. Its

Fig. 6.63. House Wren.

ruby-colored crown is seldom visible. It can be found countywide in wooded vegetation but primarily in the winter. It takes practice to distinguish it from a vireo.

Wrens, for the most part, are small brown birds. When they are seen on a perch they often rest with their tails vertically cocked. Many of them are recognized by long melodic songs. The **House Wren** (fig. 6.63) is fairly common along streams and in the canyons during the spring, where its melodic song is familiar to hikers and residents. After the breeding season it seems to move into suburban areas where it inhabits dense foliage. The **Canyon Wren** is recognized by its long descending trill that echoes off of canyon walls (fig. 6.64). Though not common, it inhabits the undeveloped canyons of the San Joaquin Hills, the Chino Hills, and the Santa Ana Mountains. **Bewick's Wren** is rarely seen away from natural plant communities in the mountains. Slightly larger than a Canyon Wren, it can be recognized by its distinctive white eyebrow. The **Marsh Wren** is found only among Cattails and Tules on the edges of marshes, in places like Upper Newport Bay and the San Joaquin Marsh. It is a small

stocky species that also has a white eyebrow. The largest of the wrens, up to 8 inches in length, is the **Coastal Cactus Wren** (fig. 6.65). It is an inhabitant of Coastal Sage Scrub, particularly in the vicinity of cactus patches. Its recent disappearance from its former range, particularly in the area of the 1993 fire in the San Joaquin Hills, is unexplained. While it does not nest in well-watered landscapes such as resorts and golf courses, its appearance there may be due to an abundance of insects. Their familiar chugging, "motorboat" call is a familiar sound in undisturbed habitat. Coastal Cactus Wrens are classified by the state as a species of special concern and according to many biologists are just as important as the California Gnatcatcher as an indicator of healthy Coastal Sage Scrub.

The **Oak Titmouse** (formerly **Plain Titmouse**) is a small, chubby gray bird with a distinctive crest (fig. 6.66). It is a very common resident of the foothills in Chaparral and Oak habitats. The **Bushtit** (fig. 6.67) is smaller, more slender, and has a longer tail than the Oak Titmouse. Bushtits often occur in flocks, calling to each other with short chipping sounds, as they move through the foliage. They are common in Chaparral and Oak Woodlands, including well-wooded landscapes in suburban Orange County. The **Wrentit** is the largest of these "tit" birds. It is highly secretive and seldom occurs outside of native Scrub habitats. This seldom-seen bird, however, has such a recognizable sound that is has been called the "voice of the Chaparral." Likened to the sound of a bouncing ping-pong ball held between the paddle and the table, the song is composed of an accelerating series of popping whistles. The term "tit," incidentally, is a British word that means "small."

Some gleaners specialize in removing insects from bark rather than leaves. The **Brown Creeper** is such a bird. These little wrenlike birds have thin, curved bills. They are mottled brown on the back and pale underneath. When they fly they reveal a bold, buffy band or flash mark on their wings. They often fly to the base of a tree and walk upward, but on occasion they can be seen walking upside down along a branch. They use their long stiff tail feathers as a brace. While not common, they can be found, primarily during the winter, in wooded areas throughout the county. The **White-breasted Nuthatch** is a year-round resident, most often associated with Oak and Pine trees from the foothills to higher elevations. These short-tailed gray birds have black crowns, and the underparts of the head and belly are white. In contrast to the Brown Creeper, the Nuthatch has the habit of walking head-down on the trunk while it forages for insects with its thin, straight bill.

Fig. 6.64. Canyon Wren.

Fig. 6.65. Cactus Wren.

Fig. 6.66. Oak Titmouse.

Fig. 6.67. Bushtit.

Warblers

Our most attractive gleaners are the various warblers, most of which are seen during migration in the spring or fall. Many species have been recorded in Orange County. These colorful birds are reminiscent of canaries, most of them bearing yellow and/or black markings. Treetop species tend to be more brightly colored, while those that remain hidden or occur on the ground are drab. Most of them have short, thin bills. The **Orange-crowned Warbler** is resident year-round, probably moving toward the coast in winter (fig. 6.68). It tends to breed in Willows. It is a fairly dull olive-green above and lightly streaked yellow below. The orange crown is rarely visible. The distinctive trill is often heard in coastal residential areas in the spring. The **Yellow Warbler** is recognizable because it is all yellow (fig.

Fig. 6.68. Orange-crowned Warbler.

6.69). Males have red streaking on the breast. These warblers breed in Riparian zones in the mountains. The **Common Yellowthroat** is a secretive year-round inhabitant of marshes and wetland shrubs. It is olive-gray above and has a bright yellow throat. The male's most distinctive feature is a black mask bordered above with white. The only bird with which it could be confused is the larger **Yellow-breasted Chat**, a rare summer visitor that breeds in Riparian zones in the mountains or around

TABLE 6.1: WARBLERS AND THEIR ALLIES LIKELY TO BE SEEN IN ORANGE COUNTY			
Species	Season	Breeding	General Location
Orange-crowned Warbler	Year-round	Yes	Summer in canyons, Winter in lowlands
Nashville Warbler	Spring	No	Coastal to foothills
Yellow Warbler	Spring, Summer	Yes	Riparian zones
Yellow-rumped Warbler	Winter	No	Countywide
Black-throated Gray Warbler	Spring, Fall	No	Coastal to foothills
Townsend's Warbler	Spring, Fall	No	Coastal to foothills
American Redstart	Spring	No	Coastal
Common Yellowthroat	Year-round	Yes	Coastal marshes
Wilson's Warbler	Spring, Fall	No	Countywide
MacGillivray's Warbler	Spring, Fall	No	Coastal lowlands
Hermit Warbler	Spring	No	Foothills
Yellow-breasted Chat	Spring/Summer	Yes	Riparian zones

Fig. 6.69. Yellow Warbler.

Fig. 6.70. Yellow-rumped Warbler.

reservoirs such as Peters Canyon or Irvine Lake. The Chat has a narrow black mask. All the other warblers (table 6.1) are migrants that may be seen nearly anywhere in lowland Orange County when they are passing through. **Wilson's Warbler** resembles the Orange-crowned Warbler, but the male has a black cap. The **Nashville Warbler** is yellow with a gray head. The **Yellow-rumped Warbler**, also known as **Audubon's Warbler**, is our most common winter visitor (fig. 6.70). It is conspicuous as it flits about in trees, often flying to grab an insect on the wing, flycatcher-style. It is a dark gray to black bird with two white wing bars and yellow patches on its throat, sides, and rump. The **Black-throated Gray Warbler** has no yellow. It is a gray bird with black and white stripes on its face and breast. Its throat is black. **Townsend's Warbler** has a gray back, with striking yellow and black stripes on its face and belly. The **American Redstart** is a recent migrant that is being seen along the coast. The female is gray and yellow, with yellow on its sides and under the tail. The male is a distinctive orange and black bird with an all-black head.

Woodpeckers

Woodpeckers are specialized gleaners. They forage for insects on the bark but are best known for drilling holes in order to access insects living beneath the bark, which they gather with a long specialized tongue. They also drill deep holes that they use for nests, typically in soft or decaying wood. Woodpeckers possess a suite of features that adapts them to their specialized lives. A woodpecker's bill is vertically chisel-shaped at the tip, and the brain has special padding to absorb the shock of pecking. The tongue has an elongated cartilaginous support that rolls back into the bird's skull like a window shade. The feet, with two toes aiming forward and two toes back, are adapted for grasping vertical surfaces, and the tail feathers are stiff and pointed, specialized to be used as a brace. When they fly, most woodpeckers flap a few times and then glide, which gives them a distinctive up-and-down flight path. Finally, most woodpeckers have distinctive calls that make them fairly easy to identify even when they are not seen.

Fig. 6.71. Acorn Woodpecker.

Our most conspicuous woodpecker is the **Acorn Woodpecker** (fig. 6.71). This clownish-looking bird is black with a white eye ring, a white throat, a white rump, and a small red cap. When it flies, large white flash marks are conspicuous on its wings. It is highly vocal, making a distinctive "whacka, whacka" sound. These birds are found wherever there are Oak trees. They will fly out of the trees and catch insects in flycatcher fashion, but acorns are their primary food. Acorns are gathered by the hundreds and stored in holes that are drilled for that purpose. In our area, Western Sycamore trees, some Palms, and power poles are favored sites. Large numbers of acorns are stored at a single site known as a granary. Acorn Woodpeckers can drill so many holes in a power pole that it looks like Swiss cheese. Utility companies paint the poles with a green "woodpecker repellent," but it only works temporarily. At Irvine Regional Park, screens were wrapped around the poles in attempt to stop the drilling, but the woodpeckers figured out how to store acorns under the screening, producing instead, huge bags of acorns high up on the power poles. Apparently the urge to fill a hole with an acorn is instinctive. If the hole happens to be in a cabin wall, Acorn Woodpeckers will continue to push acorns through until one sticks out or until the space inside the wall becomes filled up to the hole. When the woodpecker sees an acorn in the hole, it loses the urge to stuff another one in there. According to one tale, when a cabin in the Santa Ana Mountains was torn down, enough acorns were taken from the walls to fill two large trash barrels. Spaniards referred to these birds by the name "Carpintero" in reference to their woodworking activity.

Acorn Woodpeckers are unique among birds in our area in that they feed and breed in cooperative groups that may have 12 to 15 members. These social groups defend a territory that includes the granary. Males in the group are commonly brothers. Females also are commonly siblings but may be unrelated to the males. A group may include one to three breeders of each sex; the remainder of the birds are nonbreeding helpers. Mate sharing is common among the breeders. The helpers gather food, defend the granary, and feed the young. When the granary is full, helpers drill more holes. If the granary is not full, they spend most of their time searching for food. Young birds are fed insects, not acorns. The acorns are food for the birds that gather the insects.

If mating birds die or disappear, new breeders are not recruited from among the helpers. Rather, if all mating birds of one sex are gone, a mate vacancy appears. Groups of woodpeckers from nearby colonies will then appear at the granary, and a great deal of commotion ensues as mature birds compete, chase, and display for the privilege of filling the vacancy. When the vacancy is filled it is by new sibling breeders, which immediately begin to destroy eggs and offspring belonging to the former breeders. This behavior ensures that new breeders will contribute their genes to the next generation.

Fig. 6.72. Nuttall's Woodpecker.

Competition among females takes place over which of the sisters will lay the first egg. Females typically lay five eggs. If one of the breeding females begins to lay eggs before another, the second breeder will remove the egg and carry it to another tree, where it is broken and eaten by the group. This procedure continues until the second female begins to lay eggs. When two females are laying eggs in the same nest, the eggs cannot be distinguished, and none of them is destroyed. This process ensures that more than one female contributes genetic material to the offspring, and the bird that removes eggs will contribute more genetic material than the first to lay.

Nuttall's Woodpecker is a fairly common resident of woodlands throughout the county (fig. 6.72). It can be recognized by a pattern of horizontal white

bars across the back and narrow white stripes on the face. The back of the crown is red. Its distinctive rattle-call of loud repeated notes is fairly easy to recognize.

Some woodpeckers bear names that relate to features other than pecking wood. Sapsuckers are long-winged, slender woodpeckers that are generally quiet and inconspicuous. Their trademark is rows of shallow holes drilled in tree bark, including Eucalyptus trees. The birds return to the holes to drink sap and eat insects that are apparently attracted to it. There are four species that may occur in our area, three of which are closely related and represent gradual transitions in color. Only one form, the **Red-breasted Sapsucker**, is occasionally seen in wooded parks and neighborhoods during winter in Orange County (fig. 6.73). Adult birds have a red head and breast; the back has white bars.

Fig. 6.73. Red-breasted Sapsucker.

Fig. 6.74. Northern Flicker (Richard Bellomy).

Fig. 6.75. Song Sparrow.

Fig. 6.76. Belding's Savannah Sparrow.

Females have less white on the back. The **Northern Flicker**, also known as the **Red-shafted Flicker**, gets its name from the bright reddish color on the shafts of the wing and tail feathers that is revealed in flight (fig. 6.74). Overall it is brownish, with a white rump and black spots on the breast. The male has a broad, bright red mark extending backward from the corner of the beak. These are large woodpeckers, up to 12 $^1/_2$ inches in length, with a 20-inch wingspread. They are known ant-eaters and are sometimes seen eating ants on the ground. They also are known to hollow out citrus fruit on the tree. They nest fairly commonly in the mountains, even drilling holes in cabin walls and making nests there. They move toward the coast in the winter. Their call is an easily recognized clear, loud, high-pitched "kee."

Seed-eaters

Seed-eaters (granivores) can usually be recognized by their conical bills. The bills are fairly wide at the base and not too long, designed to be powerful seed-cracking tools. These birds can be observed gathering seeds from spent flowers or searching for them on the ground. Sparrows and finches are the textbook examples. It should be mentioned, however, that being too specialized is not a good survival strategy in a food-poor environment, and therefore these apparent seed-eaters often supplement their diets with insects, particularly during years with little precipitation or when feeding nestlings.

Many species of sparrows are migratory, making seasonal appearances in selected Orange County habitats. Many of these birds are similar in appearance, requiring a keen eye to distinguish differences. Our most common sparrow is the non-native **House Sparrow**, formerly known as the **English Sparrow**. These birds are highly successful in urban areas, where they can be seen flitting around picking up crumbs at fast-food restaurants. Males, with a gray crown, black throat, and white cheeks, are easy to recognize. Females are similar to many other sparrows. While these birds are fun to watch and common visitors at feeding stations, they are cavity nesters, and they have been implicated in the decline of various native species that nest in holes, including Western Bluebirds and various swallows.

The **Song Sparrow** is a common resident throughout Orange County, including some suburban parks (fig. 6.75). Typical of most sparrows, they have brownish streaks on their backs and sides. Usually there is a dark central spot on the breast. These birds can be heard singing their melodious song from a visible perch in a shrub or tree, usually near water. A look-alike sparrow of coastal marshes is **Belding's Savannah Sparrow** (fig. 6.76). Slightly lighter in color than the Song Sparrow, it also has a central spot on the breast but has a yellowish wash in front of its eyes. It is an inhabitant of Pickleweed Marshes and is unique among terrestrial birds in that it can drink

Fig. 6.77. White-crowned Sparrow.

saltwater. A victim of Salt Marsh destruction, this bird is listed by the state as an endangered species.

Several of our sparrows are recognized by markings on the head and face. The most common is the **White-crowned Sparrow**, found throughout the county during winter (fig. 6.77). It has a bold pattern of black and white stripes on its head and a bright orange bill. It is commonly seen at feeding stations. Immature birds might be confused with a Rufous-crowned Sparrow, but the immature White-crowned Sparrow has two white wing bars and an orange bill. The **Rufous-crowned Sparrow** is an inhabitant of Coastal Sage Scrub and Grasslands. The **Chipping Sparrow**, an inhabitant of the Santa Ana Mountains, also has a rufous crown, but it is bordered with a white stripe, and it has two white wing bars. Normally, Rufous-crowned Sparrows and Chipping Sparrows do not occur in the same habitat. The **Golden-**

Fig. 6.78. Dark-eyed Junco.

crowned Sparrow has a black crown with a yellow patch in the center. It is common in the foothills in Oak Woodlands and mountain canyons. The **Lark Sparrow**, an inhabitant of Coastal Sage Scrub and Grasslands, has the most distinctive facial markings of rufous, white, and black. The breast is white, with a black spot in the center. When it flies, white corners on the tail are conspicuous.

The Sparrow Family (Emberizidae) also includes birds that do not bear the name "sparrow." For example, the **Dark-eyed Junco, a small** gray bird with a distinctive black head, is a fairly common ground-nesting bird of the higher mountains that also winters in the foothills (fig. 6.78). The term "junco" refers to the medieval executioner, who wore a black hood. Towhees are large sparrows that spend lots of time on the ground, where they may be seen searching for food with hop-scratch behavior. The **California Towhee**, formerly **Brown Towhee**, is all brown with a cinnamon-colored throat and rump (fig. 6.79). It is common throughout Orange County, but it also comes to bird feeders in suburban areas. The **Spotted Towhee**, formerly **Rufous-sided Towhee**, has a dark head like a Junco,

but it is black on the back with white spots on the wings and rufous sides (fig. 6.80). This bird, common in Chaparral, where it spends a good portion of its time in heavy brush or on the ground, exhibits disruptive coloration—a color pattern that disrupts its appearance in silhouette. Without distinctive outlines, it is difficult to see in filtered light.

Finches are Sparrow-like but have slightly larger bills. The **House Finch** is one of our most common birds (fig. 6.81). The females look like thick-billed sparrows, but the males have a distinctive red head and breast. They nest throughout the county, even under the eaves of houses, and are common at bird feeders. House Finches have a melodious song with a sequence of repeated warbles that seems never to end. The **Purple Finch** replaces the House Finch at higher elevations. It is similar in coloration to a House Finch, but the red is more extensive on the head and the streaking on the breast is faint.

Goldfinches are warbler-like birds with thick bills. The **Lesser Goldfinch** is a common resident throughout the county (fig. 6.82). Males are olive-green on the back and otherwise yellow with a black cap. The wings are black with two white wing bars. **American Goldfinches** are elusive inhabitants of Riparian areas. Males are bright yellow with a black forehead and an orange bill but otherwise resemble Lesser Goldfinches. **Lawrence's Goldfinch** is locally abundant during spring migrations. Males are gray with a black face and yellow on the belly.

Fruit-eaters

Fruit is another important food source for birds of Mediterranean regions. Many of our local plants, particularly in Coastal Sage Scrub and Chaparral, produce berries. The bright color of the berries attracts birds to eat them. The sugar in the fruit is a reward for the bird which then distributes the seeds in its droppings. Most of these birds also eat insects that can be found in the shrubs or trees. Most of these berry-eaters have conical bills. Non-native fruit trees also supplement the diets of many species.

The **Western Tanager** is one of our most attractive and common spring migrants. It is most often seen in the spring heading northward to the mountains, where it breeds in Coniferous Woodlands; a few also breed at higher elevations in the Santa Ana Mountains. These are bright yellow birds with black backs and wings. The wings have two wing bars, one yellow and one white. Males are very distinctive, with bright red heads. Flocks of these birds move through in the spring,

Fig. 6.79. California Towhee.

Fig. 6.80. Spotted Towhee.

Fig. 6.81. House Finch.

Fig. 6.82. Lesser Goldfinch.

Fig. 6.83. Black-headed Grosbeak.

feeding on berries and insects. They also seem to gather among the red and yellow flowers of the Australian tree known as a **Silk Oak** (*Grevillea robusta*). Their song is a lilting sing-song that somewhat resembles that of a House Finch. Another attractive breeding bird is the **Lazuli Bunting**. The male is bright blue with an orange breast, but the female is a nondescript grayish brown, somewhat resembling a vireo. It is fairly common in the foothills and mountains and seems particularly to thrive in recently burned Chaparral.

Grosbeaks are fairly large birds that are recognized by their large, thick, conical beaks, powerful tools for eating fruit and pine seeds. We have three species that migrate through in the spring. The **Black-headed Grosbeak** is a striking bird (fig. 6.83). Males, like Spotted Towhees, have disruptive coloration, marked by a black hood, black back, and black wings with white markings. The body color is orange. Females look like large sparrows or finches. The song of the Black-headed Grosbeak also resembles that of the

Western Tanager. Although rarely seen in Orange County, females of the **Rose-breasted Grosbeak** are difficult to distinguish from the black-headed forms, but the males have a red triangle on a white breast. The black markings are similar to those of the Black-headed Grosbeak. There is no orange body color, although hybrids between the two species do show characteristics of both. The **Blue Grosbeak** female is a uniform reddish-brown, but the male is indigo blue with a black face and chestnut shoulders. Formerly it was a common species along canyons and Riparian corridors, habitats similar to those of the Yellow-breasted Chat, but recently it has become scarce.

Another conspicuous and attractive bird that travels through our area in the spring and fall is the **Cedar Waxwing**. Flocks of these beautiful birds can be seen feeding on berries in suburban gardens. They have silky gray bodies, buff-colored breasts, a dark eye stripe, and a conspicuous crest.

There are parrots in Orange County. Principally they are fruit-eaters, but they do take seeds, especially sunflower seeds. Most commonly they will be of the "Amazon" group that includes the **Red-crowned Parrot** and the **Yellow-headed Parrot**. Large groups of these birds will roost together in the trees of suburban areas and sometimes fly over in noisy flocks. Some of the larger parakeets, such as the **Black-hooded** or **Red-Masked Parakeets**, also have become naturalized in some areas. Their success and abundance indicates that they must be breeding in Orange County although records of breeding birds are scarce.

Nectar-feeders

Hummingbirds are our most important nectar-feeders. They are such small birds that they have a problem of losing heat. Objects with a high surface-to-volume ratio lose and gain heat rapidly. As a consequence, hummingbirds have high metabolic rates and require large quantities of high-calorie food. This also explains why hummingbirds thrive in hot weather. They can survive on less food when they do not have to be concerned about heat loss. A typical hummingbird consumes over 6,000 calories a day, most of it from sugary nectar. Hummingbirds also eat large quantities of insects. They can be seen gleaning and/or flycatching for small insects. Flowers that attract hummingbirds tend to be tubular and red or yellow. Hummingbirds are also able to see ultraviolet light, and ultraviolet lines, invisible to humans, on the petals of flowers attract them.

Anna's Hummingbird is the most common (fig. 6.84). At 4 inches in length, this is our largest species. Males have a bright red throats and heads and green backs. Females also have a small red spot on the throat. These birds have adapted well to urban settings and frequently visit hummingbird feeders. They produce tiny nests that are often decorated with bits of lichen or threads. It is not uncommon for this nest to be located where people frequently walk by. Of particular interest is that a successful female is able to maintain two nests at the same time and feed two youngsters in each nest.

Allen's Hummingbird is more common along the coast. Prior to the early 1980s this bird was seldom seen in Orange County, but it is becoming more common. Males have bright red-orange throats, orange sides, and green backs. There are two subspecies of this hummingbird. A migratory form travels through in the spring, but of greater interest is the island subspecies, which has been considered endemic to the northern Channel Islands and Santa Catalina. Apparently this bird has migrated from the islands and become established as a resident on the mainland, a pattern that is the reverse of the usual. Most of the time main-

Fig. 6.84. Anna's Hummingbird male.

Fig. 6.85. Costa's Hummingbird.

Fig. 6.86. Western Scrub Jay.

Fig. 6.87. Steller's Jay.

Fig. 6.88. American Crow.

land species become established on islands, where they may evolve into specialized forms. The **Rufous Hummingbird** looks very much like Allen's Hummingbird, but the male has an orange back rather than a bright green one. The Rufous Hummingbird is a migratory species that travels through in the spring on its way to the mountains. **Costa's Hummingbird** is a smaller species, about 3 inches in length (fig. 6.85). The male has a blackish-purple throat and crown and a green back. This species is most often seen in drier habitats such as Coastal Sage Scrub or Chaparral. Its nests are commonly found in Riparian areas.

Omnivores

Many of our local birds are omnivorous, feeding on a variety of foods including insects, seeds, and fruits. This is an important adaptation for animals in food-poor habitats. It enables them to be opportunistic, feeding on whatever type of food is abundant at any time. Typical of most birds that inhabit brushy plant communities, these birds tend to have short wings and a long tail. The beak is fairly long but not thin, a shape that is associated with an omnivorous diet. Most of these birds also have a rather drab color that tends to keep them concealed, but they make up for their drabness by having distinctive calls or songs.

Unlike most birds of scrub habitats, Corvids (Family Corvidae) such as jays, crows, and ravens include our most conspicuous birds. The **Western Scrub Jay** is bright blue with brown shoulders (fig. 6.86). Its

Fig. 6.89. Common Raven.

Fig. 6.90. Red-winged Blackbird.

raucous call is one of the familiar sounds of the Chaparral. This call is important to all the animals of the area because it is universally recognized as an alarm call. Western Scrub Jays feed on insects, spiders, berries, and acorns. They harvest a great number of acorns to bury and retrieve later. Acorns that have not been retrieved are free to germinate, and thus the birds are very important to the survival of Oaks. The **Steller's Jay** is primarily an occupant of Conifer Forests whereas the Western Scrub Jay is more common at lower elevations. Steller's Jay is blue with a black head and shoulders and has a conspicuous crest (fig. 6.87). In contrast to the Western Scrub Jay, which gets all the water it needs from its food, Steller's Jay requires liquid water. Furthermore, the Western Scrub Jay is more efficient than Steller's Jay at dissipating heat through the unfeathered portions of its legs. These are the types of adaptations that promote different habitats for the two birds, although on occasion both species may be found in suburban areas of the county where there are sufficient numbers of trees. Like the Western Scrub Jay, Steller's Jay is the alarmist in its community. It is named after George Steller, who

first discovered the bird on Kayak Island in Alaska. Steller was the physician aboard a ship in Vitis Bering's expedition, among the first white men to land on Alaskan shores.

The **American Crow** is fairly common throughout Orange County (fig. 6.88). Crows tend to occur in noisy groups, and they seem to be becoming more common all the time. Some people view them as pests. They are known to raid gardens and strip fruit trees of their ripened fruits. True to their omnivorous nature, they are common in open trash pits. The **Common Raven** is larger than a Crow (fig. 6.89). Ravens tend to be solitary or occur in pairs, and they soar like hawks. When a Raven is soaring, its tail can be seen to be rounded or wedge-shaped, whereas the Crow's tail is squared off. Ravens are more widely distributed, occurring from the coast to the desert. Crows and Ravens do not often occur together. Their calls are quite distinctive. The Raven makes a croaking sound, and Crows go "caw, caw."

Another common family of Mediterranean birds is the Icteridae, which includes the Blackbirds. **Red-winged Blackbirds** (fig. 6.90) and their close look-alike relatives **Tri-**

Fig. 6.91. Brewer's Blackbird.

Fig. 6.92. Brown-headed Cowbird.

colored **Blackbirds** are found in wetlands, where they often are seen calling from a shrub or the tops of Tules or Cattails. Their distinctive call resembles the sound of a squeaking gate. Females are heavily streaked, superficially resembling female House Finches. Males are easily recognized by their bright red wing patches. Experiments with Red-winged Blackbirds have revealed an interesting thing about the roles of color and sound in the defense of territories. If the red wing patch is covered, birds in heavy brush or forest habitats are able to defend territories with their calls, but birds in open habitats such as marshes are not. If the birds are made mute, those in open habitats are still able to defend territories, but forest birds are not. The conclusion is that in habitats with heavy vegetation vocalizations are more important than color, and in open habitats, where the birds are easy to see, the opposite is true. The wing patch on a Red-winged Blackbird has a yellow lower border, whereas that of the less common Tricolored Blackbird has a white lower border. The latter species used to be very common in Orange County but has been in decline since the 1970s.

Flocks of **Brewer's Blackbirds** are commonly seen in parks and agricultural areas (fig. 6.91). True omnivores, Blackbirds have an eclectic diet. The male Brewer's Blackbird is an iridescent black with a yellow eye. Females are dark brown with dark eyes. **Brown-headed Cowbirds** may be found mixed in with flocks of Brewer's Blackbirds (fig. 6.92). Looking very much like a Blackbird, a male Cowbird has a brown head and a dark eye; a female is brown. In the "old days," Brown-headed Cowbirds were probably more correctly referred to as "Buffalo Birds." Today they are common around pastures and corrals, where they search for insects on the ground and on the backs of the livestock; formerly they accompanied herds of Bison on the Great Plains, but they followed humans and their livestock westward. Unfortunately, they are nest parasites, laying their eggs in the nests of other songbirds, particularly in Riparian areas. When the juvenile Cowbirds hatch, they may evict the native bird's eggs or nestlings (particularly if they are smaller). The parents continue to feed the young as if they were their own. In order to protect certain endangered or threatened native birds such as Bell's Least Vireo, public officials set bird traps and remove all of the

Fig. 6.93. Hooded Oriole.

Fig. 6.94. Northen Mockingbird.

captured Cowbirds from the habitat. Birds that are commonly parasitized by Cowbirds are called "reservoir birds." The most common reservoir birds in Orange County seem to be Red-winged Blackbirds and **Hooded Orioles**. These birds, which are similar in size to Cowbirds, may abandon their nests when they see a Cowbird egg. More often the native offspring are not evicted by the Cowbird baby and are fed along with the nest parasite; thus both species survive the interaction.

There are four kinds of orioles that might be seen in Orange County. Males are bright yellow or orange with various amounts of black on the head. Females of all these orioles are similar in appearance, a pale yellow. Hooded Orioles have yellow heads with black faces (fig. 6.93). They are fairly common in the spring in suburban and rural areas. They are particularly fond of nesting in palm trees where they make pendulous nests of palm fibers. **Bullock's Orioles** have black caps and black throats. They tend to nest in Riparian areas, particularly in tall Sycamores. **Scott's Oriole** is yellow, with a black back and head. More of a desert bird, it is sometimes seen in the foothills during the winter. **Balti-**

more Orioles are rare in Orange County. They also have black heads, but their body color is orange. Formerly, Baltimore Orioles and Bullock's Orioles were lumped into a single species known as the **Northern Oriole**. Orioles are known for their melodic songs, composed of clear whistles. They feed on a variety of foods, including nectar, and they often visit hummingbird feeders.

The **Western Meadowlark** is a common inhabitant of open fields. Recognized by its distinctive song, a musical, descending warble, it is often seen perched on a fence post. It is a chubby, short-tailed bird with a bright yellow breast marked by a V-shaped black breast band. Because it nests on the ground, it requires open land with unmowed grass and/or weeds. Unfortunately for the Western Meadowlark, this sort of habitat is rapidly disappearing in Orange County.

The Family Mimidae includes birds that are well known for their elaborate songs, which often include the sounds of other birds. The **Northern Mockingbird** is a long-tailed gray bird with a black eye stripe (fig. 6.94). It is common in suburban and brushy habitats,

Fig. 6.95. California Thrasher.

Fig. 6.96. American Robin.

where it sings from a conspicuous perch, sometimes all night long, much to the dismay of light sleepers. A male Mockingbird may nest on the corner of a building and attempt to defend the area even from passing humans. More than one person walking by the nest has been surprised by an aerial attack consisting of a peck on the head or wing buffets. The **California Thrasher** (fig. 6.95) is also known for its musical call, but it is seldom seen because it spends most of its time on the ground in dense brush. It gets the name "Thrasher" from its habit of

thrashing its long curved beak in leaf litter and debris in search of seeds and insects. This is a textbook bird of Scrub habitats. It is drab brown and has short wings and a long tail, and it is omnivorous. Except for its distinctive bill, it most nearly resembles the California Towhee; they are both brown birds with orange to buff-colored rumps.

The **Loggerhead Shrike** is a Mockingbird look-alike. Close inspection, however, reveals that the shrike has a black eye mask and a slightly hooked beak, indicative of

Fig. 6.97. Hermit Thrush.

a bird of prey. Shrikes feed on insects, lizards, and mice, preying upon them from an open perch. The fact that this bird seems to kill more animals than it could eat has puzzled biologists, It now seems clear, however, that a courting male provisions a larder and displays it conspicuously to prove to the females that it is a good hunter. Lizards, grasshoppers, or mice may be pinned to sharp sticks, cactus spines, or barbed wire as testimony to hunting prowess, hence the name "Butcher Bird." The stored food will be used to feed the young. A highly successful male is able to mate with more than one female and supply enough food for more than one family. It appears that this formerly common bird is becoming scarce as open land is converted to buildings or turf. It is now being considered for official listing as rare, threatened, or endangered. In Orange County today it still occurs along the Santa Ana River and in some of our wilderness parks.

Thrushes (Family Turdidae) are well-known songsters, particularly for their beautiful fluting songs. In Orange County, our most familiar thrush is the **American Robin** (fig. 6.96). This red-breasted bird is grayish to black on the back and head, and its bill is bright yellow. Some of these birds nest in our local parks, but they are most common in the fall and winter, when they migrate through from their summer haunts in the mountains. They feed on insects and berries and pull earthworms from

Fig. 6.98. Western Bluebird.

the soil. Robins can be seen walking on suburban lawns with their heads cocked to the side, apparently listening for earthworms or insect larvae burrowing underground. Two other thrushes that are seen occasionally in Orange County are the **Hermit Thrush** (fig. 6.97) and **Swainson's Thrush**. These similar birds are brown with spotted breasts. The Hermit Thrush winters throughout the county; sometimes its flutelike song is heard before it moves on to its nesting sites in the mountains. Swainson's Thrush is seen primarily during spring and fall migration.

Bluebirds are also thrushes. Our only common bluebird is the **Western Bluebird**, characterized by its bright blue color and rufous breast and sides (fig. 6.98). These cavity nesters favor habitats with large trees, especially Oaks with old woodpecker holes. Unfortunately, non-native **European Starlings**, which are becoming increasingly

Fig. 6.99. Mourning Dove.

Fig. 6.100. Band-tailed Pigeon.

Fig. 6.101. California Quail.

Fig. 6.102. Greater Roadrunner sunning.

common, are evicting and replacing Blue-birds. The one saving grace for Bluebirds has been the strategic placing of artificial nest boxes (with holes too small for Star-lings), particularly in parks, on golf cours-es, in picnic grounds, and in cemeteries. Orange County leads the state in helping Western Bluebird populations to recover. Starlings look like short-tailed Blackbirds. They often occur in large aggregations and often spend the night in a particular tree, where their squeaks and creaking sounds advertise their presence.

Doves and Pigeons are in the Family Columbidae. Our most common dove is the **Mourning Dove**, which gets its name from the sorrowful sound of its "whooing" (fig. 6.99). Like many birds that feed on insects and seeds they are often seen on the ground and will forage on suburban lawns and at bird feeders. They also are often seen perched on overhead wires. They are easily recognized by their brown-ish-gray color and the black spots on their wings. They have long pointed tails with white edges that are visible when they fly. They can fly very fast, and their wings make a whistling noise in flight. Doves are very drought-tolerant, able to lose up to 50% of their body weight through dehydration. They are unique among birds in their ability to drink dew. Unlike other birds, they can pick up water and swallow it without tilting back their heads. During the heat of a summer day, Doves may fly a considerable distance to water in the morning and may spend the heat of the day perched in a shady tree.

The **Common Ground-dove** was once rare in Orange County but has expanded its range in recent years. This small 6-inch dove superficially resembles a Mourning Dove, but it has a short tail and when it flies reveals rufous outer wing feathers. It can be seen in urban areas north of the Santa Ana River and is fairly common in Huntington Central Park.

Our only other common native member of the Dove Family is the **Band-tailed Pigeon** (fig. 6.100). This large pale-gray bird was once hunted nearly to extirpation. In the absence of hunting in recent years it has recovered remarkably and is now a common sight in Orange County's foothills, where it perches in Sycamores and Oaks. It can be recognized by its large size and the broad white tip of its tail. It also has a white ring around the back of its neck and a yellow bill and legs. It should not be confused with the non-native **Rock Pigeon (Dove)** or **Domestic Pigeon**, a bird of urban areas characterized by many color patterns but with a dark bill and pink legs. Two other non-native doves may, on occasion, be spotted in Orange County, but they are increasingly scarce. These are the **Spotted Dove** and the **Ringed Turtle Dove**, also known as the Ring-necked Dove. The Spotted Dove gets its name from a dark patch with white spots on the back of its neck, and the **Ringed Turtle Dove** has a black ring on the back of its neck. These are domesticated birds that have escaped from captivity and became naturalized. The Spotted Dove was once common in coastal Orange County but is now seldom seen.

Our state bird is the **California Quail** (fig. 6.101). Easily recognized by the prominent teardrop-shaped plume on top of the head, it is very common in our brushlands and foothills. It occurs in flocks and spends most of its time on the ground. Even when it cannot be seen, it announces its presence by a distinctive call that sounds like "Ah-háh-hah" (or "Chi-cá-go"). Also very drought-tolerant, it can stand losing 50% of its body weight by dehydration. Quail spend the hot summer days in the shade and fly toward water in the evening.

The **Greater Roadrunner**, a member of the Cuckoo Family, is a large bird, nearly 2 feet in length, and clearly prefers running to flying. It is streaky brown and has a very long tail and short wings. It occurs throughout brushy lands and deserts. Its presence in Chaparral has earned it the nickname "**Chaparral Cock**." It is well adapted to hot dry climates, getting most of its water by eating moist food such as lizards and snakes. It avoids overheating by remaining in the shade during the heat of the day, and at night it conserves energy by lowering its body temperature. Often on sunny mornings it can be seen basking in the sun with the feathers of its back raised so that the dark-colored skin underneath is exposed to the sun (fig. 6.102). Contrary to the cartoon, it makes a strange low-pitched "glub-glub-glub" sound during the breeding season and distinctive bill clacks during any season.

Fig. 6.103. Deer Mouse.

Fig. 6.104. Meadow Vole.

SMALL MAMMALS

The small mammals of Orange County are mostly nocturnal rodents. Foraging at night helps them escape the summer heat and also provides some protection from diurnal predators such as hawks. Most rodents are seed-eaters. Technically they compete with certain birds and ants for the seed supply, but experiments show that they partition the seed resource by feeding on different-sized seeds in different locations. The small mammals of our public lands are as follows:

Native Mice, Rats, Voles (Family Cricetidae)

The **Deer Mouse** (*Peromyscus maniculatus*) is tan above and white below (fig. 6.103). It has a relatively short tail that is white on the underside. It differs from the House Mouse by having hair on its tail. Its large ears also differentiate it from some of the other native mice, such as the Harvest Mouse and the Vole. The Deer Mouse is distributed from the desert floor to the high mountains, one of the widest ranges of any native small mammal. One of its significant behavioral attributes is hibernating every day. By lowering its body temperature

and metabolic rate while it is in its burrow during the day, it conserves significant energy, an important strategy for survival in a food-poor ecosystem. This lowered metabolic rate also serves to extend its life span. Deer Mice live about five years, longer than most other small rodents. (Most mice live only a year or so.) They eat a large variety of foods including seeds, fungi, and insects. Less common relatives of the Deer Mouse include the **Brush Mouse** (*Peromyscus boylii*), the **Cactus Mouse** (*Peromyscus eremicus*), and the **California** or **Parasitic Mouse** (*Peromyscus californicus*). The Cactus Mouse occurs near the coast but is seldom found during the summer because it tends to retreat to its burrow and go dormant during the hot summer months. The other mice tend to occur in Chaparral at higher elevations than the coast. The California Mouse is a large, dark-colored mouse with a long tail and is also found in Oak Woodland. The Brush Mouse is distinctive in that it commonly climbs in the branches of large shrubs such as Manzanitas. The **Western Harvest Mouse** (*Reithrodontomys megalotis*) is found primarily in Grasslands and Coastal Sage Scrub. It is smaller than the Deer Mouse, and its long tail is nearly hairless. Rather than living underground, it usually makes a ball-like

Fig. 6.105. Desert Wood Rat (Greg Stewart).

Fig. 6.106. Pocket Mouse.

nest of grasses on the ground. The **California Meadow Vole** (*Microtus californicus*) is a stocky, dark-colored mouse with a short tail (fig. 6.104). Its preferred habitat is Grasslands if water is nearby (irrigated fields will suffice). It will live in Coastal Sage Scrub if water is nearby. Its diet consists primarily of green forbs and grasses; it seldom eats seeds or insects.

The **Desert Wood Rat** (*Neotoma lepida*) (fig. 6.105) is the common Wood Rat that lives in patches of Prickly Pear. It appears to be a large, light-colored version of a Deer Mouse. It may build a home of sticks, but it frequently includes mounds of Coastal Cholla. It does not hibernate but remains active all summer, feeding on a variety of foods. It obtains water by gnawing on cactus. The **Dusky-footed Wood Rat** or **Pack Rat** (*Neotoma fuscipes*) occurs more commonly in Chaparral. This large dark-colored rat is about the size of the non-native **Black Rat** but has a hairy tail. It builds a large stick nest on the ground or even in a shrub. It is known to include sprigs of sage in the nest, perhaps as a deodorant. The nest has numerous entrances, but usually only one is active, the others being dead ends. The name "Pack Rat" comes from its habit of picking up small, shiny objects and adding them to its nest.

Pocket Mice and Kangaroo Rats (Family Heteromyidae)

The **Pacific Kangaroo Rat** (*Dipodomys agilis*) has large muscular hindlegs and small front legs that it uses to sort through sandy soil in search of seeds. It stores these seeds temporarily in fur-lined cheek pouches and then in its burrow. Larger than a Mouse but smaller than a Wood Rat, a Pacific Kangaroo Rat is easily recognized by its long tufted tail and small round ears. It is dark with a white spot at the base of each ear and a black tuft at the tip of its tail. Kangaroo Rats never need to drink water; they get all the water they need from the waste product of metabolism.

The **San Diego Pocket Mouse** (*Chaetodipus fallax*) is a small version of a Kangaroo Rat (fig. 6.106). It is brownish on its back with buff-colored lines running down its sides. It has conspicuous white spiny hairs on its back and sides and black spines on its rump. The tail is white underneath and has a crest of long hairs on its upper surface. Pocket Mice and Kangaroo Rats are so efficient at gathering seeds that they often clear bare spots in grasses on the edges of shrubs.

Fig. 6.107. Pocket Gopher.

Fig. 6.108. California Ground Squirrel.

These areas become conspicuous when seeds germinate after winter rains. The **California Pocket Mouse** (*Chaetodipus californicus*) is larger and has a mixture of yellow and black hairs on its back. It also has spiny hairs on its rump and sides. This species is less common and is never seen during the winter because it hibernates. The **Pacific Pocket Mouse** (*Perognathus longimembris pacificus*) is rare in Orange County. Its only known locality of abundance is on the Dana Point headlands, where it inhabits sandy soil. Plans for development of the Dana Point headlands have included a portion of undisturbed habitat for preservation of the species, currently listed as endangered.

Pocket Gophers (Family Geomyidae)

The **Botta's Pocket Gopher** (*Thomomys bottae*) is so named because of its fur-lined cheek pouches (fig. 6.107). It is seldom seen above ground, but its dirt piles and burrows are conspicuous in grassy areas. If it is observed above ground, it can be recognized by its enlarged front feet, yellow front teeth, and small eyes and ears. These animals are active all year long.

Squirrels (Family Sciuridae)

The **California Ground Squirrel** (*Spermophilus beecheyi*) is the common burrowing squirrel that is frequently seen wherever there is abundant open space, particularly weedy areas where they thrive on seeds of non-native plants and the fruits of irrigated crops (fig. 6.108). It is conspicuous because it is diurnal. The **Western Gray Squirrel** (*Sciurus griseus*), the bushy-tailed tree squirrel that occurs in Oaks and Conifers, is larger than the California Ground Squirrel (fig. 6.109). It eats primarily acorns, which it buries in small stashes all over the forest and relies on to survive the winter.

Hares and Rabbits (Family Leporidae)

Hares and Rabbits are not rodents. They are in a separate order, the Lagomorpha, characterized by having two pairs of incisors (buck teeth) in their upper jaws. The long-legged, large-eared **Blacktail Jackrabbit** (*Lepus californicus*) is a familiar sight in grassy open habitat in interior Orange County (fig. 6.110). These animals do not live in burrows but take shelter in shrubs. They are good at conserving water because they do not perspire. They cool themselves by sitting in the shade, aiming their ears at open sky; heat escapes as the blood passes near the surface in their large ears. **Audubon's Cottontail** (*Sylvilagus auduboni*) is the common little bunny with the white tail that comes out at night to feed on well-watered lawns (fig. 6.111). In its native habitat it tends to occur in open areas. Cottontails raise their young in a burrow. Two to six helpless young are nursed in a nest lined with soft belly hair of the mother. The **Brush Rabbit** (*Sylvilagus bachmani*) may co-occur with the Cottontail, but it seldom strays from dense cover. It can be distinguished from the Cottontail by its tail, which is brown above and white below.

Shrews (Family Soricidae)

Although they are mouselike in appearance, Shrews are in the order Insectivora. They are the smallest mammals. They are carnivores and have a very high metabolic rate. Shrews usually consume many times their own weight in prey every day. They are the only mammals that have venomous saliva, which they use to subdue prey larger than themselves. They are nocturnal and very secretive. When they are found by humans it usually is because they have fallen into a container from which they were unable to escape. The **Desert Shrew** (*Notiosorex crawfordi*) is a fairly common little nocturnal predator in Coastal Sage Scrub (fig. 6.112). It has a very long pointed nose. It preys primarily on rodents and insects. The **Ornate Shrew** (*Sorex ornatus*) also occurs in our area but is not common. It occurs primarily in Grassland areas, particularly if water is nearby.

Fig. 6.109. Gray Squirrel.

Fig. 6.110. Blacktail Jackrabbit.

Fig. 6.111. Audubon's Cottontail.

Fig. 6.112. Desert Shrew.

Fig. 6.113. Mule Deer.

Fig. 6.114. Mountain Lion.

LARGE MAMMALS

The only large native herbivore in Orange County is the **Mule Deer** (*Odocoileus hemionus*) (fig. 6.113). It is remarkably common in Orange County, as testified by frequent sightings of its two-toed tracks. Mule Deer are about 3–3 ½ feet tall at the shoulder. Females may weigh 150 pounds and large bucks up to 400 pounds. They are called Mule Deer because of their very large ears. They can be distinguished from the eastern White-tailed Deer by their tails, which are black at the tip, and the fact that the antlers branch dichotomously (that is each branch can branch again). These deer are fairly common throughout Orange County's brushlands, including Coastal Sage Scrub, where they occur in a relatively undisturbed state (such as the San Joaquin Hills and Chino Hills). Mule Deer are browsers, feeding on twigs and herbs. The new growth following a fire is fairly important browse for them. They are not considered to be grazers, seldom feeding on grasses. They tend to be most active in the morning and evening, taking cover during the heat of the day in Oak Woodlands or thick brush. Mat-

ing occurs in the fall, at which time bucks will fight over the females. The dominant buck, in harem style, will mate with several females. The antlers are lost during winter and regrow in the spring. New antlers are covered with skin and hair, which ultimately dry up and are scraped off. The does are pregnant for about seven months, and spotted fawns appear from May to July. One fawn is common, although when food is abundant a female may bear triplets. The major threat to Mule Deer in Orange County is motor vehicles.

Our largest predators are **Mountain Lions** (*Panthera [= Felis] concolor*), also known as **Cougars**, **Catamounts**, or **Pumas** (fig. 6.114). Habits and distribution of Mountain Lions in Orange County have been fairly well studied. Because they are large predators, they require a very large home range, approximately 100 square miles. Habitat fragmentation is the major cause of reduced numbers of large predators. Every highway is a barrier to dispersal. Not only are Lions killed trying to cross roadways, but each road constitutes a barrier of pavement, noise, odors, and light.

Fig. 6.115. Bobcat.

Fig. 6.116. Coyote scat with seeds of Holly-leaf Cherry.

Studies using remote telemetry with collared animals show that populations of large animals are divided into subgroups on either side of a road. In an attempt to mitigate this problem, large undercrossings are built into highways that pass through otherwise undisturbed habitat. When the Highway 73 and 241 toll roads were built, these undercrossings were part of the design. Highway 91, however, was built before this problem was addressed. The Coal Canyon underpass at Highway 91 was closed to traffic, and pavement was removed to make the undercrossing more natural. Although crossings are not common, examination of footprints indicates that there is some movement of deer and other animals between lower Coal Canyon and the Chino Hills. Lion crossings are not well documented. One study of road kills on Harbor Boulevard in the Whittier Hills indicated that the number of dead animals on the road was the same before and after a large culvert was built to accommodate their movements. Wildlife biologists believe that fences have to be built along the highways in order to direct animals to use the undercrossings.

Bobcats (*Felis [= Lynx] rufus*) are more common than Mountain Lions because they are smaller and can survive on smaller patches of undisturbed land (fig. 6.115). Some evidence indicates that there could be up to two Bobcats per square mile. Bobcat footprints resemble those of a Mountain Lion but of course are smaller. Whereas a Lion's paw is nearly 4 inches across, that of a Bobcat is half that size. Cat tracks can be distinguished from those of a dog because the central pad of a cat has three lobes in the back whereas that of a dog tends to be flattened or indented at the back. Dog tracks often show claw marks as well. The other way to verify the presence of a Bobcat is to examine feces or scats. Bobcats tend to produce lumpy and tapered scats, and, in true cat style, they may attempt to bury them.

Coyotes (*Canis latrans*) are fairly common. They will never be as common as herbivores, but by virtue of their varied diet (they are omnivores) (fig. 6.116) they outnumber Bobcats in appropriate habitat. Cameras placed in the highway undercrossings designed to accommodate wildlife indicate that Coyotes are the most common animals using them, and along with Skunks, Raccoons, and Opossums they are the most common animals killed on roads. They have become acclimated to the urban/wildland interface and will raid trash cans and eat pet food. Normally they do not eat Domestic Cats, but they do view Domestic Cats and Domestic Dogs as competition and aggressively chase them away. When House Cats disappear, as they often do, Coyotes usually are blamed. By climbing trees and scaling fences, however, Cats are fairly adept at escaping the threat of a Coyote. When one is killed, it seems that it is the result of cooperative behavior on the part of two or more Coyotes working together to corner it.

Gray Foxes (*Urocyon cinereoargenteus*) are much smaller than Coyotes (fig. 2.20). Whereas Coyotes weigh 20 to 40 pounds, a large Gray Fox weighs only about 15 pounds. Gray Foxes are gray on the back

but considerably more brown on the head and neck than a Coyote, and their ears are noticeably large. When Coyotes are abundant they chase Foxes just as they chase Cats and Dogs. When patches of undisturbed habitat are too small to support a family of Coyotes, however, Gray Foxes become much more common, an example of mesopredator release (see chapter 2). Gray Foxes are also omnivores, but they eat insects and small rodents as well as birds. Gray Foxes can climb into shrubs and small trees and feed on birds in their nests or while they are asleep on a perch. So, ironically, when Coyotes are scarce, Domestic Cats and Foxes become more common, and since they eat birds, the birds seem to disappear.

Red Foxes (*Vulpes vulpes* [= *V. fulva*]) are not native to Orange County, although there is a native population in California in the northern Sierra Nevada (fig. 6.117). The Red Foxes introduced to Orange County were probably originally from the eastern United States. They were introduced initially to the foothills of the Santa Ana Mountains for hunting purposes, but they are believed to have been extirpated from that habitat if for no other reason than Coyotes that will not tolerate their presence. Red Foxes were also introduced at the Seal Beach Naval Weapons Station, and for a time their presence there was implicated in the demise of the Light-footed Clapper Rail and a population of Least Terns at nearby Bolsa Chica. The Navy began trapping the Red Foxes in 1986, and by 1989 it had removed 250 of the animals. They are believed to be rare or absent in the county today.

Fig. 6.117. Red Fox.

The Family Mustelidae includes Weasels, Skunks, Minks, and Otters, all of which are known for producing musky odors. The **Long-tailed Weasel** (*Mustela frenata*) is common but seldom seen (fig. 6.118). This small predator has a voracious appetite, being capable of eating more than its body weight in mice every day. There are two kinds of Skunks locally. The **Striped Skunk** (*Mephitis mephitis*) is a familiar sight in suburban areas that are near wildlands. It is nocturnal and omnivorous, eating all sorts of food including grubs and snails in suburban gardens, and it will raid pet food that is left out overnight. Where Skunks are common, their diggings can make a nicely tended garden look like a mine-field. They are also very commonly killed on roads. A Skunk's odor is a defense mechanism that is used to deter predators. When it is threatened, it stomps its feet and raises its tail, which is like a warning flag. Most animals know to avoid a Skunk, but a Domestic Dog may not be aware of the significance of the warning and may get sprayed. Striped Skunks are about Cat-sized, weighing about 3–10 pounds. They look larger because they have so much fur. **Western Spotted Skunks** (*Spilogale putorius*) are much smaller than Striped Skunks. They are much less common as well, although they have similar habits and diet, and they are not as likely to invade suburban gardens. Spotted Skunks have large black and white patches on their bodies. Their defense posture is quite strange; instead of simply raising their tails they do a handstand and, turning their backs to the threat, use their whole bodies and tails as a signal.

Raccoons (*Procyon lotor*) are familiar suburban raiders. Their ringed tails and black eye masks are unmistakable marks of recognition. Like Striped Skunks they are nocturnal, digging in gardens and eating pet food. They are known to "wash" their food before eating. They are good climbers, so they can climb into trash cans and also will climb on roofs, and for inexplicable reasons they have been known to tear off shingles and invade attics. Raccoons weigh up to 40 pounds, and in a fight are easily a match for most Domestic Dogs. Their front paws are like hands, and they are very dexterous. A raccoon in a fight with a Dog may climb onto its back, hanging on with its teeth and using its paws to gouge at its eyes. Footprints of Skunks and Raccoons are fairly recognizable because they show all five digits on the front and hind feet. Furthermore, Raccoon prints look a bit like handprints because the digits are fairly long.

Another familiar suburban raider is the **Opossum** (*Didelphis virginiana*). Weighing up to 15 pounds, Opossums look like large white-faced rats. They are mostly gray with coarse hair, small ears, long pointed noses, and prehensile hairless tails. Like Skunks and Raccoons, they are omnivorous. Opossums are marsupials, the only North American members of that group of primitive mammals. They are native to the eastern United States but have been introduced into California. Up to 25 young are born at a time, after which they must crawl up into the pouch and attach themselves to one of 9 to 17 nipples. After about three months in the pouch, 9 young, on average, emerge. The young remain with the mother for some time and can be seen clinging to her back while she wanders through some suburban garden. Opossum footprints also show all five digits, but the hind foot is significantly larger than the front foot, and the big toe is opposable like a human thumb. They are even better climbers than Raccoons because of the grasping ability of their hind feet and their prehensile tails. The phrase "playing possum" refers to the animal's habit of feigning death. Perhaps this behavior, when it rolls over, lolls its tongue, and drools, somehow startles a potential predator, or perhaps it is a submissive posture that defuses the aggression of an attacker.

Chapter 7

The Intertidal Region

The intertidal region is where the land meets the sea. Because of its scenic nature, this is the most highly visited region in Orange County. As far as human impact is concerned, humans are loving it to death. Yet, by virtue of the foresight of citizens and public agencies, our beaches, estuaries, and headlands are primarily in public hands. They are available for public use, but their resources are largely protected. The intertidal or littoral zone is characterized by three major habitats, **sandy beaches, rocky headlands,** and **estuaries**.

This region, influenced by the daily ebb and flow of tides, is one of the best examples of **edge effect** in the world. This is because the area retains characteristics of both ocean and terrestrial habitats and contains organisms associated with both. Rates of primary production (photosynthesis) also are quite high, providing a rich source of food for intertidal organisms. In the surf zone, kelps produce the food, and in estuaries most of the organic matter comes from Cord Grass, but the greatest contribution to the food chain comes from decaying

material and dissolved organic matter in the water. Offshore, **Giant Bladder Kelp** (*Macrocystis pyrifera*) grows to lengths of 200 feet, reportedly the fastest-growing plant in the world (fig. 7.1). The diversity of species and habitats within 10 vertical feet is greater in the intertidal zone than in any other habitat on earth.

SANDY BEACHES

Sands of beaches are derived primarily from weathering of rocks in the mountains. The sand is delivered to the ocean by rivers and then carried southward by the action of waves and currents. Additional materials are added to beaches by erosion of shore-line cliffs. The bulk of the material that makes up sand is quartz, a hard insoluble mineral sorted into particles that usually range between 0.06 and 2 millimeters in size. Particle size determines the water-holding capacity of the beach, a feature that has a profound influence on the nature of creatures that live there. Sands that remain soft are the most habitable.

Food for sand-dwelling organisms comes primarily from planktonic or detrital particles suspended in seawater. An-other important source of food is organic molecules that adhere to the sand particles themselves, and a third is broken-up kelp and other debris washed up on the beach by high tides or storms. Of course, beach-dwelling organisms also eat each other.

Fig. 7.1. Giant Bladder Kelp.

Fig. 7.2. Pacific Mole Crab (Peter Bryant).

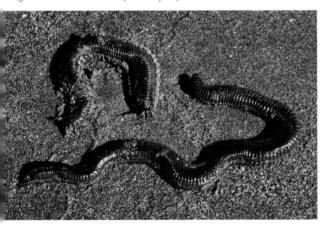

Fig. 7.3. Clam Worms.

Fig. 7.4. California Grunion (Peter Bowler).

One of the most common animals of sandy beaches is the **Pacific Mole Crab** or **Western Sand Crab** (*Emerita analoga*) (fig. 7.2). These crustaceans, about an inch in length, are shaped like small flattened chicken eggs. Their small appendages can be used for swimming or digging. Mole Crabs move up and down the beach in the surf line, feeding on detritus and plankton. Every time a wave recedes, they burrow backward into the soupy sand and therefore are seldom seen. People wading in the surf may feel them as a tingling sensation on their bare feet. Between molts, when the carapace is soft, Mole Crabs are prized bait for surf fishermen.

Among the filter-feeding inhabitants of sandy beaches are several varieties of clams. When the tide is in, these organisms pass a current of water through their bodies and extract small organisms and particulate organic matter from the water. The **Pacific Razor Clam** (*Siliqua patula*), one of the most common of these clams, is narrow and elongated, about 3 inches in length. Similarly to Mole Crabs, they move in and out with the tides. They are surprisingly motile, fast-digging organisms. During the lowest of tides, many people search the low-tide line for these clams, which are considered a delicacy. A large, thick-shelled clam known as the **Pismo Clam** (*Tivela stultorum*) can be found outside of the surf zone, particularly where the beach is fairly flat. It is not particularly tasty, but its large size makes it sought after. On days of the lowest tides, thousands of people visit Pismo

Beach in San Luis Obispo County and dig up the clams with shovels and pitchforks. In Orange County Pismo Clams can be found at beaches in Huntington and Newport.

Bloodworms (*Glycera* spp.) and **Lugworms** (*Arenicola* spp.) also live buried in beaches with fine sand. These segmented worms (Phylum Annelida) feed like earthworms, by ingesting sand and digesting suspended organic material. The undigested material passes through their bodies. These worms, belonging to a group known as polychaete worms, have small bristly paddles on their sides, one pair per segment. They are usually about an inch long, although in some habitats they may be much larger. Their red color comes from hemoglobin, the same pigment that carries oxygen in the blood of vertebrate animals. The hemoglobin of these worms enables them to store oxygen while buried in the sand. When the tide is out they bury themselves deeply, up to a depth of 18 inches. Larger polychaete worms, up to a foot in length, are active predators. When the tide is in, they emerge from the sand to prey upon other sand dwellers. They have a pair of curved jaws that resemble the fangs of a spider. There are several species, but among the most common are the **Clam Worms** (*Nereis* spp.) that also are found in the musssel beds of rocky intertidal areas (fig. 7.3).

Detritus feeders live in the piles of kelp and other organic debris that line the upper tide line. One of the most common is the **California Beach Flea or Beach Hopper** (*Orchestoidea californiana*). Sunbathers lying near kelp piles often feel these small amphipod crustaceans hopping on their legs. Isopod crustaceans, similar to Sow Bugs, prefer to eat meat such as dead fish that may wash up on the beach. One form, known as **Harford's Greedy Isopod** (*Cirolana harfordi*), occurs in swarms large enough to clean the skeleton of a dead fish in a matter of hours.

One of the most interesting inhabitants of sandy beaches is a fish that lays its eggs on land. This the **California Grunion** (*Leuresthes tenuis*) (fig. 7.4). This member of the Silversides family (Atherinidae) is a sardine-sized fish about 8 inches in length. Grunion have in common with human females that their reproductive cycles are lunar rhythms, keyed to the phases of the moon. California Grunion lay their eggs primarily on beaches in southern California; they are seldom seen north of Morro Bay. In the spring of the year, on nights following the full moon, Grunion migrate by the thousands to beaches. Females burrow tail first into the soupy sand at the upper limits of high tide waves. Males wrap their bodies around the females and release sperm into the burrows as the females lay their eggs. Fertilized eggs incubate in clusters in the wet sand. Two weeks later, during the new moon, tides once again rise high on the beach. At this time--the dark of the moon--the eggs hatch, and the tiny fish swim out to sea under the cover of darkness. Dates of the high tides and the Grunion runs are listed in most coastal newspapers and in a number of free publications. On nights of predicted runs, hordes of people swarm to dark beaches, such as Huntington, Newport, Corona del Mar, or Laguna, where Grunion are known to spawn. Grunion do not always behave according to schedule, but if they do,

TABLE 7.1 MARINE ECOSYSTEMS		
Stress	**Adaptation**	**Example**
Wave shock	Adherent threads	Mussels
	Stick tightly	Chiltons, limpets
	Conical shape	Barnacles, limpets
	Flexible stalks	Goose barnacle, kelps
	Hide in cracks	Crabs
	Motility	Periwinkles
Dehydration	Motility	Starfish
	Operculum	Turban shells
	Stick tightly	Abalone, limpets
	Seal openings	Barnacles
	Valved shells	Mussels
Temperature extremes	Motility	Crabs
	Evaporative cooling	Mussels
	Tolerance	Barnacles
	Nocturnal behavior	Rock lice
Salinity extremes	Tolerance	Periwinkles
	Motility	Crabs
Feeding	Filter feeding	Mussels, barnacles
	Grazing	Chiltons, limpets
	Detritus feeding	Sea hares, crabs
	Absorption of DOM	Sea urchins
	Predation	Octopi, starfish
Predation	Hard shells	Barnacles, mussels
	Motility	Crabs
	Toxins	Nudibranchs, kelps
	Protective coloration	Tidepool sculpin
Competition	Aggression	Crabs, octopi
	Rapid growth	Barnacles
	Opportunistic larval establishment	Mussels, barnacles
	Large numbers of offspring	Sea urchins, barnacles
	Good dispersal	Planktonic larvae

After A.A. Schoenherr, 1999. *Natural History of the Islands of California*. University of California Press

people catch them with their hands (a fishing license is required). Many people enjoy eating them, but unfortunately too many folks are there for the party, and the Grunion that are caught wind up fertilizing the rose bushes.

Most of the predators of the sandy beaches are the birds that probe the sand for prey items mentioned above. Included here are various kinds of Gulls and several species of long-billed shorebirds such as **Willets** (fig. 7.5), **Marbled Godwits** (fig. 7.39), and **Sanderlings**.

ROCKY HEADLANDS

For many visitors to the coves of Laguna Beach and Little Corona del Mar, the trip is not complete without a walk to the tide pools during low tide (fig. 7.6). The rocky intertidal habitat is one of the most diverse in the world. It is extremely harsh, but this is where most higher animals are believed to have evolved. Representatives of every major group (phylum) of animals are found in this region.

Fig. 7.5. Willet probing in sand.

Fig. 7.6. Rocky headland at Little Corona del Mar.

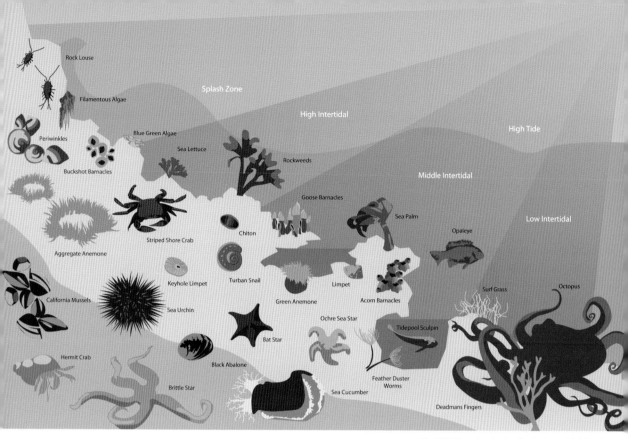

Fig. 7.7. Zonation in the Rocky Intertidal Region.

The rocky intertidal region has five zones based on the length of time that organisms are out of the water: the **splash zone**, the **upper intertidal zone**, the **middle intertidal zone**, the **lower intertidal zone**, and the **subtidal zone** (fig. 7.7). Each zone has its own combination of stresses, including wave shock, exposure, temperature extremes, and predation. Adaptations to the stresses are varied (table 7.1). Although there is some controversy over the precise boundaries of each zone and the organisms that inhabit each, the zones do occur in distinct bands on the rocks. The reasons for this zonation represent some of the most interesting concepts in ecology.

Splash Zone

The source of water in the splash zone is that which splashes up on the rocks as the surf crashes against the shore. This is primarily a terrestrial community that gets limited amounts of water. Photosynthetic organisms in the zone are drought-tolerant, crustose forms such as **Cyanobacteria (Blue-green Algae)** and black **Lichens**. This is an extremely harsh habitat, subject to prolonged drying. Few species of animals live here, and those that do either hide in cracks during daylight hours or take refuge in shallow tide pools. Most common among dwellers in the cracks is a nocturnal isopod crustacean about an inch long known as the **Rock Louse** (*Ligia* spp.)

Fig. 7.8. Rock Louse.

Fig. 7.9. Periwinkles.

(fig. 7.8). Venturing out at night, it feeds on attached algae or kelp that is deposited on the rocks by the surf. Biologists have studied these small animals to get a better understanding of innate biological clocks or circadian rhythms. Rock Lice change color during the 24 hours of a day; they are dark during daylight hours and lighter at night.

In the shallow tide pools, the most common animals are small snails known as **Periwinkles** (*Littorina* spp.) (fig. 7.9). There are several species of these snails, and all are tolerant of exposure. When the tide is in they creep about grazing on attached algae. When the tide goes out they take refuge in tide pools, where they continue feeding. If the rocks become too dry they retreat into their shells, sealing the entrance with a circular bit of shell known as an operculum. These small snails are particularly well suited to life in the splash zone. They can breathe in or out of water, and they can also tolerate submersion in freshwater when it rains during low tide. They stick tightly to the rocks during periods of high surf, but even so they may be knocked off their perches and carried away into deeper water. Periwinkles have an interesting set of reflexes that brings them back to their normal habitat in the upper tidal zones. When they are underwater, they respond negatively to gravity. This instinct, known as negative geotaxis, causes them to crawl upward toward the surface. In addition, if the snail crawls into a crack right side up, it has a negative reaction to light, while if it is upside down it has a positive reaction to light. These instincts, known as negative and positive phototaxes, cause it to crawl into cracks and back out again, always moving upward. Once a snail emerges from the water it "knows" that it is home. As long as the rocks are moist it will move only to feed.

Upper Intertidal Zone

The upper intertidal zone is covered by nearly every high tide and exposed by most low tides. The area is characterized by attached **Green Algae** (*Chlorophyta*) such as **Sea Felt** (*Enteromorpha* spp.) and **Sea Lettuce** (*Ulva* spp.), which are heavily grazed upon by animals in this zone. These particular algae are found in intertidal zones all over the world. Sea Felt is thin and fragile, while Sea Lettuce is usually larger, up to 4

Fig. 7.10. Shore Crab.

Fig. 7.11. Chitons.

inches in length, with a wavy margin. Sea Lettuce is gathered by humans and may be sold under the name of "Iceland Sea Grass" or "Green Laver" as rich in vitamins and minerals.

The animals of this surf-splashed zone, mostly grazers and filter-feeders, are active primarily when the tide is in, although there may be hundreds of snails, particularly **Black Turban Shells** (*Tegula funebralis*) that graze in the tide pools. Some of the snail shells in these upper tide pools may appear to lurch along in a very un-snail-like fashion, and close inspection may reveal that they are occupied by Hermit Crabs, the most common of which is the **Hairy Hermit Crab** (*Pagurus hirsutiusculus*). While these crabs usually occupy snail shells, they will use any unoccupied container of the appropriate size, even an abandoned lipstick tube or film can. As they grow, they must find a larger container, so their life consists of incessant scavenging, either for food or for a home with a proper fit. The other common crab is the **Striped Shore Crab** (*Pachygrapsus crassipes*), a squarish, flattened crab with big claws that is well

designed to back into cracks and cling there to avoid being carried off by the surf (fig. 7.10). For the most part these crabs are active at night, but any bit of food that becomes available will lure them out of hiding. Fights between crabs are common, and usually the larger one wins.

Periwinkles visit this zone, but the more common grazers are **Limpets** and **Chitons** (fig. 7.11). Limpets are snails with a flattened cone shape that helps to deflect the energy of the waves and during low tide helps to seal water under the edge of the shell. These grazers inhabit a depression or home site when the tide is out and feed when the tide is in. Their biological clock causes them to move away from home when the tide is in and return when the tide goes out. They know where home is by following a slime trail to their home depression. **Keyhole Limpets** (fig. 7.12) are a large species with a hole in the top. Chitons have a hinged shell made up of eight plates. Because the shell is hinged they are able to move over uneven surfaces. If one becomes dislodged, it can roll up to protect its vulnerable underside from drying or predators.

Filter feeders of the upper intertidal zone consist mostly of attached small barnacles (*Chthamalus* spp.). There is confusion over the common names for these barnacles, but the term **Buckshot Barnacles** seems to suit them as well as any. These are small crustaceans that live as adults in volcano-shaped shells. When the tide is in they feed on plankton by means of a feather-like hind appendage. The shell, made up of several plates, contracts to seal in water when the tide is out. Forming a nearly solid gray band in the upper intertidal zone, these animals are able to tolerate desiccation for a long period of time. At the lower margin of this zone is a belt of larger barnacles known as **Acorn Barnacles** (*Balanus* spp.) They are unable to tolerate as much drying as Buckshot Barnacles, but they grow faster and larger and are able to pry the smaller barnacles off the rocks. Therefore the two kinds of barnacles seldom grow together anywhere in the world.

Middle Intertidal Zone

The middle intertidal zone becomes covered by every high tide and is uncovered by most low tides. This is a zone particularly of filter-feeding animals and resilient small kelps such as **Rockweeds** (*Pelvetia, Pelvetiopsis, Fucus, Hesperophycus*). The most conspicuous animals of this zone are the mussels, which are bivalve molluscs (Pelecypoda). These black clams adhere to the rocks by strong tendrils known as byssal threads. They feed when the tide is in by passing a current of water through their bodies and filtering out plankton. When the tide is out they close

Fig. 7.12. Keyhole Limpet.

tightly to seal in the water. On hot days when the tide is out, they may remain partly open to cool themselves by evaporation. There are two kinds of mussels here. The smaller **Bay Mussel** or **Blue Mussel** (*Mytilus edulis [= M. trossulus]*) is more tolerant of desiccation and therefore tends to occur at the upper fringes of the mussel beds. The larger **California Mussel** (*Mytilus californianus*) is dominant in areas with stronger wave shock. The byssal threads of the Bay Mussel are thinner, and therefore they are less firmly attached to the rocks. In protected areas, however, the Bay Mussel dominates. Bay Mussels are better able to tolerate quiet water because they are motile. They can grow new byssal threads and detach the old ones, which enables them to move upward out of sedimentation that might clog their filters. These adaptations also suggest seasonal changes in dominance within the same "wads" of mussels, particularly on pier pilings. During periods of quiet surf, usually in the summer, Bay Mussels may be more common because they are able to move to the outer edges of the clumps. During winter, when the pounding of the surf is more severe, Bay Mussels get carried away and the California Mussels, with their stronger byssal threads, prevail.

Fig. 7.13. Black Oystercatcher.

Mussels are common intertidal organisms throughout the world and are important in the diets of many nations. Because they grow rapidly, they are one of the world's most important cultured seafoods, and in many nations they may be the most important cultured source of protein. In Spain they are grown commercially on floating rafts where they are not subjected to tides. Remaining under water continuously, they never stop feeding and grow rapidly to harvestable size. Harvesting of mussels (and other shellfish) is illegal throughout most of Orange County, but constant policing of our marine reserves is necessary.

Goose Barnacles (*Pollicipes polymerus*) commonly occur mixed in with the mussels. These strange-looking barnacles occur on a flexible stalk, and the arrangement of the enclosing plates resembles a goose in profile. In Europe there is an ancient legend related to Goose Barnacles. In the North Atlantic, along the west coast of Europe, there is a bird known as the **Barnacle Goose**, which resembles the **Canada Goose** of North America. As the story goes, the leaves of certain trees fell into the sea and became barnacles. After a time the barnacles fell off rocks, logs, or ships' timbers and became Barnacle Geese. This is actually an expression of changes in seasonal abundance. Furthermore, in the thirteenth century, Irish priests, believing that Barnacle Geese arose from barnacles, considered them to be seafood, not fowl, and so they were eaten during Lent. Pope Innocent III was not convinced and issued a decree in 1215 that forbade the eating of Barnacle Geese during Lent. Meanwhile a prominent rabbi in France concluded that if Barnacle Geese arose from Goose Barnacles, Jews could not eat them because they were shellfish, which were forbidden under religious dietary laws.

An interesting predatory bird that frequents the intertidal zone is the **Black Oystercatcher** (fig. 7.13). It is easily spooked by humans, but if one has the chance of observing an inaccessible rocky shore there is a good chance of seeing one of these strange-looking birds at work feeding in the mussel beds. They are completely black except for pink legs and a bright red bill, looking as if they were assembled from spare parts. The long bill, which is compressed laterally, is used to open mussels. They also feed heavily on juvenile mussels and other sedentary prey species such as barnacles. Their activity, along with that of gulls and other predatory birds such as **Whimbrels**, is very important to the formation of bare areas that are constantly being recolonized by larval mussels and barnacles.

Fig. 7.14. Surfgrass at low tide.

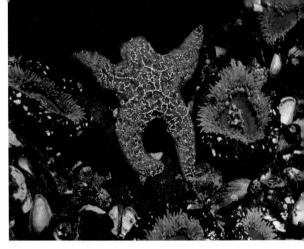

Fig. 7.15. Ochre Sea Star and Green Sea Anemones.

Lower Intertidal Zone

The lower intertidal region is exposed only during the lowest of low tides, known as the "spring" tides (a name referring to upwelling not the season). The upper margin of this zone is considered to be the average sea level, the line from which the height of a tide is measured. A minus tide drops below this line. During a 6-foot high tide, this line would be 6 feet underwater.

This zone is characterized by certain kelps such as the **Feather Boa Kelp** (*Egregia menziesii*). Farther north, the **Sea Palm** (*Postelsia palmaeformis*) is common in this zone, although this is an annual species and often disappears in the fall and winter when the surf tears it from the rocks. Conspicuous in this area, forming a bright green mass of hairlike tendrils during the lowest tides, are the **Surfgrasses** (*Phyllospadix* spp.) (fig. 7.14). Plants in this family (Zosteraceae) are unique in that they are terrestrial plants adapted to living underwater. These plants actually have roots and flowers. Surfgrasses produce millions of filamentous pollen grains that

are shed into the water. These microscopic slimy threads become entangled with the stigmas of flowers on female plants, which produce a sticky secretion that adheres like glue to the pollen and holds it in place in the surf. The bond does not form with pollen of the wrong species, and this specificity prevents hybridization when different kinds of surfgrass pollen are shed simultaneously into the surf.

Tide pools of the lower intertidal zone are often coated with Red Algae (Rhodophyta) known as **Coralline Algae** (*Corallina* spp.), which resemble coarse, pinkish lace. The coarse texture is provided by a coating of calcium carbonate secreted by the plant, a deterrent to grazing by most herbivores.

Most of the animals of the lower intertidal zone take refuge in or are attached to the plants. They are not well suited to long periods of time out of water. Included are many species of worms, snails, and limpets. The "spiny-skinned" animals (Echinodermata) are common here. This is an entirely marine phylum of animals which includes **Sea Stars (Starfishes)**, **Sea Urchins**, **Sea**

Fig. 7.16. Sandcastle Worms.

Cucumbers, and **Sand Dollars**. They are unique in the animal world in that they circulate seawater through their bodies, and they use this mechanism to distribute nutrients, excrete wastes, and operate their hydraulic tube feet. The most common Starfish of this zone is the **Ochre Sea Star** (*Pisaster ochraceus*) (fig. 7.15). Formerly this was one of the most conspicuous animals at low tide, but over the years curious children and collectors of memorabilia have decimated the population. These days they are seldom exposed during low tide. Their usual habit is to migrate during high tide in the middle intertidal zone in order to feed on Mussels or sometimes Acorn Barnacles and then retreat before the tide goes out.

Different species and/or sizes of Sea Stars feed on different kinds of prey. For example, the lower limit of the Mussel bed is regulated by Starfish predation. The regulating factor is the length of time it takes for a Starfish to digest the flesh of a Mussel. When a Starfish feeds, it uses its tube feet gradually to open a Mussel shell by exerting relentless suction. Then it inserts its stomach between the halves of the shell and

secretes digestive enzymes, breaking down the soft tissues and absorbing the nutrients through its stomach. The length of time it takes to complete this procedure is the critical factor that enables Mussels to dominate the middle intertidal zone. This type of feeding strategy may seem inefficient, as some of the digested material may be carried away. There is a small polychaete worm, *Ophiodromus pugettensis*, that lives within the tube feet that are arranged in grooves on the undersides of each arm of the Starfish. This worm lives on the "table scraps," but it does not harm the Starfish, a form of symbiosis known as **commensalism**.

Predatory snails that live in this zone are the **Unicorns** and **Dogwinkles**. The **Emarginate Dogwinkle** or **Rock Thais** (*Nucella [= Thais] emarginata*) has a rasp-like drill that it uses to make a hole in another shelled animal such as a Mussel or Limpet. Other snails sometimes escape predation by riding on top of the Dogwinkle. These sometimes are called **Purple Snails** in reference to a purple dye that may be extracted from the flesh.

Filter-feeding organisms in this zone often live in tubes. In areas protected from the crashing surf there may be honeycombed masses of tubes that belong to polychaete worms known as **Sandcastle Worms** (*Phragmatoma californica*) (fig. 7.16). They form tubes by cementing together many particles of sand. When the tide is out they close the opening of the tube with an operculum. These tubes should not be confused with those of **Scaly Tube Snails** (*Serpulorbis squamigerus*)

Fig. 7.17. Scaly Tube Snails.

Fig. 7.18. Black Abalone.

Fig. 7.19. Purple and Red Sea Urchins.

Fig. 7.20. Sea Otters.

(fig. 7.17). These limey tubes, looking as if they had been squeezed out like toothpaste, are secreted by a true snail that has taken up a filter-feeding way of life. Both of these tube-dwelling organisms may also be found in protected regions in the middle tidal zone.

Grazers of the lower intertidal zone feed primarily on kelp. They are seldom seen out of water. Along with many obligate aquatic animals, they may take refuge in tide pools in some of the upper intertidal zones, and this is often the best place to see them. For example, the **Brown Sea Hare** (*Aplysia californica*) is often observed in the tide pools of the middle intertidal zone. This is a sluglike mollusc with two longitudinal folds along its back. It may be up to 15 inches in length and weigh 15 pounds. It is primarily a detritus-feeder and may be seen creeping along, grazing on detached bits of kelp. When it is disturbed it emits a cloud of deep purple ink, presumably so that it can escape or at least distract a predator.

There are three species of Abalone that graze in the lower intertidal zone, although they are becoming increasingly scarce in this area. These are actually large flattened snails (Gastropoda). A close look will reveal that the shell is spiraled but flat like a cinnamon roll. A number of open holes in the shell carry away wastes. The edible part, which brings a high price in gourmet restaurants, is the large muscular foot. The **Black Abalone** (*Haliotis cracherodii*) is the most commonly seen (fig. 7.18). It is seldom over 6 inches in diameter and has five to nine open holes. It is not prized for human consumption. The **Green Abalone** (*Haliotis fulgens*) averages about 8 inches in diameter and has five to seven open holes. Not often seen in the lower intertidal zone, it is fairly common in deeper water. The **Red Abalone** (*Haliotis refescens*) is up to 11 inches in diameter and is the most important commercial species. It has only three to four open holes. It lives in water up to 500 feet deep and is rarely found in the intertidal zone.

There are two common species of Sea Urchin in our tide pools (fig. 7.19). The smaller **Purple Sea Urchin** (*Strongylocentrotus purpuratus*) is very common. Freshwater is lethal to Sea Urchins. Sometimes during heavy rainstorms, mortality of Purple Sea Urchins may be as high as 90%. Sea Urchins also have the ability to absorb dissolved organic matter from seawater, and therefore some species of Sea Urchin aggregate near sewer outfalls. Careful inspection of these animals while they are in the water reveals that there are long flexible tube feet between the movable spines. If the surf turns them over they can, by means of these tube feet, right themselves in a few minutes. They are not likely to be turned over, however, because they usually rest in depressions that they enlarge by abrasion from their spines and gnawing. They have five jaws that form a structure known as Aristotle's lantern that they use to graze on kelp or carrion. Gnawing by Sea Urchins on the holdfast that anchors a kelp can cause the kelp to be carried away by the surf. Predators such as a large **Sheephead** (*Semicossyphus pulcher*), a fish that feeds in the intertidal region during high tide, can keep the number of Sea Urchins under control. Formerly, **Sea Otters** (*Enhydra lutris*) lived in southern California waters (fig. 7.20), and with their extirpation Sea Urchins became so common in some areas that entire kelp beds were washing away. In this case, the Sea Otter could be called a keystone species.

The **Red Sea Urchin** (*Strongylocentrotus franciscanus*) may have a body 5 inches in diameter with spines extending beyond that. It is more common farther north and on some of the Channel Islands. In these areas there is a thriving business in the export of Sea Urchin gonads, known as "uni" or "frutta del mare," for consumption in sushi bars. This delicacy brings such a high price that it is profitable to extract the gonads and ship them overseas to countries such as Japan or Italy. The rest of the animal, the bulk of its biomass, is simply discarded, often winding up in landfills.

In the bottoms of tide pools or on lower cliff faces, rocks may be found with holes and tunnels bored in them. These tunnels, up to an inch in diameter, are carved by boring clams known as **Piddocks**. There are several species separated by size and the hardness of the rock into which they are able to bur-

Fig. 7.21. Rough Piddocks.

Fig. 7.22. Bat Star.

Fig. 7.23. Green Anemone (Peter Bryant).

row. They live many years, but many species stop boring when the burrow is complete. The **Rough Piddock** (*Zirfaea pilsbryi*) usually bores into heavy clay or mud throughout its seven to eight years of life (fig. 7.21). Its foot, which is modified into a sucker, holds onto the substratum while the shell is moved up and down and rotates slightly. Thirty-two turning movements and 70 minutes are required to make a complete revolution, after which the direction is reversed.

The intertidal zone also has surge channels lined with rocks under which other animals take refuge. **Brittle Stars** or **Serpent Stars** (Ophiuroidea) move about by moving their serpentlike arms. They feed in a unique way by cleaning up fine particulate organic matter that collects between sand grains. **Bat Stars** or **Sea Bats** (*Patiria miniata*) are small red Sea Stars with a webbing between their arms (fig. 7.22). They feed in typical Starfish fashion on small Mussels and Barnacles. Flatworms (Phylum Platyhelminthes) are primitive creeping animals that spend most of the daylight hours under rocks. At night they come out and feed by grazing on attached algae and detritus. The **Common Flatworm** (*Notop-*

lana acticola) looks like a one-way sign, a fat, gray arrow about $1/2$ inch long. The **White Flatworm** (*Pseudoceros luteus*) is larger and roughly circular. It is actually able to swim gracefully with lateral undulations of its body, looking like a miniature Bat Ray.

Among the most conspicuous members of the lower tide pools are the Sea Anemones (Anthozoa), a name that refers to their flower-like appearance. These Coelenterates (Phylum Cnidaria) have a body plan like a two-layered bag with a single opening into the digestive cavity. A ring of tentacles around the mouth gives them the appearance of a flower. The tentacles bear sting cells known as nematocysts. Any small object that touches the tentacles is instantly pierced by toxic barbs. The tentacles fold toward the mouth, and cilia carry the object inward until it drops into the mouth. Digestion is rapid, and indigestible parts are regurgitated in a surprisingly short time. These are opportunistic predators. They lie in wait with their tentacles open wide waiting for small organisms that may walk carelessly across them. Among the food items that may fall in are pieces of Mussel or Barnacle dropped by a

Fig. 7.24. Common Sea Cucumber.

sloppy eater in the zone above them. The largest of the Anemones is known as the **Green Anemone** (*Anthopleura xanthogrammica*), which may be up to 10 inches in diameter, although half that size is more common (fig. 7.23). Its bright green color is due to photosynthetic single-celled algae that live in the tissues. The algae use the Anemone for support and protection, and the Anemone apparently derives a portion of its nutrients from the algae, an example of mutualism.

Fig. 7.25. Wavy Top with Gorgonion growing on it.

Among the carnivores of these lower tide pools is a group of sluglike molluscs known as **Nudibranchs**, a name that refers to naked gills. These are shell-less snails with exposed gills. Nudibranchs are often brightly colored, but most are smaller than 2 inches in length. They are seldom conspicuous. One interesting species, *Phidiana (= Hermissenda) crassicornis*, is white with bright blue stripes on the center of its back. This species feeds on Sea Anemones and their relatives. Sting cells are ingested intact and are translocated to the tips of the exposed gills, technically known as cerata, where they provide protection for the Nudibranch. Once again, it may be seen that a brightly colored animal need not fear predators.

Sea Cucumbers are related to Sea Stars and Sea Urchins. The **Common Sea Cucumber** (*Parastichopus californicus*) is bright orange (fig. 7.24). A Sea Cucumber maintains its shape by filling its body with seawater. Its tube feet are reduced to a ring of tentacles around its mouth that are used to gather detritus. It does not have many enemies, but when disturbed it eviscerates itself, expelling most of its internal organs through its anus. Presumably a would-be predator is so disgusted that it moves off in revulsion.

There also are large snails in these pools. The **Wavy Top** (*Lithopoma undosum*) is a slow-moving algae-eater that often has other organisms growing on its back (fig. 7.25). The largest predator of this zone is the **Two-spotted Octopus** (*Octopus bimaculatus*) (fig. 7.26). It may be up to 3 feet across but is

Fig. 7.26. Two-spotted Octopus.

while it lies in wait for its prey. In the tide pools it usually remains out of sight under an overhanging ledge, but even in the open it is difficult to see.

There are several species of small fishes in these lower tide pools. Many are kelplike in appearance, cryptically colored to remain nearly invisible. Most common is the **Woolly** or **Tidepool Sculpin** (*Clinocottus analis*), sometimes known as a **Tidepool Johnny** (fig. 7.27). These fish remain motionless on the bottom most of the time. When they move, they often crawl with their large pectoral fins, and when they swim it is in short bursts. They feed primarily on detritus that accumulates in the tide pools.

more likely to be half that size. An Octopus grasps its prey with its tentacles and immobilizes it with its venomous saliva. The saliva may be emitted into the water, in which case it acts as an anesthetic, relaxing the prey. Crabs are trapped and eaten in this way. An Octopus can also drill a hole into an abalone shell with a filelike radula and inject the venom. The Two-spotted Octopus is capable of producing a painful bite when grabbed by a human, but apparently this is a rare occurrence. It is known for its ability to change color instantly, a trait that enables it to match its background perfectly

Superficially similar to the Woolly Sculpin is the **California Clingfish** (*Gobiesox rhessodon*). This little fish has an adhesive sucker on its underside so that it can cling upside down under rocks of the lower tideal zone. Among the kelps, a diligent observer may notice the **Spotted Kelpfish** (*Gibbonsia elegans*). This is an elongated, kelp-colored fish with a long dorsal fin running almost to its tail and a prominent eyelike spot above and behind the gill cover (operculum). This shy little fish so resembles the kelp in which it hides that it is seldom seen. Numerous species of sculpin also inhabit

Fig. 7.27. Sculpin.

Fig. 7.28. Blenny.

California's kelp beds. The **Rockpool Blenny** (*Hypsoblennius gilberti*) and its relative the **Bay Blenny** (*Hypsoblennius gentilis*) resemble the kelpfishes, but they are rounded rather than flattened in cross section (fig. 7.28). They have short, stubby noses and long, continuous dorsal fins. They are common in the lower intertidal zone but are seldom seen because they hide in the kelp.

A unique eel-like fish of the rocky intertidal region is the **Monkeyface Prickleback** or **Monkeyface-eel** (*Cebidichthys violaceus*). It and the **Rock Prickleback** or **Rock-eel** (*Xiphister mucosus*), an algae-eater, are in the Prickleback Family (Stichaeidae). The Rock Prickleback may grow large enough to be confused by skindivers with the **California Moray** (*Gymnothorax mordax*) (fig. 7.29). What makes the Monkeyface Prickleback unique is that it is an air-breathing fish. When the tide is out, through a mechanism that is not completely understood, it can absorb oxygen from the air. Large specimens have been known to survive for 24 hours out of water.

The most conspicuous fishes of the lower tide pools are juveniles of those that are common in the offshore kelp beds. Most common of these is the **Opaleye**

(*Girella nigricans*), which gets its name from the opalescent blue of its eyes. In the tide pools Opaleyes move about in active schools. They are easily identified by their dark color and a distinctive white spot on each side of their dorsal fins. They remain in the tide pools until they reach about 2 inches in length, after which they migrate to the kelp beds. Adults, which are primarily herbivorous, can reach a length of 15 inches.

The **Garibaldi** (*Hypsypops rubicundus*) is the official state saltwater fish (fig. 7.30). The name is probably a reference to a loose-fitting garment by that name that was popular in the 1890s. The garment was named for Giuseppe Garibaldi, an Italian patriot who wore such a shirt as a uniform. These are the brilliant orange fishes that are sometimes quite visible in offshore waters. Goldfish Point in La Jolla is named for these fishes. The juveniles are usually present in the tide pools in the spring and early summer. As juveniles they are bright orange with brilliant blue spots. It is illegal to harm or capture them at any age. Typical of bright-colored members of the Damselfish family (Pomacentridae), they are fairly pugnacious, defending territories in the rocks.

Fig. 7.29. California Moray.

Fig. 7.30. Garibaldi (courtesy of California Department of Fish and Game).

Fig. 7.31. Habitat zonation at Upper Newport Bay.

ESTUARIES

Estuaries are places where freshwater mixes with seawater. There are two prominent estuaries in Orange County, Newport Bay and Bolsa Chica. The origin of these bays is often associated with a barrier beach bar or sand spit formed by the southward drift of the longshore current. The towns of Newport Beach and Balboa occupy the sand spit that shelters Newport Bay, and Bolsa Chica State Beach occupies the spit at Bolsa Chica. Wetlands are among the most endangered habitats in California, victims of residential developments and marinas. South of San Francisco about 90% of this habitat has been destroyed. At 740 acres, Upper Newport Bay (figs. 1.12) is the largest "natural" estuary in southern California, and the 1,200-acre Bolsa Chica Ecological Preserve (fig. 1.13) is the largest estuary that is undergoing restoration.

While it appears to be relatively featureless, this habitat is extremely productive. It provides a source of food for millions of animals. Birds are particularly conspicuous. Most of them travel thousands of miles migrating from arctic habitats where long summer days promote abundant photosynthesis and thus an abundant source of food. During the winter months these birds travel southward to equally productive habitats including our coastal wetlands. While an estuary may appear monotonous to the eye, the capacity of the area to support life rivals that of a tropical forest, and it appears that there would be tremendous competition for food with so many bird species and so little diversity in habitat. An estuary, however, is a classic example of niche partitioning by birds. These birds feed in different ways and in different locations, aided by different sizes and shapes of their beaks, legs, and feet (fig. 7.32). On the basis of the duration of submergence, five major habitats (fig. 7.31) are present in an estuary:

Open water refers to the area offshore. Progressing toward the coast or the mouth of the bay, an estuary changes gradually from freshwater to a completely marine environment. It is a rather harsh environment for intertidal invertebrates that live in the mud because there is a profound change from freshwater to saltwater every

Flycatcher
catching insects in midair

Sparrow
crushing seeds

Curlew
probing in the mud

Hawk
tearing flesh

Cormorant
grasping fish

Heron
spearing fish

Duck
filtering mud

Avocet
swishing on surface of mud

Raptor
grasping prey

Quail
walking, scratching

Perching Bird
grasping perch

Duck
swimming, walking on mud

Fig. 7.32. Functions of beaks and feet.

Fig. 7.33. Topsmelt.

Fig. 7.34. Forster's Tern.

Fig. 7.35. Least Tern.

Fig. 7.36. Ruddy Duck, a diving duck.

time the tide goes in or out. Fishes such as **Topsmelt** (*Atherinops affinis*) (fig. 7.33) and **Striped Mullet** (*Mugil cephalus*) feed on plankton and themselves provide food for birds. **Pelicans**, **Terns** (figs. 7.34, 7.35), **Kingfishers**, and **Black Skimmers** dive on their prey from the air and catch the food in their mouths, whereas **Ospreys** (fig. 6.45), which are fish-eating hawks, catch their food with their feet. **Cormorants**, **Grebes**, and Diving Ducks such as **Scaups**, **Buffleheads** and **Ruddy Ducks** (fig. 7.36) dive under from a swimming position and chase their prey underwater. These diving birds are heavy-bodied, so they ride low in the water and do not experience difficulty remaining underwater.

Mud Flats become exposed at low tide (fig. 7.37). At this time many of the invertebrates retreat to burrows or shells to avoid drying. As the tide goes in and out, a myriad of shorebirds and bay ducks wade or swim in the shallow water to capture worms, snails, and crustaceans that may still be on or near the surface. Shorebirds are waders: they follow the tide out and in and by virtue of different leg-lengths and bill sizes feed at different water depths and probe to different depths in the mud. **Long-billed Curlews** (fig. 7.38) have long decurved bills, **Marbled Godwits** (fig. 7.39) have long slightly upturned bills, and **Willets** (fig. 7.5) have fairly short, straight bills. Most birds probe in the mud, but **American Avocets**, with long upturned bills, swish their bills in the mud from side to side. Bay Ducks are very buoyant, hence

Fig. 7.37. Mud Flats of Upper Newport Bay.

Fig. 7.38. Long-billed Curlew.

they do not dive under for their food. Instead, they bob under to feed on the mud they can reach by floating tail up in the water, and many of them, such as **Northern Shovelers** (fig. 7.40), aided by their webbed feet, simply walk about on the mud, sifting algae and invertebrates with their broad beaks. Because of their light weight, Bay Ducks such as **Mallards**, **Pintails** (fig. 7.41), and **Widgeons** can take off straight up from a floating position, whereas heavy-bodied Diving Ducks must run along the surface of the water in order to get up enough speed to be airborne.

Fig. 7.39. Marbled Godwit, Western Sandpiper.

Fig. 7.40. Northern Shovelers feeding on mud.

Fig. 7.41. Pintail Duck, a Bay Duck.

American Coots or **Mud Hens** are also Mud Flat birds, but they are able to dive under to feed on the mud or use their large, flattened toes to walk about on the mud.

Salt Marsh is a habitat that fringes the bay (figs. 7.42, 7.43). It is composed primarily of **Cord Grass** (*Spartina foliosa*), a salt-tolerant plant that provides most of the food for the estuary system. Because it is one of the few terrestrial plants that can tolerate periodic inundation by saltwater, it is extremely common and successful in its habitat. Its photosynthetic contribution to the estuary environment is the major source of food for this highly productive ecosystem. Cord

Fig. 7.42. Salt Marsh zones.

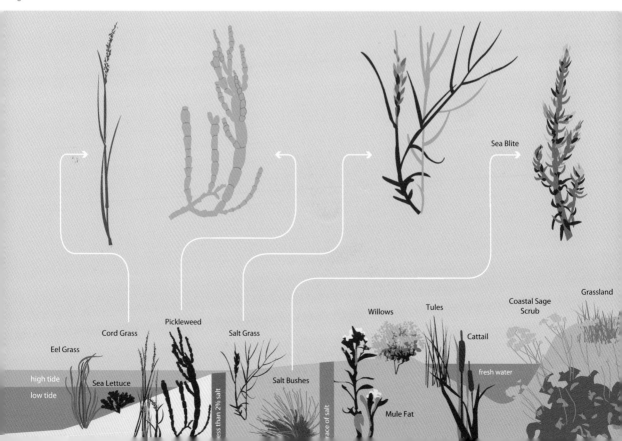

Grass roots absorb salt and water, but the salt is excreted upon its leaves, making them inedible to most herbivores. The stems of these grasses are hollow and air-filled, and therefore they can carry gases to and from the roots. Nitrogen-fixing bacteria living in the roots convert nitrogen gas to the proteins that are important for the plants and therefore for the entire ecosystem. Finally, Cord Grass possesses a special kind of photosynthesis, known as C-4 photo-synthesis, that provides a large amount of food (glucose) per unit of time. Rather than making its contribution to the ecosystem in the usual way, it does so through detritus. Few animals can eat the salty foliage, but

Fig. 7.43. Salt Marsh zonation at Bolsa Chica Ecological Reserve.

the tips of the grass blades are constantly breaking off and falling into the mud that becomes trapped by the root system. Microorganisms consume the detritus and contribute to the dissolved organic matter that enters the water. Worms and snails also feed directly on the detritus while fishes and birds feed on them and thus the entire estuary food web is based largely on the detritus produced by Cord Grass. Other Salt Marsh plants such as **Pickleweed** (*Salicornia* spp.) (fig. 7.44), **Sea Blite** (*Suaeda californica*), and **Salt Grass** (*Distichlis spicata*) occur farther from the water and tolerate shorter periods of flooding. When the tide comes in, fishes such as the **California Killifish** (*Fundulus parvipinnis*) (fig. 7.45) move among the submerged stems and feed on detritus and invertebrates. It is in this habitat that the large members of the Heron Family, such as the **Great Blue Heron** (fig. 7.46), **Common Egret** (fig. 7.47), and **Snowy Egret** (fig. 7.48), can often be seen wading and feeding. While there are not many bird species that are identified as marsh birds, a number of our endangered species, such as the **Light-footed Clapper Rail**, the **Long-billed Marsh Wren**, and **Belding's Savannah Sparrow** (fig. 6.76) are inhabitants.

Freshwater Marsh is composed of plants such as **Sedges** and **Cattails** that are intolerant of saltwater but capable of being inundated by freshwater (fig. 7.49). Upstream from the Upper Newport Bay Ecological Reserve, along San Diego Creek in the vicinity of the Uni-

Fig. 7.44. Pickleweed.

Fig. 7.45. California Killifish.

Fig. 7.49. Cattails in Freshwater Marsh.

Fig. 7.46. Great Blue Heron.

Fig. 7.47. Common Egret.

Fig. 7.48. Snowy Egret.

Fig. 7.50. Coastal Sage Scrub on bluffs at Newport.

versity of California at Irvine, are the San Joaquin Marsh (fig. 1.26) and the San Joaquin Wildlife Sanctuary. This is Orange County's largest complex of Freshwater Marsh and its component of marsh birds. Small patches of this habitat also occur along Back Bay Drive where irrigation water from bluff-top homes percolates down to the base of the cliffs.

Coastal Sage Scrub is the plant community of the coastal bluffs (fig. 7.50). It is not a wetland community but is similar to the terrestrial community that occurs in undisturbed areas throughout Orange County.

TABLE 7.2: COMMON BIRDS OF ESTUARIES

Open Water

Diving Ducks: Ruddy Duck, Bufflehead, Canvasback, Surf Scoter, Lesser Scaup, Red-breasted Merganser

Grebes: Western Grebe, Pied-billed Grebe, Eared Grebe

Water Birds: Common Loon, Brown Pelican, White Pelican, Double-crested Cormorant, Osprey, Ring-billed Gull

Terns: Forster's Tern, Least Tern, Caspian Tern, Black Skimmer, Kingfisher

Mud Flats

Dabblers (Surface-feeding Ducks): Mallard, Pintail, Green-winged Teal, Blue-winged Teal, Cinnamon Teal, American Widgeon, Shoveler

American Coot (Mud Hen)

Shore Birds (Waders): Long-billed Curlew, Marbled Godwit, Willet, Lesser Yellowlegs, Knot, Semipalmated Plover, Black Turnstone, Western Sandpiper, Least Sandpiper, Short-billed Dowitcher, American Avocet, Black-necked Stilt

Marshes

Herons: Great Blue Heron, Common Egret, Snowy Egret, Black-crowned Night Heron, Green Heron, American Bittern

Rails: Light-footed Clapper Rail, Sora, Moorhen

Shorebirds: Killdeer, Wilson's Snipe

Songbirds: Belding's Savannah Sparrow, Song Sparrow, Black Phoebe, Red-winged Blackbird, Yellowthroat, House Finch, Long-billed Marsh Wren, Northern Harrier

REFERENCES

Alden, P., F. Heath, R. Keen, A. Leventer, and W. B. Zomlefer. 1998. *National Audubon Society Field Guide to California*. Alfred A. Knopf, Inc., New York. 447 pp.

Barbour, M., B. Pavlik, F. Drysdale, and S. Lindstrom. 1993. *California's Changing Landscapes*. California Native Plant Society, Sacramento. 224 pp.

Barbour, M. G., T. Keeler-Wolf, and A. A. Schoenherr (Editors). 2007. *Terrestrial Vegetation of California*. University of California Press, Berkeley. 712 pp.

Belzer, T. J. 1984. *Roadside Plants of Southern California*. Mountain Press, Missoula. 157 pp.

Brown, E. M. 2007. *Back Pocket Field Guide: An Introduction to Orange County Wildlands*. Laguna Greenbelt, Inc., Laguna Beach. 143 pp.

Chilcote, R. H. 2003. *Nature's Laguna Wilderness*. Laguna Wilderness Press, Laguna Beach. 96 pp.

Clarke, O. F., D. Svehla, G. Ballmer, and A. Montalvo. 2007. *Flora of the Santa Ana River and Environs*. Heyday Books, Berkeley. 495 pp.

Croker, K. S. 1985. *Santa Ana Mountains Trail Guide*. Whale and Eagle Publishing Co., Costa Mesa. 12 pp.

Dole, J. W. and B. B. Rose. 1996. *Shrubs and Trees of Southern California Coastal Region and Mountains*. Foot-loose Press, North Hills. 184 pp.

Eder, T. 2005. *Mammals of California*. Lone Pine Publishing International, Auburn. 344 pp.

Gallagher, S. R. 1997. *Atlas of Breeding Birds: Orange County, California*. Sea and Sage Audubon Press, Irvine. 264 pp.

Goodson, G. 1988. *Fishes of the Pacific Coast*. Stanford University Press. 267 pp.

Hall, C. A. Jr. 2007. *Introduction to the Geology of Southern California and Its Native Plants*. University of California Press, Berkeley. 493 pp.

Halsey, R. W. 2005. *Fire, Chaparral, and Survival in Southern California*. Sunbelt Publications, Inc., San Diego. 188 pp.

Hamilton, R. A. and D. R. Willick. 1996. *The Birds of Orange County California: Status and Distribution*. Sea and Sage Audubon Press. 150 pp.

Hickman, J. C. (Editor). *The Jepson Manual: Higher Plants of California*. University of California Press, Berkeley. 1,400 pp.

Hinton, S. 1987. *Seashore Life of Southern California*. University of California Press, Berkeley. 217 pp.

Hogue, C. L. 1993. *Insects of the Los Angeles Basin*. Natural History Museum of Los Angeles County, Los Angeles. 446 pp.

Jameson, E. W. Jr. and H. J. Peeters. 2004. *Mammals of California*. University of California Press, Berkeley. 429 pp.

Keeley, J. E. (Editor). 1992. *Interface Between Ecology and Land Development in California*. Southern California Academy of Sciences, Los Angeles. 297 pp.

Keeley, J. E., M. Baer-Keeley, and C. J. Fatheringham (Editors). 2000. *2nd Interface Between Ecology and Land Development in California*. U. S. Geological Survey Open-File Report 00-62, Sacramento. 300 pp.

Latting, J. (Editor). 1976. *Plant Communities of Southern California*. Special Publication No. 2, California Native Plant Society, Berkeley. 164 pp.

Lemm, J. M. 2006. *Field Guide to Amphibians and Reptiles of the San Diego Region*. University of California Press, Berkeley. 326 pp.

Lozinsky, R. P. 2006. *Our Backyard Geology in Orange County California*. McGraw-Hill Custom Publishing, Boston. 72 pp.

Mitchell, P. 2006. *Santa Ana River Guide*. Wilderness Press, Berkeley. 246 pp.

Munz, P. A. 1974. *A Flora of Southern California*. University of California Press, Berkeley. 1,086 pp.

Munz, P. A. and D. D. Keck. 1959. *A California Flora*. University of California Press, Berkeley. 1,681 pp.

McGuinnis, S. M. 2006. *Field Guide to Freshwater Fishes of California*. University of California Press, Berkeley. 538 pp.

McKinney, J. 2001. *Day Hiker's Guide to Southern California*. Olympus Press, Santa Barbara. 335 pp.

Norris, R. M. and R. W. Webb. 1990. *Geology of California*. John Wiley and Sons, Inc., New York. 541 pp.

Orsak, L. J. 1978. *The Butterflies of Orange County, California*. Museum of Systematic Biology, University of California, Irvine. 349 pp.

Pavlik, B. M., P. C. Muick, S. Johnson, and M. Popper. 1991. *Oaks of California*. Cachuma Press, Los Olivos. 184 pp.

Powell, J. A. and C. L. Hogue. 1979. *California Insects*. University of California Press, Berkeley. 388 pp.

Roberts, F. M. Jr. 1995. *Illustrated Guide to the Oaks of the Southern Californian Floristic Province*. F. M. Roberts Publications, Encinitas. 112 pp.

Quinn, R. D. and S. C. Keeley. 2006. *Introduction to California Chaparral*. University of California Press, Berkeley. 322 pp.

Rundel, P. W. and R. Gustafson. 2005. *Introduction to the Plant Life of Southern California*. University of California Press, Berkeley. 316 pp.

Sawyer, J. O. and T. Keeler-Wolf. 1995. *A Manual of California Vegetation*. California Native Plant Society, Sacramento. 471 pp.

Schad, J. 1993. *Afoot and Afield in Orange County*. Wilderness Press, Berkeley. 126 pp.

Schoenherr, A. A. (Editor). 1989. *Endangered Plant Communities of Southern California*. Southern California Botanists Special Publication No. 3, Fullerton. 114 pp.

Schoenherr, A. A. 1992. *A Natural History of California*. University of California Press, Berkeley. 772 pp.

Schoenherr, A. A. 1999. *Natural History of the Islands of California*. University of California Press, Berkeley. 491 pp.

Schoenherr, A. A., D. Clarke, and E. M. Brown (Editors). 2005. *Docent Guide to Orange County Wilderness*. Laguna Greenbelt, Inc., Laguna Beach. 142 pp.

Sexton, C. W. and G. L. Hunt, Jr. 1979. *An Annotated Checklist of the Birds of Orange County, California*. Museum of Systematic Biology, University of California, Irvine. 95 pp.

Sharp, R. P. 1972. *Geology; Field Guide to Southern California*. W. C. Brown, Dubuque. 181 pp.

Sharp, R. P. and A. F. Glazer. 1993. *Geology Underfoot in Southern California*. Mountain Press Publishing Co., Missoula. 224 pp.

Sibley, D. A. 2004. *The Sibley Field Guide to Birds of Western North America*. Alfred A. Knopf, New York. 471 pp.

Small, A. 1994. *California Birds: Their Status and Distribution*. Ibis Publishing Co., Vista. 342 pp.

Stebbins, R. C. 2003. *A Field Guide to Western Reptiles and Amphibians*. Houghton Mifflin Co., Boston. 531 pp.

Stephenson, J. R. and G. M. Calcerone. 1999. *Southern California Mountains and Foothills Assessment: Habitat and Species Conservation Issues*. Pacific Southwest Research Station, Forest Service, U. S. Department of Agriculture, Albany. 402 pp.

Thelander, C. G. (Editor). 1994. *Life on the Edge: A Guide to California's Endangered Natural Resources: Wildlife*. BioSystems Books, Santa Cruz. 550 pp.

Vogel, R. 1999. *Best Easy Day Hikes: Orange County*. Falcon Publishing, Inc., Helena. 86 pp.

Zedler, Z. B. 1982. *The Ecology of Southern California Coastal Salt Marshes: A Community Profile*. U. S. Fish and Wildlife Service, Biological Services Program, FWS/OBS-81/54.

LIST OF FIGURES

CHAPTER 7

LIST OF TABLES

INDEX